A Personal Invitation

from Author

Mark Nolting

Before Booking ... *Contact Us at*

The Africa Adventure Company

to request a complimentary copy of our easy-to-use
SAFARI PLANNER and to discuss the many options
we have to offer. Call today - my expert staff and I
would love to assist you in planning your safari!

2601 East Oakland Park Boulevard, Suite 600
Fort Lauderdale, Florida 33306
U.S.A
Tel: 800.882.9453 * 954.491.8877
* Fax: 954.491.9060

THE
AFRICA ADVENTURE
COMPANY   EST. 1986

Dear Adventurer,

The Africa Adventure Company is the passport to the safari of your dreams. Our team is managed and directed by Mark and Alison Nolting, two people whose combined experience and knowledge of Africa is unsurpassed in the safari business.

We are proud of the reputation we have earned on the African continent over the past 30 years. We were recognized again by **Travel+Leisure's "World's Best Awards"** *on the Top Safari Outfitters list. And* **National Geographic** *honored us as one of the* **"Best Adventure Travel Companies on Earth".**

Mark is the author of **Africa's Top Wildlife Countries,** *an award-winning guide book that is considered the quintessential guide for planning a safari by the travel industry. He has also authored the* **Safari Planning Map: East & Southern Africa,** *and this, the* **African Safari Field Guide.** *He has received the* **Conde Nast Traveler** *magazine award as one of the* **World's Top African Travel Specialists** *for over a dozen years and has been on* **Travel+Leisure's** *A-List for many years as well. Born and raised in Zimbabwe, Alison managed a safari camp for several years, hosting guests in the bush, and worked in the travel industry in England before joining Mark in 1991.*

We specialize only in Africa and bring an educational and experiential aspect to each trip – opening doors to the wildlife and people of this magical continent. All of our safari consultants travel frequently to Africa – providing first-hand knowledge when designing your safari. We offer a refreshing assortment of over 100 unique and exciting itineraries – most of which can be further adapted to your personal interests – to craft your "dream safari" into reality!

Please contact us so that we may send you our **SAFARI PLANNER** *that concisely summarizes the safari experience and includes our "When's the Best Time to Go" chart and other valuable information, and to speak to of one of our safari consultants so that we may assist you in planning your African Adventure. The value we offer and our personalized service will exceed your expectations!*

Best Regards,   *Mark and Alison Nolting*

AFRICAN SAFARI
FIELD GUIDE

Mark W. Nolting

with illustrations and natural history texts by
Duncan Butchart

Copyright © 2016 by Mark W. Nolting

Requests should be addressed to Global Travel Publishers Inc.,
2601 E. Oakland Park Blvd., Suite 600, Ft. Lauderdale, FL 33306, USA
Email: info@globaltravelpublishers.com
www.globaltravelpublishers.com

African Safari Field Guide
(Seventh edition, completely revised and updated, 2016)
ISBN: 978-0-939895-22-9
Cover photo credit: Lions in tree by Michael Peterson (michaelrenniephotography.com);
Black Rhinoceros, Leopard cub and African Elephant all by Duncan Butchart
Publication Design by Nature Works, South Africa
Printed by RR Donnelley, USA.
Illustrations © Duncan Butchart
Edited by Sarah H. Taylor
Proofread by Monica C. Kowalski

Publisher's Notes
Although every effort has been made to ensure the accuracy of the information in this book, the author and publisher do not assume and hereby disclaim any liability to any party for any loss or damage caused by errors, omissions, misleading information or any potential travel problem caused by information in this book, even if such errors or omissions are a result of negligence, accident, or any other cause.

Also Available in E-Book Version in All Formats.
ISBN: 978-0-939895-23-6   US$22.95

SPECIAL SALES

Discounts for volume purchases.

For details please contact the publisher at:
phone: 954-491-8877 or 1-800-882-9453, fax 954-491-9060
e-mail: info@globaltravelpublishers.com
or write to
Global Travel Publishers, 2601 E. Oakland Park Blvd., Suite 600,
Ft. Lauderdale, FL 33306, USA
www.globaltravelpublishers.com

FOREWORD

Dear Safarier,

For more than three decades I have had the privilege of exploring Africa on countless safaris. Having spent hours of preparation for each of my earlier safaris, and in the end having to carry with me several heavy resource books on mammals, reptiles, birds and trees, as well as maps, phrase books and a diary, the idea of consolidating all this into one book was formed.

Why do so many people wish to go to Africa? Many seek the wonderful wilderness of a still largely undeveloped African continent, where wildlife in its natural and exciting environment still abounds. Others seek contact with wild spaces and traditional African cultures which can have a meaningful effect on the human spirit – stirring and stimulating the senses, relaxing and revitalizing the mind.

Visiting Africa means getting back to basics and feeling the thrill of experiencing something entirely different from the developed world in which we live.

The main allure of the continent is that you can find adventure there. When you go on safari, you never know what you're going to see or what is going to happen. Each safari is unpredictable and exciting. With the right planning, there's no finer adventure!

Taking an ecotourism trip to Africa is an investment in protecting this incredible continent's amazing wildlife for future generations, while having the vacation of a lifetime.

There is no better time to venture to Africa than the present. Go now, while Africa can still deliver all that is promised – and more!

Sincerely,

Mark W. Nolting

Lion cub

5

African Elephant in Damaraland, Namibia

CONTENTS

African Facts at a Glance

Area:
11,635,000 square-miles
(30,420,000 km²).

Approximate Size:
More than three times the size of the
United States; larger than Europe, the
United States and China combined;
the second largest continent, covering
20% of the world's land surface.

Largest Waterfall:
Victoria Falls (the world's largest
waterfall by volume), twice the height
of Niagara Falls and one-and-a-half
times as wide.

Longest River:
Nile River (world's longest), 4,160
miles (6,710 km).

Largest Crater:
Ngorongoro Crater (largest intact
caldera/crater in the world), 12 miles
(19 km) wide with its rim rising 1,200
to 1,600 feet (366 to 488 m) off its
expansive 102 square-mile (264 km²)
floor.

Highest Mountain:
Mt. Kilimanjaro (highest mountain in
the world that is not part of a range),
19,340 feet (5,895 m).

Largest Lake:
Lake Victoria (world's third largest),
26,828 square miles (69,485 km²).

Largest Freshwater Oasis:
Okavango Delta (Botswana), over
6,000 square miles (15,000 km²).

Largest Desert:
Sahara (world's largest), larger than the
continental United States.

Largest Land Mammal:
African Savannah Elephant (world's
largest), over 15,000 pounds (6,800 kg).

Largest Bird:
Common Ostrich (world's largest), over
8 feet (2.5 m) tall.

Deepest Lake:
Lake Tanganyika (world's second deepest),
over 4,700 feet (1,433 m).

Longest Lake:
Lake Tanganyika (world's longest),
446 miles (714 km).

Longest Rift Valley:
The Great Rift Valley, a 5,900 mile
(9,500 km) gash from the Red Sea to
Lake Malawi, with 30 active volcanoes.

Lake With Most Fish Species:
Lake Malawi (500 species).

Tallest People:
The Dinka of southern Sudan (world's
tallest) generally reach on average 5'11"
(180 cm).

Shortest People:
The Pygmies of the Congo (world's
shortest) reach only 4'11" (125 cm).

Human Population:
1,166,000,000 (source: United Nations
Population Fund, 2015).

HOW TO USE THIS BOOK

The *African Safari Field Guide* differs from other books on the wildlife of the continent in that it is designed for you to write down your experiences and observations while you are traveling. While there is a great deal of interesting and useful information on the following pages, the book will really come to life when you add your own notes and stories. Most travelers have become used to recording their safaris and other holidays through photographs, but there is nothing quite like the immediacy of a personal **travel diary** to complement these images. This book has been designed in such a way that it will encourage and help you to record the highlights, events and dramas of your African safari, as well as providing a means of noting activities and lists of the mammals and birds which you encounter.

Introductory information on the landscapes and habitats of Africa will set the scene for your own notes. The **descriptive accounts of the animals** mention interesting behavior which you should look out for, as well as identification tips, while the **comprehensive checklist of mammals and birds** will allow you to fully document all the species you encounter on safari.

The detailed **Map Directory** will help you to orientate yourself and follow the route of your safari, while the brief **language section** has some key words and phrases that provide a stepping-stone into local conversation. A list of recommended books for further reading is also provided, and there is a **glossary** of unfamiliar terms that you will hear on safari.

Bushbuck

Note: In this book the common names of all species are capitalized in line with the recommendations of the International Ornithological Committee (Union). The unique vernacular names given to biological entities (species) should be regarded as proper nouns in order that they can be distinguished from simple descriptions. Examples of this method of capitalization can also be found outside the animal kingdom as with the "Rocky Mountains" which distinguish this North American range from any "rocky mountains".

Preparing for Safari

While on safari, you will enjoy the attention and input of one or more guides whose job is to make sure that you have a safe, fun and enlightening experience. Although you will be in capable hands, the more you know before setting off, the more you will get out of your adventure.

Background reading is perhaps the most important, although speaking to somebody who has been to the area you intend to visit can be invaluable. The *African Safari Field Guide* is aimed at providing you with an advance overview, as well as being a guide and field book to record your observations.

Your desire to visit Africa may well have been triggered by National Geographic documentaries or Animal Planet. This is all very well, but you should not expect to see everything in the way in which these films depict. The best wildlife films take years to create, and involve weeks or months of waiting for action to unfold. Part of enjoying your safari is having a realistic expectation, and you should always remember that wildlife is just that – wild! With the exception of the most common birds and herbivorous mammals, nothing can be guaranteed on safari – and that, really, is the thrill of it. It is the anticipation and chance that makes getting up early each morning, and driving around each bend in the road, so enthralling.

It is vital to develop a good relationship with your guide from the outset. Bear in mind that he or she will not only know the area and its wildlife, but also the best ways to reveal this to you. Make sure that you state your expectations clearly from the word "go", and don't be shy to get involved in each day's routine. If you have seen enough lions for one day, for example, let your guide know that you would like to focus on seeking out other species.

Cheetah

Rather than spending your whole safari in search only for big game, aim to get an understanding and appreciation for the whole ecosystem, of which termites and fig trees play as important a role as elephants and lions. Developing an interest in birds, reptiles and trees means that you'll have a captivating experience even when relaxing at your lodge or being transferred from one locality to the next.

Sensitivity toward wildlife is paramount at all times. Your guide will know the correct distance to approach each individual species without causing stress, but in the rare instances where this may not be so, it is always best to be over-cautious. The most enthralling wildlife encounters are often those in which the animals that you are viewing are unaware or unafraid.

Being on safari generally puts you at less risk than you would be when traveling on busy roads in your own neighborhood, but many animals are potentially dangerous and some simple precautions are advisable. A good guide will naturally try to avert any risky situations, but as already mentioned, respecting animals' space by not attempting to get too close is paramount. Almost all large mammals are frightened of humans and generally run or move off when confronted with the upright form of a person. This can never be taken for granted, however, and you should not be tempted to leave the safety of a safari vehicle to approach an animal unless in the company of an armed guide. It is equally important to remain seated while in open safari vehicles, because lions, for example, appear to regard safari vehicles as one entity, rather than a collection of edible primates! Many of the best wildlife lodges are not fenced and allow free movement of all wildlife, so you can expect to be escorted to and from your room or tent before and after dinner by an armed guard. Large mammals may explore camp and lodge surroundings after dark, but typically keep well clear during daylight hours. Exceptions include elephant, impala, bushbuck and some other herbivores which realize that the lodge offers protection from predators. Opportunistic monkeys, and sometimes baboons, frequently raid kitchens and table fruit. Primates can become aggressive once they are accustomed to handouts, so the golden rule is to never feed them, or any other animal.

Naturally, most people will want a record of their safari, so some photography tips are provided on page 26. Perhaps the most important piece of equipment, however, is a pair of binoculars which are not only essential for watching birds but also for looking at larger mammals in detail. Apart from the usual casual clothing one would pack for a holiday in a warm region, you should bear in mind that morning and night game drives in open vehicles can be cool to very cold, so it is advisable to pack a good jacket and woollen hat. A baseball cap and a wide-brimmed hat are also recommended, along with sun protection cream, and anti-malarial medication (check with your doctor).

AFRICA: A CONTINENT OF DIVERSITY

Africa is a continent of incredible diversity. Straddling the equator, and stretching beyond both the Tropic of Cancer and Capricorn, almost every conceivable landscape and climate is present on the giant landmass. From snow-capped peaks to parched deserts, and from dripping rainforests to expansive savannahs, each habitat has its own particular community of plants and animals. No other parts of the world contain as much unaltered habitat, and nowhere are large mammals still so numerous and widespread. All African countries have extensive networks of protected areas and – in many cases – these are actually increasing in size as nature-based tourism becomes an ever more important component of local economies. Nevertheless, Africa's wild places face innumerable threats and challenges as human populations increase, and development goes unchecked. The impacts of man-induced climate change is of growing concern here, as it is around the world.

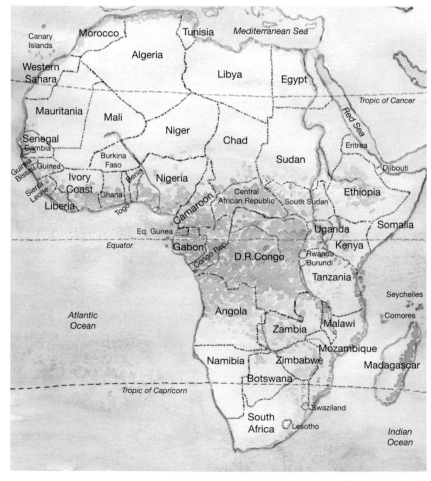

TOPOGRAPHY - HIGH AND LOW

Altitude above sea level is a major factor in terms of Africa's climate, as it determines the vegetation types and distribution of wildlife, as well as the patterns of human settlement. The continent can be divided into "high" and "low" regions, with the land above 3,200 feet (1,000 meters) being more temperate even on the equator. European colonists chose to establish settlements on the higher plateaus, where wheat, tea and livestock such as cattle and sheep were able to thrive. Malaria and most livestock diseases are prolific in hot lowlands, so these areas were spared from much development and still contain some extensive wilderness areas. The Congo Basin and most of West Africa is a steamy wet lowland, while the majority of countries of eastern and southern Africa enjoy the benefits of both temperate and tropical or sub tropical climates. The South African highveld plateau experiences bitterly cold night temperatures during winter (May to August), while high-lying towns such as Nairobi experience cool nights throughout much of the year.

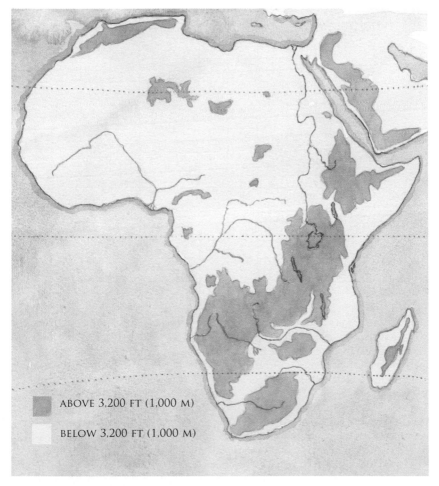

ABOVE 3,200 FT (1,000 M)

BELOW 3,200 FT (1,000 M)

Africa's Climate

Average monthy temperatures min/max in Fahrenheit (white) and Celcius (fawn) for some main cities and wildlife reserves. Actual temperatures may vary more than 10°F (7°F) from the averages below.

LOCALITY	JAN	FEB	MAR	APR	MAY	JUN	JUL	AUG	SEP	OCT	NOV	DEC
Addis Ababa	42/73	48/75	54/77	54/75	54/76	52/68	52/64	52/68	52/75	50/72	48/73	51/73
	6/23	9/24	12/25	12/24	12/24	11/20	11/18	11/20	11/24	10/22	9/22	8/23
Antananarivo	62/82	62/79	61/78	59/77	55/73	51/70	51/68	50/69	52/72	55/73	59/79	61/78
	17/28	17/26	16/25	15/25	13/23	11/21	10/20	10/21	11/23	13/25	15/26	16/26
Brazzaville	70/88	70/90	70/91	72/91	70/90	64/84	63/82	64/84	68/88	70/90	70/88	70/88
	21/31	21/32	21/33	22/33	21/32	18/29	17/28	18/29	20/31	21/32	21/31	21/31
Cape Town	61/79	59/79	57/77	54/73	50/68	46/64	45/63	45/64	46/66	50/70	55/75	59/77
	16/26	15/26	14/25	12/23	10/20	8/18	7/17	7/18	8/19	10/21	13/24	15/25
Hwange	64/85	64/85	62/85	56/83	47/80	42/76	40/76	45/81	54/88	61/90	64/89	64/85
	18/29	18/29	17/29	14/29	9/27	5/24	5/25	7/27	12/31	16/32	18/32	18/30
Kampala	65/84	65/84	64/82	61/81	63/79	63/78	63/78	62/78	63/81	63/82	62/81	62/81
	18/28	18/28	18/27	18/26	17/25	18/26	18/26	17/26	17/27	17/27	17/27	17/27
Kigali	43/68	48/68	46/68	43/68	41/68	37/68	41/68	39/70	37/70	38/68	37/68	39/68
	15/26	15/26	15/25	15/25	14/25	13/24	16/27	15/28	15/28	15/27	13/24	15/24
Kruger	67/89	67/87	63/85	62/85	54/81	48/77	48/77	52/78	55/84	62/85	63/87	67/88
	20/32	20/30	18/29	16/29	12/27	9/25	9/25	11/26	14/28	16/29	18/30	20/31
Mana Pools	71/89	71/89	70/89	67/88	62/85	57/81	56/81	59/86	66/92	73/97	74/95	72/91
	22/32	21/32	21/32	20/31	17/29	14/27	13/27	15/30	19/34	23/36	23/35	22/33
Mombasa	75/88	76/88	77/89	76/87	75/84	75/83	71/81	71/81	72/83	74/85	75/86	76/87
	24/32	24/32	25/32	24/31	23/28	23/28	22/27	22/27	22/28	23/29	24/29	24/30
Nairobi	55/78	56/80	58/78	58/76	58/73	54/70	51/70	52/71	53/76	55/77	56/74	55/75
	12/25	13/26	14/25	14/24	13/22	12/21	11/21	11/21	11/24	14/25	13/24	13/24
Okavango	66/90	66/88	64/88	57/88	48/82	43/77	43/77	48/82	55/91	64/95	66/93	66/93
	19/32	19/31	18/31	14/31	9/28	6/25	6/25	9/28	13/33	18/35	19/34	19/34
Serengeti-Mara	63/86	65/86	65/86	65/82	64/82	64/82	62/82	62/84	64/86	64/86	64/84	64/84
	17/30	18/30	18/30	18/28	17/28	17/28	16/28	16/29	17/30	17/30	17/29	17/29
South Luangwa	68/90	68/88	66/90	64/90	66/88	54/86	52/84	54/86	59/95	68/104	72/99	72/91
	20/32	20/31	19/32	18/32	19/31	12/30	11/29	12/30	15/35	20/40	22/37	22/33
Swakopmund	54/77	54/73	54/73	59/77	59/77	64/82	59/82	59/82	54/77	54/77	54/77	54/77
	12/25	12/23	12/23	15/25	15/25	15/28	15/28	15/28	12/25	12/25	12/25	12/25
Victoria Falls	65/85	64/85	62/85	57/82	49/75	42/76	42/76	47/82	55/89	62/91	64/90	64/86
	18/29	17/29	17/29	14/28	9/24	6/24	6/24	8/28	13/32	17/33	18/32	18/30
Windhoek	63/86	63/84	59/81	55/77	48/72	45/68	45/68	46/73	54/79	57/84	61/84	63/88
	17/30	17/29	15/27	13/25	9/22	7/20	7/20	8/23	12/26	14/29	16/29	17/31
Zanzibar	77/89	77/89	75/89	74/87	72/85	68/85	66/84	66/84	68/84	68/86	73/88	75/88
	25/32	25/32	24/32	23/31	22/29	20/29	19/28	19/28	19/28	21/29	23/31	24/31

Rainfall is seasonal over most of Africa, even at the equator where there are two dry and two wet seasons each year. The East African highlands (including Nairobi and the Serengeti-Mara) receive the highest rainfall between March and May (6.2 inches/160 mm per month) with another peak in October-November (4.5 inches/115 mm per month). In much of southern Africa, there is virtually no rain between May and September, with a monthly average of around 3.5 inches/90 mm in the wet summer (November to March); the southwestern Cape experiences a reverse pattern with an average of 3.3 inches/85 mm per month between May and August. Brazzaville, on the Congo River, has heavy rain from October to May (7 inches/180 mm average per month) but it is comparatively dry from June to August. Namibia's desert coast receives so little rain in any month it is difficult to measure.

AFRICA'S VEGETATION ZONES

Africa can be divided into several broad categories of landscape which are determined by climate (particularly rainfall), altitude, topography and soils - all of which arc interlinked. Geographers refer to these landscapes as vegetation zones (or biomes), and they include well-known types such as forest, desert and grassland. In most cases, these and other vegetation zones do not have well defined boundaries but merge to create zones of transition. On the following pages, the more conspicuous vegetation types are described.

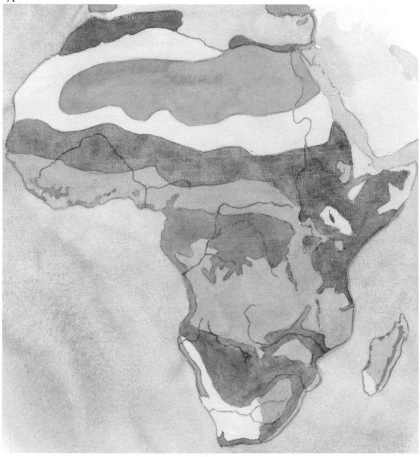

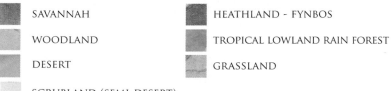

SAVANNAH

WOODLAND

DESERT

SCRUBLAND (SEMI-DESERT)

HEATHLAND - FYNBOS

TROPICAL LOWLAND RAIN FOREST

GRASSLAND

Savannah

The African landscape so often depicted in films - and imagined by travelers - is a park-like vista of grassland dotted with flat-topped trees. This is the savannah, a mosaic of woodland and grassland. The ratio of trees to grass and the species of trees present is determined by rainfall and soil type. This is the dominant habitat in most of the large wildlife reserves in southern and eastern Africa, with thorn trees being conspicuous. Seasonal grass fires are an important mechanism in the maintenance of savannah ecosystems, as they encourage grass growth and limit the spread of woody plants. Large herbivores including giraffe, elephant, zebra, buffalo and wildebeest favor savannah which also supports the highest density of lions and other large predators. Bird diversity is high, with eagles, vultures, bustards, rollers, hornbills, larks, shrikes, starlings and weavers among the conspicuous families.

Woodland

Woodland generally occurs in higher rainfall areas than savannah but often merges with it. Trees are taller and more closely spaced, sometimes with their canopies touching. Much of southern Tanzania, Zambia and Zimbabwe is blanketed in moist *miombo woodland*, while swathes of dry *mopane woodland* occur in northern Botswana and the low-lying parts of Zimbabwe and northeastern South Africa. Browsing herbivores such as Greater Kudu live in woodlands, while Roan and Sable favor grassy clearings. Elephant may be seasonally abundant in mopane woodland. Birds such as woodpeckers, cuckoos, orioles, warblers and sunbirds are often common in woodlands.

SCRUBLAND (SEMI-DESERT)

In low rainfall areas such as the Karoo, Kaokoveld and northern Kenya, short spiny shrubs and occasional small trees (particularly *Acacia*, *Boscia* and *Commiphora*) are interspersed with hardy grasses. Bands of taller trees occur along seasonal streams (drainage lines) where they typically tap into an underground water supply. Aloes, euphorbias and other succulents may proliferate. These landscapes are transformed after good rainfall and typically explode with life for short periods. Springbok, Gerenuk and Cheetah as well as various species of oryx, dikdik and jackals are well-adapted for semi-deserts, while gerbils and other rodents can be seasonally abundant. Bustards, sandgrouse, doves and larks are typical birds, while eagles, goshawks, falcons and other raptors are well-represented.

DESERT

Africa has two true deserts. The Sahara is undoubtedly the world's most famous but it is not known for its wildlife and is not dealt with here. In contrast, the Namib Desert (after which the country of Namibia is named) is an extraordinary wilderness with a host of unique arid-adapted plants and animals. Deserts are characterized by extremely low annual rainfall, although brief periods of bounty follow rare thunderstorms. Large mammals are few and mostly nomadic, but a variety of interesting arid-adapted birds and reptiles are present.

GRASSLAND

On the highveld plateau of South Africa, a prairie-like grassland once dominated the landscape but sadly, intensive agriculture and coal mining have reduced this to a fragment of its former extent and many grassland specialist species are now endangered. Native tree species are largely absent due to winter frosts and regular fires, but invasive alien species such as *Eucalyptus* and Weeping Willow may be locally abundant. Ground orchids and bulbous plants are characteristic, with tree ferns in damp gulleys.

The upland regions of Ethiopia, Kenya, Malawi, Zimbabwe and Tanzania have smaller but often more pristine areas of high altitude grassland. Large mammals are few but birds may be abundant and conspicuous.

HEATHLAND - FYNBOS

This biome is characterized by small- or medium-sized bushes growing on sandy, low-nutrient soils of mountains and flats. In the southwestern Cape it is known as "fynbos" and one of only six "botanical kingdoms" on the planet with over 8,000 unique plant species. Proteas, ericas and restios are key elements along with numerous lilies and bulbs. Mammal and bird diversity is low but there are many endemic species.

A similar-looking heathland exists on the summit of the Drakensberg chain, and the upper reaches of Kilimanjaro, Mount Kenya and the Rwenzoris, but plant diversity is nowhere near as rich as in the Cape Fynbos. Giant Lobelia and Giant Senecio are characteristic plants of these "alpine" heaths and moors.

Temperate Forest

Forest is a community of trees whose canopies interlock such that reduced sunlight inhibits the growth of grass. Cool, temperate forest occurs from the southern Cape into the foothills of the Drakensberg, Rift Valley, Ethiopian Highlands and on the moist slopes of Kilimanjaro, Mount Kenya, Ngorongoro, Usambara and Gorongosa (to name some examples). Palms are absent, but conifers such as *Podocarpus* occur. Mosses, ferns and epiphytic orchids abound, with the height of trees being shorter at higher elevations. Duikers, monkeys and squirrels are typical mammals, with greenbuls, trogons and turacos among the many birds. Mountain Gorillas inhabit the cool, misty forests of the Virungas.

Tropical Lowland Rain Forest

The Congo Basin is the second largest rainforest on the planet, after the Amazon. To the west, the once extensive Guinea forests of the coast have been reduced to fragments between Senegal and Ivory Coast due to human impacts. To the east, however, there are numerous, albeit small, outlying forest patches containing Congo Basin flora and fauna. Uganda's Kibale Forest and the Kakamega Forest of Kenya reveal the former extent of equatorial forest during a wetter era. Equatorial lowland forest is characterised by tall, straight-boled trees with a dense canopy. Larger trees have wide buttresses, and palms are characteristic. Clearings (bais) are a feature of Odzala in the Congo Republic where Forest Elephant, Lowland Gorilla and Bongo are regularly seen. Large mammals are otherwise hard to see, although monkeys of several species are conspicuous and Chimpanzee occurs. Hornbills, barbets, turacos and the strange picathartes are among the birds, while butterflies abound.

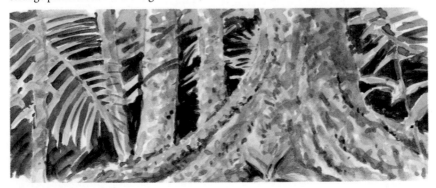

RIVERS, LAKES AND WETLANDS

Africa has several major rivers, including the north-flowing Nile – the world's longest – which empties into the Mediterranean. The Congo River is second only to the Amazon in terms of volume as it drains west into the Atlantic. The Zambezi, Limpopo, Ruvuma, Rufiji, Galana and Tana are the major river systems draining from southern and eastern Africa into the Indian Ocean. The Orange River rises in the Lesotho highlands to drain west across the width of South Africa and into the Atlantic Ocean. These rivers are all fed by smaller tributaries, many of which are seasonal. All of these waterbodies are essential for people and wildlife but many are threatened by inappropriate agriculture, deforestation and erosion of catchments and the impacts of climate change.

A chain of magnificent lakes occurs in the two arms of the Rift Valley, with Turkana, Baringo, Naivasha, Nakuru, Natron, Eyasi and Manyara in the eastern Great Rift Valley, and Albert, Edward, Kivu and Tanganyika in the western Albertine Rift. Africa's largest, Lake Victoria, is set in between the two Rift Valley arms while Lake Malawi is situated where the two arms meet.

Botswana's impressive Okavango Delta is formed by the river of the same name that rises in the Angolan highlands and spills out into the Kalahari Basin. The great Sudd Swamp of South Sudan is largely inaccessible to tourists (although still rich in wildlife) but Zambia's Bangweulu is a similarly productive wetland.

Hippopotamus, Sitatunga and Red Lechwe are restricted to wetlands but most larger mammals depend on fresh water throughout their lives. Pelicans, flamingos, storks, herons, geese, ducks, cormorants, kingfishers, jacanas and migratory sandpipers inhabit various wetland types.

Healthy mountain catchments are vital to ensure the ongoing flow of freshwater into these aquatic systems. Conservation of montane grassland and forest habitat is therefore critical for a wide range of species including our own.

Coasts and Ocean

The shore and seas off Africa's coast support diverse wildlife communities in habitats ranging from kelp beds and coral reefs, to mangroves and pristine beaches. The deep pelagic waters beyond the continental shelf are home to whales, dolphins, sea turtles and sharks, as well as birds such as albatrosses, petrels and shearwaters.

There is a vast difference between the east and west coasts of the continent. The cold Benguela current sweeps north from the Antarctic to bring cool, nutrient-rich water to the western Cape and Namibia, with large numbers of fur seals and gannets thriving in the productive waters. In contrast, the Indian Ocean is warmed by equatorial waters, with coral reefs off the Kenyan, Tanzanian and Mozambican coasts, and palm-fringed islands such as Zanzibar and Seychelles. Fish and other wildlife have been heavily harvested along this tropical coast which has been exploited and fought-over by traders, settlers and locals for centuries. Fortunately, marine reserves in Kenya, Tanzania and elsewhere protect extensive areas.

A few days on an island or beach is a perfect way to end an African safari, with the splendor of a healthy coral reef surpassing most terrestrial habitats in terms of biodiversity and color.

HISTORY OF SAFARI

The modern safari has its origin in the expeditions of European hunters and naturalists who traveled to hitherto uncharted parts of the continent in search of unusual animals for scientific description, or as trophies, during the early part of the nineteenth century. Among the better known explorers and hunters of the 1800s were William Burchell, Cornwallis Harris and Frederick Courtney Selous. Although Selous was undoubtedly in pursuit of macho adventure, thrill and bounty, he eventually proposed that wanton destruction of large mammals ought to be tempered with the British concept of "sportsmanship"; this was in contrast to the African hunters armed by Arab merchants, and the Boer settlers in South Africa, who had set about decimating virtually all large mammals. Within a few decades of the publication of Selous' famous book, *A Hunter's Wanderings in Africa,* the first game control laws were established in most African countries which, in the early part of the 20th century, were European colonies. It is perhaps fitting that one of Africa's largest reserves – the Selous Game Reserve in Tanzania – should be so named, although many conservationists remain horrified at the number of rhino and other animals Selous "bagged" over the years.

It was Kenya and other parts of East Africa that attracted a growing number of American and European trophy hunters. The extravagant and glamorous expeditions of Theodore Roosevelt and others became legendary, as did the often eccentric antics of the foreign and colonial participants. Safari outfitting companies such as Ker & Downey sprung up to service the industry, and professional hunters became established. Needless to say, overland safaris relied heavily upon unheralded gun-bearers and porters until the introduction of motorized transport.

By the 1970s, the idea of a safari based on looking at and photographing game, as opposed to shooting and skinning, had become established. In many national parks and other protected areas, overland safaris were organized, tented camps erected, and lodges constructed. Over time, these tours and facilities have become increasingly sophisticated both in terms of the guided interpretation and the quality of meals, accommodation and transportation which may rival a five-star luxury hotel.

Interestingly, many of the best wildlife-watching experiences still rely on the very same acute observational skills of trackers and patient naturalists upon which the early explorers were dependent. Another thing that has not changed about the safari is the marvelous sense of adventure and wondrous anticipation that comes with every walk or drive in Africa's wild places.

The word "safari" is an Arabic verb which means "to make a journey". This word was infused into the Swahili language where it refers to an expedition or voyage, and subsequently into the English language.

SAFARI TIPS

✸ Read the "Safari Terms" glossary to become familiar with the terminology used in the bush. Once on safari, you will notice that when you ask people what animals they saw on their game drive, they might reply, "elephant, lion, leopard and oryx," when in fact they saw several members of each species. This use of the singular form, when more than one of that species was seen, is common. However, one exception to this rule is saying crocs for crocodile. This form of "Safaricsc" will be used throughout this guide to help separate you from the amateur.

✸ Carry your valuables with you or put them in a room safe or safety deposit box at your lodge or hotel.

✸ Do not call out to a person, signaling with an index finger. This is insulting to most Africans. Instead, use four fingers with your palm facing downward.

✸ During daytime game viewing activities, wear colors that blend in with your surroundings (brown, tan, light green or khaki).

✸ Do not wear perfume, cologne or bright colored clothing while game viewing. Wildlife can detect unnatural smells for miles and unnatural colors for hundreds of yards (meters), making close approaches difficult.

✸ The very few tourists who get hurt on safari are almost always those travelers who ignore the laws of nature and most probably the advice and warnings of their guides. Common sense is the rule.

✸ Do not wade or swim in rivers, lakes or streams unless you know for certain they are free of crocodiles, hippos and bilharzia (a snail-borne disease).

✸ Never walk along the banks of rivers at dawn, dusk or at night. Those who do so may inadvertently cut off a hippo's path and it may charge.

✸ Do not walk close to the edge of a river or lake due to the danger of crocodiles.

Nile Crocodile

✸ Malaria is present in almost all the parks and reserves covered in this guide. Malarial prophylaxis (pills) should be taken and must be prescribed by a physician in the USA but are available without prescription in some countries. Because most malaria-carrying mosquitoes come out from dusk until dawn, during this period you should use mosquito repellent and wear long pants and a long-sleeve shirt or blouse, shoes (not sandals) and socks. For further information see the section on "Health" in the "Resources" section of this book.

✸ Because of the abundance of thorns and sharp twigs, wear closed-toed shoes or boots at night and also during the day if venturing out into the bush. Bring a flashlight and always have it with you at night.

✸ Never venture out of your lodge or camp without your guide, especially at night, dawn or dusk. Remember that wildlife is not confined to the parks and reserves in many countries, and, in fact, roams freely in and around many camps and lodges.

✸ Resist the temptation to jog or walk alone in national parks, reserves or other areas where wildlife exists. To lion and other carnivores, we are just "meat on the hoof" like any other animal – only much slower and less capable of defending ourselves.

"SAFARI TERMS" - A GLOSSARY

4wd: Abbreviated term standing for 4-wheel drive vehicle.

Acacia: Common, dry-country trees and shrubs armed with spines or curved thorns; most have tiny, feathery leaflets.

Adaptation: Structural or functional characteristics that enable an animal or plant to flourish in a particular habitat.

Aloe: A succulent plant of the lily family with thick, pointed leaves and spikes of red or yellow flowers.

Arboreal: Living in trees.

Avifauna: The birdlife of a region.

Bais: A large open area surrounded by equatorial rain forest.

Banda: A basic shelter or hut, often constructed of reeds, bamboo or dry grass.

Bathroom, open-air: A bathroom attached to a chalet or permanent tent that is enclosed on all sides, and does not have a roof.

Boma: A place of shelter, a fortified place, enclosure, community (East Africa).

Browse: To feed on leaves.

Bum crawl: To move while sitting on the ground by using your arms for propulsion – used primarily to approach wildlife more closely while on a walk.

Calving season: A period during which the young of a particular species are born. Not all species have calving seasons. Most calving seasons occur shortly after the rainy season begins. Calving seasons can also differ for the same species from one region to another.

Camp: Camping sites; also refers to lodging in chalets, bungalows or tents in a remote location.

Canopy: The uppermost layer of a tree.

Caravan: A camping trailer.

Carnivore: An animal that lives by consuming the flesh of other animals.

Carrion: The remains of dead animals.

Charter flight (private): An air charter booked from one point to another for a private party. The plane is not available for the guests for the entire day – only for the route for which they have paid.

Charter flight (scheduled): An air charter that is used by different parties of guests. Most scheduled air charters make multiple stops on a route, picking up and dropping off passangers. Travelers preferring not having stops should consider booking a private charter.

Crepuscular: Active at dusk or dawn.

Diurnal: Active by day.

Dung: Feces, or "droppings" of animals.

Dung midden: A pile of animal droppings, used as a territorial marker.

Aloe

En suite: Refers to a bathroom that is within a room, chalet or tent.

Endangered: An animal that is threatened with extinction.

Endemic: Native and restricted to a particular area.

Estrus: A state of sexual readiness in a female mammal when she is capable of conceiving.

Fixed tented camp: (also known as "permanent" tented camp) Applies to a safari camp that is not moved.

Fly Camp: A mobile tented camp, generally with small tents and separate shower and toilet tents that can easily be transported to remote areas. Fly camps can also be of a "luxury" standard.

Game: Large mammals.

Gestation: The duration of pregnancy.

Grazer: An animal that eats grass.

G.R.: An abbreviation for "Game Reserve."

Habitat: An animal's or plant's surroundings that offers everything it needs to live.

Habituated: An animal that has been introduced to and has accepted the presence of human beings.

Herbivore: An animal that consumes plant matter.

Hide: A camouflaged structure (blind) from which one can view or photograph wildlife without being seen.

Home range: An area familiar to (utilized by) an adult animal but not marked or defended as a territory.

Kopje (pronounced kopee): Rock formations that protrude from the savannah and are not part of a range.

Koppie: Same as kopje (East Africa).

Kraal: Same as boma (southern Africa).

LBJ: "Little brown job" referring to a small nondescript bird.

Mammal: A warm-blooded animal that produces milk for its young.

Migratory: A species or population that moves seasonally to an area with predictably better food, grazing or water.

Midden: Usually, an accumulation of dung deposited in the same spot as a scent-marking behavior.

Mokoro: A traditional-style canoe, which is used for exploring the shallow waters of the Okavango Delta.

Nocturnal: Active during the night.

N.P.: An abbreviation for "National Park".

N.R.: An abbreviation for "Nature Reserve".

Omnivore: An animal that eats both plant and animal matter.

Pan: A shallow depression that seasonally fills with rainwater.

Pelagic: Ocean-dwelling.

Permanent tented camp: Safari camps that are not moved. The tents are normally very large with en suite bathrooms, and often set on raised decks.

Predator: An animal that hunts and kills other animals for food.

Prey: An animal hunted by a predator for food.

Pride: A group or family of lions.

Raptor: Bird of prey such as an eagle or hawk.

Resident: Not prone to migration; present in a given area throughout the year.

Rondavel: An African-style structure for accommodation.

Ruminant: A mammal with a complex stomach and which chews the cud.

Rutting: The behavioral pattern exhibited by the male of the species during a time period when mating is most prevalent, e.g., impala, wildebeest.

Sala: An additional private lounge area located off a tent's deck and features comfortable seating or a bed for relaxing.

Savannah: An open, grassy landscape with widely scattered trees.

Scavenger: An animal that feeds on carrion or the remains of animals killed by predators.

Shower, bush, bucket or safari: (Usually associated with a mobile tented camp) Upon request by the guest, water is heated by a campfire and then placed in a raised container over a shower tent.

Species: A group of plants or animals with specific characteristics in common; in particular, the ability to reproduce among themselves.

Spoor: A track (i.e., footprint) or trail made by an animal.

Symbiosis: An association of two different organisms in a relationship that may benefit one or both partners.

Tarmac: An asphalt-paved road.

Termitarium: A mound constructed by termite colonies.

Terrestrial: Ground living.

Kopje/Koppie

Territory: An area occupied, scent-marked and defended from rivals of the same species.

Toilet, long-drop: A permanent bush toilet or "outhouse" in which a toilet seat has been placed over a hole that is dug about 6 feet (2 m) deep.

Toilet, safari or short-drop: A temporary bush toilet, usually a toilet tent used on mobile tented safaris in which a toilet seat is placed over a hole that has been dug about 3 feet (1 m) deep.

Tracking: Following and observing animal spoor by foot.

Traversing Area: The land used by a particular lodge or safari operator.

Tribe: A group of people united by traditional ties.

Troop: A group of apes or monkeys.

Ungulate: A hooved animal.

Veld: Southern African term for open land.

Vlei: An open grassy area, usually along a drainage line and with trees along the edge.

Wallow: The art of keeping cool and wet, usually in a muddy pool (i.e., rhinoceros, buffalo and warthog).

PHOTOGRAPHY ON SAFARI

You are going to see some beautiful and amazing things on safari, and it has never been easier to document those moments and to share them with others. Your safari will be filled with photographic opportunities but many animals will be seen just once, and interesting events usually occur unpredictably whether in terms of action or dramatic lighting.

To document your safari fully, you should aim to take photographs of the landscapes that you travel through (both inside and outside protected areas) as well as the wildlife that you get close to. Many people return from safari with super close-up shots of lions or gorillas but no record of the savannahs or forests that these animals inhabit.

In terms of equipment, there are two basic kinds of digital cameras (as there are conventional film cameras). One kind with a built-in lens (comparable to the old "instamatic") and the other kind with detachable lenses. For photographing wildlife, it is important to be able to zoom close to your subject, so you'll need a minimum of 10x "optical zoom", or in the case of digital SLR, a lens of at least 300 mm. Larger magnifications will be required for photographing birds. Most quality equipment has "image stabilization" technology which reduces blur caused by slight movement, and this is very valuable on safari.

Many digital cameras (including SLRs) have a video option and the quality offered is constantly improving. There is also a bewildering variety of dedicated camcorders. Many camcorders have optical zoom of 20x or more which is ideal for shooting wildlife, but don't be fooled by high "digital zoom" statistics as these exaggerated magnifications may produce images that are highly pixelated (broken up into small squares) and unsatisfactory.

The quality of any still photograph is dependent upon lighting. For this reason, the best wildlife photographs are taken in the early morning or late afternoon when sunlight comes at an angle. In the middle of the day, sunlight comes from directly overhead which creates hard black shadows on and around your subject matter.

Choosing where to place your subject in the viewfinder of your camera is known as composition. This is the most vital aspect of photography and separates great images from ordinary ones. Things to avoid are chopping off part of your subject (for example, feet), zooming in too tightly, or placing your subject in the very center of your frame. It is much more pleasing on the eye if an animal is pictured off center and thus "looking into" a space. Likewise, placing the horizon of your landscape pictures in the bottom or top third of the frame (depending on whether the sky or foreground is of more interest), rather than in the very center, will create a more interesting perspective.

Malachite Kingfisher

Duncan Butchart

As already mentioned, many cameras have "image stabilization" technology. Blurred photographs are caused mostly by camera shake, which is the result of not holding the camera firmly, or not selecting the correct exposure options and thus using long shutter speeds. The use of a tripod is hard to beat but this is not very practical on a safari. Some travelers will extend one leg of a tripod or use a monopod. Alternately, use a soft "beanbag". Simply pack a small cloth bag in your travel kit and then fill it with dry beans (or rice) when you get to Africa. This will then provide you with a flexible yet solid support for your camera. In the absence of a tripod or beanbag, a rolled-up jacket or sweater placed on a window ledge or vehicle rooftop will provide decent support.

Vehicle vibration is probably the major cause of blurred images, so ask your guide to turn off the vehicle engine when you wish to take photographs so as to avoid this.

It is obviously necessary to have all the required battery chargers for your equipment when you travel. An electrical adaptor will also be important for connecting to local power supplies. Even the most remote safari camps usually have a generator capable of charging batteries. Consider taking two batteries for each camera, so that you always have a backup.

Take two or three memory cards and consider copying the data (i.e. your images) onto a backup device. Many travelers now carry tablets or laptops for copying image files onto; these instruments also allow you to better preview and edit photographs or video clips on the spot. It is wise to store cameras and lenses in plastic ziplock bags to protect them from dust and humidity.

Conservation in Africa

Africa is blessed with some of the most extensive wilderness areas on planet Earth – the Serengeti, Okavango and Congo Basin are among the most spectacular. A look at any map will show that a large proportion of land has been set aside as national parks or game reserves in many countries, with Botswana (39%) and Tanzania (15%) among those with the greatest percentage of land devoted to wildlife.

In most cases, these national parks were founded by colonial governments prior to 1960; although there are some notable exceptions such as in Uganda where three new national parks were established in 1993. Many of the national parks were initially set aside as hunting reserves for settlers. Rural people, most of whom were dependent upon wildlife for their sustenance, were deliberately excluded. It was because wildlife was primarily seen as something to pursue, hunt and kill that the word "game" (as in "fair game") came into use, and that is why wildlife reserves are still today known as game reserves (even though hunting is prohibited). In time, hunting came to an end in the national parks because the wildlife resource was seen to be finite, and a "conservation" ethic took root.

Most early national parks were run along military lines, and local people who attempted to capture "game" were regarded as the enemy – poachers to be punished and jailed. This approach to national parks undoubtedly safe-guarded large areas of wild land (for which modern-day conservationists can be grateful), but, at the same time, it alienated local communities which came to regard the reserves – and sometimes even the animals themselves – as symbols of repression.

In the 1990s, conservation philosophy in Africa swung toward initiatives that brought communities and wildlife closer together. Two things had become obvious. First, even the largest national parks contained only portions of ecosystems; many species extended their range beyond the boundaries. Second, a protectionist approach dictated to local people by governments or enthusiastic foreign environmentalists would have very little chance of succeeding in the absence of any real incentives.

While the borders of most national parks remain intact, innovative community-based programs encourage local people to develop sustainable resource utilization in adjoining areas. This concept serves to maintain natural ecosystems beyond the borders of protected areas, as opposed to the establishment of marginal farming activities that generally destroy or displace all wildlife.

Non-consumptive utilization, such as ecotourism, provides jobs and financial returns to communities, while the harvesting of thatching grass, honey, wood and wildlife, such as antelope and fish, provides direct sustenance. In essence, these programs set out to restore ownership and responsibility for wildlife to the local

White Rhinoceros are under intensive pressure from poachers

Duncan Butchart

people. In areas of low seasonal rainfall (much of eastern and southern Africa) the financial returns from wildlife have proven to exceed most forms of agriculture or livestock farming.

Perhaps the most interesting development in recent years are the so-called transfrontier initiatives, such as Peace Parks, which link existing protected areas across national boundaries. These potentially massive areas not only allow for greater expansion of wildlife but also provide developing countries with growth points for ecotourism and stimulate greater economic cooperation between neighbors.

There can be little doubt that ecotourism has made a significant contribution to the conservation of wildlife in Africa, through job creation and the stimulation of local economies. Another important benefit is that many young African people have been reconnected to the wildlife that their grandparents interacted with and depended upon, because they have become skilled and articulate guides, hosts and hostesses.

There is much to be positive about for the future of African wildlife. As many governments recognize the value of ecotourism, many rural people are deriving real benefits from sustainable resource use, and protected areas are actually increasing in size. But conservation is not just about elephants and other large mammals – it is about the land itself. Much still has to be achieved outside of Africa's savannah biome, because rainforests, temperate grasslands and specialized ecosystems such as mangroves shrink daily and rare, geographically isolated species face extinction. Taking a safari to Africa in itself is a significant donation to conserving wildlife!

AFRICAN WORLD HERITAGE SITES

The United Nations Educational, Scientific and Cultural Organization (UNESCO) has a focused goal to protect and embrace the past for future generations to enjoy. World Heritage Sites are chosen based on their unique and diverse natural and cultural legacy. The preservation of these sites around the world is considered to be of outstanding value to humanity. Below is a list of World Heritage Sites in eastern, central and southern Africa as well as in Madagascar and Seychelles.

BOTSWANA
Tsodilo Hills.

ETHIOPIA
Simien N.P.
Rock-Hewn Churches, Lalibela.
Fasil Ghebbi, Gondar Region.
Aksum.
Lower Valley of the Awash.
Lower Valley of the Omo.
Tiya.
Harar Jugol: Fortified Historic Town.

KENYA
Lake Turkana N.P.
Mt. Kenya N.P. / Natural Forest.
Fort Jesus, Mombasa.
Great Rift Valley Lake System.
Lamu Old Town.
Sacred Mijikenda Kaya Forests.

MADAGASCAR
Rainforests of Atsinanana.
Royal Hill of Ambohimanga.
Tsingy de Bemaraha N.R.

MALAWI
Lake Malawi N.P.
Chongoni Rock Art Area.

MAURITIUS
Aapravasi Ghat.
Le Morne Cultural Landscape.

MOZAMBIQUE
Ilha de Mozambique.

NAMIBIA
Twyfelfontein.

SEYCHELLES
Aldabra Atoll.
Vallee de Mai N.R.

SOUTH AFRICA
Fossil Hominid Sites of Sterkfontein,
   Swartkrans, Kromdraai and Environs.
iSimangaliso Wetland Park.
Robben Island.
uKhahlamba/Drakensberg Park.
Mapungubwe Cultural Landscape.
Cape Floral Region Protected Area.
Vredefort Dome.
Richtersveld Cultural & Botanical Landscape.

TANZANIA
Ngorongoro Conservation Area.
Ruins of Kikwa Kisiwani and Ruins of
   Songo Mnara.
Serengeti N.P.
Selous G.R.
Kilimanjaro N.P.
Stone Town of Zanzibar.
Kondoa Rock Art Sites.

UGANDA
Bwindi Impenetrable N.P.
Ruwenzori Mountains N.P.
Tombs of Buganda Kings at Kasubi.

ZAMBIA
Mosi-oa-Tunya / Victoria Falls.

ZIMBABWE
Mana Pools N.P., Sapi and Chewore.
Great Zimbabwe National Monument.
Khami Ruins National Monument.
Mosi-oa-Tunya / Victoria Falls.
Matobo Hills.

AFRICAN MAMMALS

Africa has the greatest mammal diversity of any continent with over 1,000 species south of the Sahara. Over half of these are bats, rodents and shrews but the diversity of larger mammals is still unrivalled.

Today, wild populations of large mammals are confined to 'protected areas' which include national parks and game reserves as well as the sometimes vast "hunting concessions" of Tanzania, Zambia and elsewhere. Big mammals need big ranges, not only for themselves but for the dispersal of their offspring.

In recent years, there has been much research on the classification and naming of mammals, with molecular studies based on DNA analysis. In many cases, however, these molecular results are controversial because they are not reflected by morphological data (body structure) and thus not accepted by all ecologists and scientists. Taxonomy is the science of defining groups of biological organisms on the basis of shared characteristics and giving names to these animals and plants. Taking antelope as an example, several species are divided into local races (sub-species) and some taxonomists now regard these forms as distinct species. In this new edition, we revert to a more traditional and conservative arrangement of the African mammals, largely following the six volume *Mammals of Africa* by Jonathan Kingdon *et al* (Bloomsbury, 2013).

MAMMAL WATCHING

The savannahs of Africa are blessed with the greatest assemblage of large mammals of any region on Earth. But in addition to the spectacular and charismatic lion, giraffe, elephant and others, there are a host of smaller, but no less fascinating mammals which make every safari a revelation.

Larger mammals are best watched from inside a safari vehicle, as the majority of animals in national parks regard this as non-threatening. It is for this reason that your guide will typically advise you to remain seated when watching lion, cheetah and other species which have learned to avoid people and will usually panic and bolt when confronted with an upright human figure. Viewing from a boat or "pop-top" vehicle roof is also non-threatening to most mammals.

Finding mammals to watch and photograph is a combination of luck and awareness of a particular species' preferred habitat and habits. Skilled local trackers often display remarkable abilities to find and follow the footprints and other signs left by mammals, so it is wise to make use of their abilities where possible. In national parks and other protected areas, larger mammals often allow a close approach for photography as they are used to seeing safari vehicles. This is not the case in some of the more remote wilderness regions, where wildlife is less habituated to human presence and is more difficult to approach closely.

It is important to bear in mind that sensitivity is paramount with all wildlife watching to ensure that animals are not unduly disturbed, threatened or forced to behave in an unnatural way. Virtually every instance of a large mammal harming a human is a result of not allowing space for an animal to retreat. One of the most productive and exciting situations in which to watch mammals is at a waterhole; it is here that various species come together and where predators frequently lie in wait to ambush their prey.

Smaller, mostly nocturnal mammals pose a different challenge and it is often necessary to employ a wait-and-watch approach. Again, the expertise of a guide who may know the whereabouts of an active burrow or den site, might afford the chance to see fascinating creatures such as Aardvark, Honey Badger or Springhare. These and other denizens of the African night may also be encountered on wildlife reserve "night drives" when the sensitive use of a spotlight picks up their reflective eyes.

On the following pages are illustrations and descriptive texts on the mammals which you are most likely to encounter on a safari in east and southern Africa, as well as several species characteristic of the tropical rainforests of the Congo Basin and the island of Madagascar.

GALAGOS (BUSHBABIES)

Related to the lemurs of Madagascar, Africa's smallest primates are arboreal and strictly nocturnal. Most species have loud calls, some resembling the wail of a human baby and this has given them their alternate name of "bushbaby". All galagos have exceptional eyesight and are able to see up to 100 feet (30 m) using starlight alone. These agile primates have prodigious leaping abilities and can cover over 6 feet (2 m) in a single, elastic bound. Like most other primates, bushbabies are omnivorous, feeding on acacia gum, berries, insects, and the eggs and nestlings of small birds. Galagos live in small family groups led by mature females, with territories being advertised by calling and scent-marking - a process where individuals urinate on their hands and feet to leave distinctive odor trails on favored pathways. Night drives offer the best chance of seeing these interesting mammals, the eyes of which reflect strongly in spotlight.

There are around 20 species of galago, but with little overlap in range among members of the same genus, most parts of Africa have no more than two species in one locality. The similarly nocturnal but short-tailed Potto is a strange and rarely-seen nocturnal primate of the Congo basin, the range of which extends into Uganda and western Kenya.

LESSER GALAGO
Galago senegalensis
L:16 in. (40 cm)
W: 6-9 oz (150-250 g)

GREATER GALAGO
Otelemur crassicaudatus
L: 30 in. (76 cm)
W: 2-3 lb (1-1.4 kg)

BABOONS

Baboons are terrestrial monkeys and among the most entertaining of African animals to watch, perhaps because they exhibit many behaviors rather similar to our own. Troops typically number between 20 and 80 individuals, although bigger aggregations of over 100 members are not uncommon. A troop consists of several kinship groups of adult females and their offspring, as well as a number of mature, sexually-active males. There is a strict hierarchy among the females and the males, with individual males generally having exclusive mating rights to certain kinship groups. Immature males are tolerated within the troop until they reach five years of age, after which they attempt to join neighboring troops.

Individual male baboons are formidable animals armed with large canine teeth, and fear only Lions and large male Leopards. When two or more male baboons are together, even these predators usually give them a wide berth. This partial immunity from predation has allowed baboons to develop a terrestrial lifestyle, although constant vigilance is required to keep the young out of danger. Baboons frequently forage alongside antelope as the acute hearing of these herbivores provides an early warning against predators. At night, baboons gather to roost in large trees along watercourses or on steep rock faces.

Like other primates, baboons are omnivorous. The troop forages in a loose group, digging up succulent roots, turning over rocks in search of insects and scorpions, gorging themselves on fruit and berries, or wading into shallow pools for waterlily tubers. The newborn fawns of gazelle and antelope may be preyed upon by adult male baboons. Baboons can become a pest in agricultural areas as they raid orchards and feed on crops, so they are often persecuted by farmers. They can even become a menace around safari lodges, where "baboon chasers" are sometimes employed to discourage them.

Most baboon species favor open savannah or grassy hillsides, but the Mandrill and Drill (confined to Cameroon where it is critically endangered) occur in primary rainforest.

OLIVE BABOON
Papio anubis
L: 34-62 in. (85-150 cm)
Wm: 46-96 lb (21-43 kg)

Rear
foot
print

Front
foot
print

CHACMA BABOON
Papio ursinus
L: 34-62 in. (85-150 cm)
W: 46-96 lb (male) (21-43 kg)

HAMADRYAS BABOON
(SACRED BABOON)
Papio hamadryas
L: 35-54 in. (80-130 cm)
W: 25-48 lb (10-20 kg)

GELADA BABOON
Theropithecus gelada
L:42-48 in. (105-120 cm)
W:30-45 lb (14-20 kg)

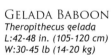

MANDRILL
Mandrillus sphinx
L:42-48 in. (105-120 cm)
W:30-45 lb (14-20 kg)

Monkeys

Monkeys occur throughout the wooded regions of Africa, with the greatest diversity of species living in the forests of central and eastern Africa. These primates are strictly arboreal and although some spend part of their time foraging on the ground, they quickly retreat into trees when disturbed.

There are two primary groups of African monkeys – the colobus and the so-called "cheek-pouch monkeys" which are represented by the guenons (typical monkeys), the mangabeys and the baboons (featured on the previous pages).

The Vervet Monkey is the most widespread of the guenons, occurring in savannah woodland rather than forest. Vervets live in troops of between eight and fifty individuals which comprise several family groups in a strict hierarchy. The offspring of high ranking females are accorded a position in the troop just below their mothers and gain priority for food above adults of a lower ranking family. One or more adult males – immigrants from other families – are key members of the troops. Young males transfer to other troops to prevent inbreeding with their siblings. The diet consists of berries, seedpods, tree sap, flowers, insects, reptiles and nestling birds. Vervets quickly adapt to human settlements and learn to raid orchards and kitchens. Visitors to wildlife reserves should not feed monkeys as this encourages them to live on easy handouts and they rapidly become real pests.

The forest-dwelling Blue, Sykes' and Samango Monkeys are closely related and regarded as a single, regionally variable, species by some authors. The Samango and Sykes' occur on the eastern coastal lowlands, while the Blue Monkey occupies higher altitudes on northern Tanzania, Kenya and Ethiopia. The agile and attractive Red-tailed Monkey lives in lowland rainforest of the Congo basin, but extends east to Uganda and western Kenya. The relatively short-tailed Bale Monkey is a vulnerable species endemic to Ethiopia, while the Golden, Le Hoest's and De Brazza Monkeys are confined in East Africa to relict forests of the Rift Valley. The terrestrial, long-limbed Patas Monkey is primarily a species of the semi-arid Sahel belt south of the Sahara, but small populations exist in northern Uganda, Kenya and Tanzania.

Colobus are entirely vegetarian and are unique among African primates in lacking a thumb. Their five forward-facing digits are unable to grasp moving objects such as live prey while the complex stomach can hold a third of their body weight in undigested leaves. With chemicals able to break down cellulose and detoxify plant compounds, colobus are browsers of the forest canopy. In eastern Africa, the Black-and-White Colobus has two distinct forms, with the short-coated subspecies (with white-tipped tail) in the lower altitudes surrounding Lake Victoria, and the longer-coated subspecies (with completely white tail) in high-altitude forests of Mount Kenya, Meru and Kilimanjaro. The smaller Zanzibar Red Colobus occurs only in the Jozani Forest of Zanzibar where it is readily observed although fewer than 1,500 survive.

The mangabeys are forest-dwelling monkeys of central and western Africa.

BLACK-AND-WHITE COLOBUS
Colobus guereza
L :50-60 in. (1.2-1.5 m)
W:14-32 lb (6.5-14 kg)

VERVET MONKEY
Cercopithecus pygerythrus
L:40-75 in. (1-2 m)
W:9-16 lb (4-8 kg)

BLUE MONKEY
Cercopithecus mitis
L: 42-75 in.(1-2 m)
W:9-16 lb (4-8 kg)

Rear foot print of
Cercopithecus
monkeys

RED-TAILED MONKEY
Cercopithecus ascanius
L: 42-75 in.(1-2 m)
W:9-16 lb (4-8 kg)

RED-CAPPED MANGABEY
Cercocebus torquatus
L: 42-75 in.(1-2 m)
W:11-16 lb (5-8 kg)

PUTTY-NOSED MONKEY
Cercopithecus nictitans
L:40-75 in. (1-2 m)
W:9-16 lb (4-8 kg)

37

GORILLAS

Gorillas are the largest of the apes – ground-dwelling and herbivorous residents of evergreen forest. Mountain Gorillas are among the world's most critically endangered mammals, with only around 800 surviving in two isolated populations: some 400 on the forested slopes of the Virunga Volcanoes (shared by Rwanda, Uganda and the Democratic Republic of Congo) and a similar number in the Bwindi Impenetrable Forest of western Uganda. These are the only suitable habitats remaining for the species and they occur at maximum density. The priority for conservationists is therefore to safeguard the Virunga and Bwindi forests in perpetuity.

Gorillas live in troops led by a dominant adult male, whose massive size inspires respect and confidence among the family members. This so-called 'silverback' leads the family troop, deciding where to forage, rest and sleep within their home range. Unlike the closely-related Chimpanzee (and us humans, for that matter) the gorilla is entirely vegetarian, favoring a few selected leafy plants such as wild celery and bamboo shoots.

Over the past two decades, various Mountain Gorilla troops in the Virunga and Bwindi forests have been sensitively habituated to researchers, wildlife-guards and small groups of ecotourists. Watching gorillas in their natural habitat is not only one of the most enthralling wildlife experiences imaginable, it is also a way of ensuring the conservation of gorilla habitat, as local communities and national governments derive tangible economic benefits from ecotourism.

Up to 200,000 Western Gorillas occur in the forest of the Congo Basin, but their habitat is shrinking and they are hunted for the "bushmeat" trade.

MOUNTAIN GORILLA
Gorilla beringei
H:5-6 ft (1.4-1.8 kg)
Wf:187 lb (85 kg) Wm:352 lb (160 kg)

WESTERN GORILLA
Gorilla gorilla

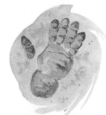

Rear foot print

CHIMPANZEE

Chimpanzees are the closest relatives of humankind and geneticists have determined that our two species share 98% of their DNA. It is not surprising then, that these muscular primates display numerous behaviors which make them fascinating to observe. They have been the subject of intense study for over three decades at Gombe Stream in Tanzania, and primatologists have observed and monitored them at numerous other localities in central and eastern Africa.

Chimps live in communities which usually number up to ten but may be very much larger depending upon habitat and food resources. The communities are dominated by mature males which spend their whole life in an ancestral home range. Sexually mature female offspring must move to neighboring troops. Infants are born after an eight month pregnancy, weaned at five years and become sexually active at around eight, although they cannot conceive until the age of 12 or 13.

Forest of one kind or another is the habitat of Chimpanzees and they may also be seen on the fringe of savannah in riverine forest. They are omnivorous, feeding on fruit as well as insects (especially termites), bird eggs and nestlings, small mammals and even monkeys, which are pursued and trapped in a carefully coordinated hunt. Social grooming is important group behavior that maintains the hierarchy among adults. Facial expressions are as varied as our own, and over 30 recognizable sounds are made. Young chimps laugh, tickle each other and cry.

CHIMPANZEE
Pan troglodytes
H:4-5 ft (120-152 cm)
W:66-120 lb (30-55 kg)

Rear foot print

The Bonobo (*Pan paniscus*) was formerly known as the Pygmy Chimpanzee although it is not significantly smaller than the "true" chimp. It is distinguished by its longer limbs, dark face and tail tuft. The Bonobo is restricted to the Congo Basin rainforest south of the Congo River with fewer than 50,000 surviving.

LEMURS

Lemurs are 'primitive primates' or prosimians – related to the galagos (bushbabies) of Africa, and the lorises and tarsiers of tropical Asia. Unlike their relatives, however, many of the lemurs are diurnal – active by day – and readily observed.

Lemurs are confined to the island of Madagascar, where up to 100 species are now recognized. Many more have become extinct since humans found and colonized the huge island about 2,000 years ago; the fossil remains of one of these was a giant lemur about the size of a gorilla! The clearing of forests for cultivation and hunting for food subsequently caused the extinction of this and numerous other lemur species.

The surviving diversity of lemurs range in size from the 17 lb (8 kg) Indri to the tiny Pygmy Mouse-Lemur at less than an ounce (25 g). The majority of species are arboreal, but the Ring-tailed Lemur and Verreaux's Sifaka are terrestrial - the sight of them bounding along the ground is a highlight for many ecotourists. All lemurs are incredibly agile and capable of prodigious leaps and jumps.

Interestingly, and in contrast to monkeys and apes, lemur social groups are led by dominant females rather than males. Territories are scent-marked but some species are very vocal; the haunting song of the Indri is an unforgettable sound. The sense of smell is highly developed in lemurs and may explain the long, dog-like snouts of most species. In general, smaller lemurs are primarily insectivorous, while larger species are vegetarian. Most lemurs are opportunistic, however, and will feed on termites, berries and so on, when these are available. The strange Aye-aye feeds primarily on beetle larvae.

VERREAUX'S SIFAKA
Propithecus verreauxi
L:3.2 ft (100 cm) incl.tail
W:7.5 lb (3.5 kg)

RING-TAILED LEMUR
Lemur catta
L:3.5 ft (110 cm) incl.tail
W:4.5 lb (2.5 kg)

Rear foot print

GRAY
MOUSE-LEMUR
Microcebus murinus
L:6 in (14 cm)
W: 1-3 oz (30-70g)

INDRI
Indri indri
L:2.4 ft (75 cm)
W:17 lb (8 kg)

AYE-AYE
Daubentonia
madagascariensis
L:3 ft (95 cm)
W:4 lb (2 kg)

BLACK-AND-WHITE
RUFFED LEMUR
Varecia variegata
L:4 ft (120 cm) incl.tail
W:8 lb (4 kg)

RED-FRONTED
BROWN LEMUR
Eulemur rufus
L:3.2 ft (100 cm) incl.tail
W:5 lb (2.3 kg)

41

JACKALS

Close relatives of coyotes and foxes, jackals are intelligent and highly adaptable carnivores. In addition to carrion which is scavenged from kills made by larger predators or natural mortalities, rodents, reptiles, frogs, ground birds, beetles and other insects are all preyed upon. In parts of East Africa, Golden Jackals regularly capture and eat Lesser Flamingos. Jackals frequently follow hunting Lion and Cheetah, shadow Spotted Hyena clans, or rush to a site where vultures are descending from the sky. At the huge seal colonies on Namibia's coast, large numbers of Black-backed Jackals survive on natural mortalities and seal pups.

Jackals are a great advertisement for monogamy. Pairs stay together for life, share duties in raising litters of pups in underground dens, and put themselves at risk to defend one another. Pairs defend their territory rigorously against rivals of their own species. Both sexes are vociferous, maintaining contact and warding off rivals with howling cries and echoing calls.

In the Serengeti-Ngorongoro ecosystem, all three species of jackal may be seen together. In areas where humans have encroached into wild habitats, jackals are able to flourish by living on farmlands and the outskirts of cities.

BLACK-BACKED JACKAL
Canis mesomelas
L:40-54 in. (1-1.3 m)
W:20-28 lb (9-14 kg)

GOLDEN JACKAL
Canis aureus
L:40-54 in. (1-1.3 m)
W:20-28 lb (9-14 kg)

SIDE-STRIPED JACKAL
Canis adustus
L:40-54 in. (1-1.3 m)
W:20-28 lb (9-14 kg)

Foxes and Ethiopian Wolf

Both the Bat-eared Fox and Cape Fox are small members of the canine family which prey largely upon insects although they will occasionally take small rodents and reptiles. They are most active after dark, but are frequently seen during the daytime in cooler weather.

The Bat-eared Fox occurs in two widely separated parts of Africa – the semi-arid Kalahari-Karoo region of southern Africa, and the scrub-grasslands of eastern Africa. This attractive little fox uses its huge cup-shaped ears to detect the movements of termites and other subterranean insects which are then swiftly dug up with the front paws. Pairs raise litters of four to six pups which will remain with their parents for a year or more. These offspring sometimes help to raise their parent's next litter although they must eventually move on to establish their own territory. Leopard and Martial Eagles are feared predators.

The shy Cape Fox is found only in the southwestern part of the continent, where individuals and pairs may be encountered in the Kalahari, Karoo and Namib ecosystems.

The Ethiopian Wolf is critically endangered and now confined to just a few localities in moorland on the high plateau of Ethiopia. Although related to the true wolf, it feeds largely on rodents. Packs consist of two or more adult females and up to five related males.

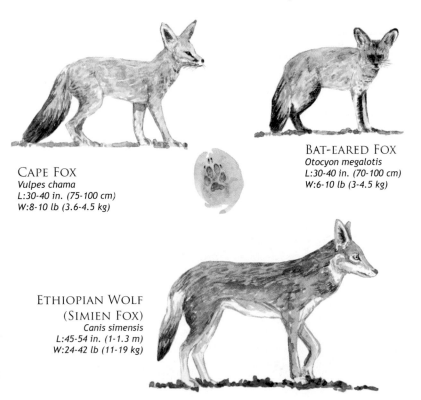

CAPE FOX
Vulpes chama
L:30-40 in. (75-100 cm)
W:8-10 lb (3.6-4.5 kg)

BAT-EARED FOX
Otocyon megalotis
L:30-40 in. (70-100 cm)
W:6-10 lb (3-4.5 kg)

ETHIOPIAN WOLF
(SIMIEN FOX)
Canis simensis
L:45-54 in. (1-1.3 m)
W:24-42 lb (11-19 kg)

43

AFRICAN WILD DOG (PAINTED DOG)

This fascinating, sociable carnivore lives in packs averaging ten adults and their offspring. The lineage of the pack is split along gender lines, with all females usually being related, and all males typically being siblings. An "alpha" female is the only pack member which gives birth, but all help to feed and safeguard her litter of pups. This dominant female seems to dictate pack movements and the selection of a den site.

Litters of up to 16 pups are born blind and helpless in an underground burrow, usually at the coldest time of the year (May to July in southern Africa). The pups spend the first three months within the den, but the timing is perfect, for when they are at their most demanding in terms of food provision, the invariably abundant Impala have dropped their lambs, which makes hunting easy for the adults.

Few predators are as efficient as the Wild Dog which enjoys a hunting success rate of around 80%, due to pack cooperation and individual stamina. Impala are the most frequent prey species over much of the dogs' range.

Northern Botswana, Zambia, Zimbabwe and southern Tanzania support the greatest number of Wild Dog, which is considered one of Africa's most threatened larger mammals with fewer than 5,000 individuals surviving. Good numbers also occur in South Africa's Kruger National Park and packs have been successfully introduced to other South African reserves. Direct persecution by stock farmers, wire snares, and diseases such as canine distemper and rabies threaten wild dogs throughout their range. Because feral dogs are often a significant problem outside of protected areas, some conservationists argue that renaming the species as the "Painted Dog" might help to eliminate confusion and unnecessary persecution of these endangered animals in rural districts adjacent to protected areas.

AFRICAN WILD DOG
Lycaon pictus
L: 42-56 in (75-110 cm)
W:45-55 lb (20-25 kg)

Pup

SPOTTED HYENA

Few animals have attracted such disparagement from humans as the Spotted Hyena – long regarded as a cowardly scavenger dependent upon the leftovers of Lion. In reality, the Spotted Hyena is an efficient predator with highly advanced social behavior.

Hyenas live in clans of up to 30 or 40 individuals, led by a dominant female known as the matriarch. Females remain in the clan of their birth but males leave the group when they mature at around the age of three. A communal den, often an enlarged warthog burrow at the base of a termite mound, is the center of clan life, with pups of all ages socializing. Hyenas demarcate their territory by defecating repeatedly in particular places and the chalky, calcium-rich droppings persist for some time. Anal pasting and nocturnal vocalization are other means of territorial advertisement.

Spotted Hyenas are most active after dark but are frequently encountered during the early morning and late afternoon. The hunting procedure of the clan is to run down prey until it becomes exhausted, usually selecting lame or young antelope. Much food is obtained by scavenging and they frequently rob Cheetah and Leopard of their prey. Powerful canines and molars allow hyenas to consume almost an entire animal carcass, from hide and flesh, to hooves and bones.

Due to its ghostly whooping call and secretive nocturnal ways, the hyena is regarded as a witch or evil spirit in many African societies. For the Maasai, Karamajong and some other tribes, the hyena was (and still is in more remote locations) used as an "undertaker", consuming the body of the deceased and delivering a person's spirit to the afterlife.

SPOTTED HYENA
Crocuta crocuta
L:5 ft (1.5 m)
W:88-176 lb (40-80 kg)

Pup

OTHER HYENAS AND AARDWOLF

Somewhat smaller than the Spotted Hyena, and only rarely encountered, are the Striped and Brown Hyenas. Both are almost entirely nocturnal, solitary, silent, shy and secretive. These animals are not as well-studied as their spotted cousins and much still has to be learned about their ecology.

The Brown Hyena occurs in desert and semi-arid habitats from Namibia's Skeleton Coast, through the Kalahari, to the dry bushveld of South Africa. Carrion and wild melons make up the bulk of its diet, and it is an ineffective predator. The similarly-sized Striped Hyena is widespread from Tanzania north to the Horn of Africa, throughout the Sahara and east into Arabia and India. This secretive hyena may be seen on the fringes of Maasai villages where it scavenges on old animal hides and other scraps. Both Brown and Striped Hyenas include ostrich eggs in their diet.

The much smaller Aardwolf lacks powerful teeth and is a specialized termite-feeder. Individuals may be seen digging for and feasting on large numbers of these social insects after dark, sometimes following behind an Aardvark which is able to excavate entire termite colonies.

BROWN HYENA
Parahyaena brunnea
L:4-5 ft (1.2-1.5 m)
W: 77-110 lb (35-50 kg)

AARDWOLF
Proteles cristata
L:30-42 in (80-90 cm)
W:18-26 lb (8-12 kg)

STRIPED HYENA
Hyaena hyaena
L:4-5 ft (1.2-1.5 m)
W:66-120 lb (35-50 kg)

SMALLER CATS

The African Wild Cat is the direct ancestor of the domestic cat and is virtually indistinguishable from a domestic cat although it has rather long legs. This adaptable carnivore occurs throughout Africa where it is secretive and largely nocturnal. It is most often encountered during daytime in semi-arid habitats such as the Kalahari and Etosha. Rodents and ground birds are favored prey.

The Serval is at least twice the size of the African Wild Cat and resembles a small Cheetah. This long-limbed predator favors areas of tall grass, often close to water, in savannah and montane grasslands. Rodents are the main prey, but ground birds are often flushed and seized in flight as they take off. Serval appear to be less nocturnal in East Africa than in the southern part of the continent.

The Caracal is about the same size as the Serval but heavier in build and similar to a Lynx (Bobcat). It is powerful for its size, capturing hyrax, hares and guineafowl as well as small antelope. The Caracal occurs throughout Africa in desert, savannah, woodland and grassland, but it avoids closed-canopy forest. This is an adaptable carnivore able to flourish on farmland where it may prey upon unguarded small livestock.

Not illustrated here are the tiny Black-footed Cat of the Karoo-Kalahari, and the Golden Cat of equatorial forest; these rare and elusive cats are seldom seen.

SERVAL
Leptailurus serval
L:40-56 in. (1-1.4 m)
W:20-40 lb (8-19 kg)

AFRICAN WILD CAT
Felis sylvestris
L:30-40 in. (78-100 cm)
W:7-14 lb (3-4 kg)

CARACAL
Felis caracal
L:30-45 in. (80-120 cm)
W:22-40 lb (10-19 kg)

CHEETAH

Built for speed, the Cheetah is the planet's fastest land mammal and has been reliably clocked at over 60 miles (100 km) per hour. These lithe cats favor open habitats where gazelle, medium-sized antelope and hares are among the principle prey. When hunting, the Cheetah targets a particular individual and then stalks as close as possible before exploding in a sudden burst of speed. Using its tail as a rudder, it rapidly gains ground on its quarry which it then attempts to trip from behind. Once the victim is grounded, the spotted cat pins it down and suffocates with a throat hold. Only around one quarter of pursuits end successfully for the Cheetah, however, and when prey is successfully captured, the hunter must feed quickly to avoid detection and possible displacement by vultures or more powerful predators.

Female Cheetah are solitary and raise litters of two to four cubs every second year. It is no easy task for the mother to provide for her family and there is usually a high mortality of cubs. Unlike Leopard, female Cheetah do not have fixed territories and wander over an extensive area, often moving to avoid contact with lion prides. Male cheetah are territorial and occupy large areas in which they have mating opportunities with a number of females. The larger the coalition of males (they are often siblings) the longer their tenure in an area of prime habitat.

Cheetah are readily distinguished from similarly-sized leopards by their proportionately longer legs, single coin-like spots, and distinctive black "tear marks" running from the eyes to the mouth. Cheetah cubs are covered in long grayish hair on their backs which may aid them in camouflage.

CHEETAH
Acinonyx jubatus
L:4.6-5.8 ft (1.5-1.8 m)
W:80-140 lb (35-65 kg)

LEOPARD

The Leopard is the most adaptable of Africa's large predators and is able to survive in virtually any habitat, being at home in forest, savannah, desert or mountain top. These secretive cats may be found in close proximity to human settlements, even on the outskirts of large cities.

Leopards are solitary, and in typical cat fashion, come together only to mate. Individuals live within home ranges in which they continually advertise their presence through calling and scent marking. All possible steps are taken to defend territories through scent, signs and signals rather than physical conflict. As a solitary hunter, a Leopard cannot afford to become injured and must avoid confrontation. The size of a territory will depend upon the terrain and the density of available prey. Prime habitat often includes rocky outcrops or well-wooded drainage lines which provide ambush opportunities as well as den sites for cubs. One to three cubs are born blind and helpless and it is six weeks before they emerge from their den. Weaning takes place at about three months but it will be a year before they are able to fend for themselves. Females range over smaller territories than males, and there is often overlap between mothers and their matured daughters.

Leopards are the ultimate opportunists, feeding on a wide range of prey from winged termites, rodents and stranded catfish, to duiker, warthog, bushbuck, impala and young zebra. Leopards are most active at night but are not strictly nocturnal and will readily slink down the trunk of a tree at midday to take advantage of a hunting opportunity.

LEOPARD
Panthera pardus
L:4-4.5 ft (1.2-1.5 m)
W:130-200 lb (60-90 kg)

LION

The Lion is the only truly social member of the cat family, with prides typically consisting of related females and their offspring. Male cubs are ejected from the pride when they approach maturity, whereas female cubs stay on as a second or third generation. Mothers help to raise one another's offspring, with litters often being synchronized. Prides are usually lorded over by adult males (normally two or three) which are often related (brothers). The males defend a territory larger in size than the home range of the lionesses and often rule over two or more prides.

Lions are the super predators of Africa. By and large, zebra, wildebeest and buffalo are the preferred prey, but this always depends upon the size of the pride, the terrain and the density of a particular prey species. Only large prides will tackle buffalo, and, even then, males are often called upon to deliver the killing bite. Some prides specialize in certain species and develop effective hunting techniques for giraffe, warthog and others. One reason for living in a pride is not only to be tackling large prey but also to defend it. The Spotted Hyena is their main rival, and large clans of these tenacious carnivores are able to dispossess the big cats of their kills. Terrific battles may ensue between these competing predators, although the involvement of a big male lion invariably swings the balance. Since any predator has to avoid injury if it is to survive, Lions will usually target the easiest available prey, preferring a limping zebra foal to a vigorous stallion. A substantial part of its diet comes from pirating prey from other carnivores (particularly Cheetah) and from scavenging off natural mortalities.

The Lion's historical range in Africa has contracted by about two-thirds, and they are now largely confined to the more extensive protected areas. A few prides have, however, been successfully reintroduced to newly-created conservation areas.

LION
Panthera leo
L:8-11 ft (2.4-3.5 m)
Wm:520 lb (240 kg)
Wf: 300 lb (130 kg)

OTTERS

Although familiar to most people, and with species in North America and Europe, otters are secretive and rarely seen. The most widespread species in Africa is the Cape Clawless Otter which occurs at low densities in highland streams, large rivers, lakes, man-made dams, and coastal estuaries. Pairs defend a fixed territory which is advertised with dung-middens and they raise pups in a waterside burrow. Crabs are the primary food for this otter, and an accumulation of crab shells at favored feeding sites is a tell-tale sign of their presence in an area. They are most active at dawn and dusk. The smaller and rarely-seen Spotted-necked Otter feeds mostly on fish and requires clear water in which to hunt.

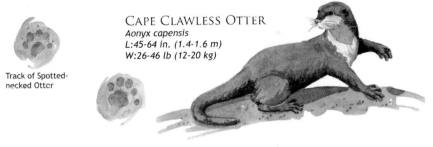

CAPE CLAWLESS OTTER
Aonyx capensis
L:45-64 in. (1.4-1.6 m)
W:26-46 lb (12-20 kg)

Track of Spotted-
necked Otter

SEALS

Seals are fish predators of cold seas, and huge numbers of Cape Fur Seals occur in the Atlantic Ocean which laps the coast of Namibia and South Africa. Colonies of up to 400,000 exist on the 'west coast' where their numbers are thought to have increased in recent years due to changes in the marine food chain caused by commercial fishing enterprises. There is constant activity at seal colonies - much of it hostile as adults compete for space, and provision their young. The Great White Shark is the main predator of fur seals, while Black-backed Jackals and Brown Hyenas scavenge around breeding colonies. There are seven species of seal in the cool waters of South Africa and Namibia.

CAPE FUR SEAL
Arctocephalus pusillus
L:5-8 ft (1.8-2.4 m)
Wm:440-770 lb (200-350 kg)
Wf:200-250 lb (90-115 kg)

MONGOOSES

As small terrestrial carnivores related to weasels and polecats, mongooses are thought to be similar in physiology and ecology to the first mammalian carnivores that appeared on the scene around 60 million years ago when the era of dinosaurs was coming to an end.

There are over 20 species of mongoose in Africa. Most are opportunistic feeders, solitary, active after dark and poorly known, but the habits of several diurnal, group-living species have been intimately studied and are well known. Beetles, spiders, scorpions and lizards are among the favored prey of most mongooses, and many are known for their brave attacks on venomous snakes.

In savannah habitats the sociable Banded Mongoose and Dwarf Mongoose are frequently encountered, and often provide entertaining viewing as they interact with one another and forage for food. Both species commonly occupy termite mounds in which they tunnel nursery chambers, sleeping quarters and hideouts. The equally gregarious Meerkat of the Kalahari and Karoo has been the subject of numerous documentary films which have highlighted the tight bonds between pack members. All-for-one, and one-for-all, seems to be the motto of group-living mongooses. The solitary Slender Mongoose is active during the day and is often seen darting across vehicle tracks with its long black-tipped tail turned upwards. The much larger, badger-sized White-tailed Mongoose is strictly nocturnal, as is the Egyptian Mongoose. The Marsh Mongoose occurs in and around wetlands.

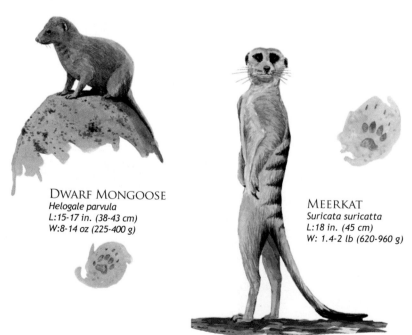

DWARF MONGOOSE
Helogale parvula
L:15-17 in. (38-43 cm)
W:8-14 oz (225-400 g)

MEERKAT
Suricata suricatta
L:18 in. (45 cm)
W: 1.4-2 lb (620-960 g)

Slender Mongoose
Galerella sanguinea
L:26 in. (64 cm)
W:28 oz (800 g)

Yellow Mongoose
Cynictis penicillata
L:22 in. (52 cm)
W:28 oz (800 g)

Banded Mongoose
Mungos mungo
L:20-26 in. (50-78 cm)
W:2-4 lb (1-2 kg)

White-tailed Mongoose
Ichneumia albicauda
L:4 ft (1.2 m)
W:7-11 lb (3-5 kg)

Track of
Marsh Mongoose

Genets and Civets

Genets and civets belong to the viverrid family of small, strictly nocturnal carnivores with distinctive black-and-white-banded tails. All are solitary, with males and females coming together only briefly to mate.

There are at least eight species of genet in Africa, with the Large-spotted (or Blotched) Genet being most common in the moister eastern half of the continent, and the Small-spotted (or Common) Genet favoring the high plateau and dryer southwestern regions. Genets are agile climbers and live primarily arboreal lives, hunting for tree rats, roosting birds, geckos and insects. These slender, cat-sized predators are often located on safari night drives when their highly reflective eyes shine back at spotlights. Genets may be residents or frequent visitors to the trees and roofs of safari camps.

The African Civet is larger than any of the genets and rarely climbs into trees. This terrestrial, racoon-sized animal has a varied diet which includes berries and wild dates, as well as rodents and nestlings of ground birds. When alarmed or confronted, the civet raises the hair on its neck and back to appear much larger in size. Civets secrete copious amounts of sticky fluid to demarcate their territorial boundaries, and this "civetone" is harvested from captive animals (of a related Asian species) in the Far East.

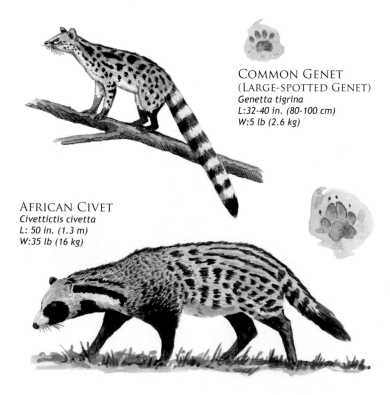

Common Genet
(Large-spotted Genet)
Genetta tigrina
L:32-40 in. (80-100 cm)
W:5 lb (2.6 kg)

African Civet
Civettictis civetta
L: 50 in. (1.3 m)
W:35 lb (16 kg)

Honey Badger and polecats

These three small carnivores are primarily nocturnal and seldom seen, although the Honey Badger is often encountered in daylight hours in the Kalahari and Okavango Delta during the dry winter season. All three belong to the mustelid family and are closely related to otters. They are mostly solitary with sexes living in distinct but overlapping territories, and coming together only to mate. Two to four pups are born in an underground burrow or den and typically accompany their mother for several months until they become independent. Invertebrates such as dung beetles and scorpions, as well as reptiles, small birds and rodents are among the preferred prey. The Honey Badger is a great opportunist and will scavenge from large carcasses and campsites.

Honey Badgers are known to be incredibly pugnacious and there are numerous observations of these muscular creatures standing their ground against Leopards and even Lions. Their powerful claws enable them to dig and climb with ease, so crocodile eggs and even vulture nestlings may feature in the diet from time to time. Honey and bee larvae are relished, and they may be led to active hives by a bird known as the Greater Honeyguide.

The skunk-like Striped Polecat and tiny Striped Weasel are shy, secretive and seldom encountered.

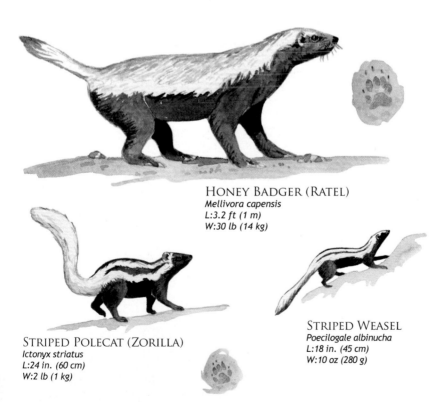

Honey Badger (Ratel)
Mellivora capensis
L:3.2 ft (1 m)
W:30 lb (14 kg)

Striped Polecat (Zorilla)
Ictonyx striatus
L:24 in. (60 cm)
W:2 lb (1 kg)

Striped Weasel
Poecilogale albinucha
L:18 in. (45 cm)
W:10 oz (280 g)

Aardvark and Pangolin

The Aardvark is an oddity among mammals. This pig-like creature has a long truncated snout, donkey-like ears, and powerful bear-like paws, which are adaptations to locating and excavating termites and ants. Thousands of these social insects may be consumed in a single night of foraging. Interestingly, the Aardvark rarely destroys an entire colony of termites, practicing a form of sustainable harvesting so as not to deplete the food supply in its home range.

The Aardvark plays an important ecological role for many other species, as its extensive underground burrows are occupied by foxes, large rodents, hyenas and others. Two birds, the South African Shelduck and Ant-eating Chat, as well as various species of swallows, commonly nest in Aardvark burrows. Unfortunately, this fascinating creature is both nocturnal and shy, so is seldom encountered. It is fairly common in some areas, however, as evidenced by the number of characteristic burrows and soil excavations.

The much smaller Ground Pangolin is primarily nocturnal, shy and increasingly rare. Individuals are killed for use by traditional healers and spiritualists, the scales being regarded as love charms among Zulu and other tribes. Like the Aardvark, it is an "anteater" with a specialized diet of ants and termites that are licked up with its long, sticky tongue. Although superficially similar to the ant-eating armadillos of America, the pangolins (there are three species in Africa) are not related but display traits of parallel evolution (a phenomenon whereby two unrelated families develop similar body forms for similar ecological niches).

Ground Pangolin
Manis temminckii
L:40 in. (1 m)
W:35 lb (16 kg)

Aardvark (Antbear)
Orycteropus afer
L:3-5 ft (1-1.5 m)
W:90-140 lb (40-65 kg)

Hyraxes (Dassies)

Hyraxes – or "dassies" as they are known in South Africa – resemble rabbits or rodents and were once commonly known as 'rock rabbits'. In fact, the eleven species of hyraxes are unique and fascinating creatures. With their rubbery-soled feet and dense coat of hair, they are adapted for life among rocks, bounding among boulders and able to withstand extremes of heat and cold. Families can typically be seen sunning themselves in the early morning and then retreating into shady crevices during the heat of the day. Hyraxes obtain all their moisture requirements from their food and rarely drink.

The three family groups of hyraxes rock, bush and tree – are named after their preferred habitats. The diurnal Rock Hyraxes (five geographically separated species) live among boulder outcrops (kopjes), rocky cliffs and boulder-strewn slopes, often in the company of Bush Hyraxes (three geographically separated species). It takes a keen observer to tell the two species apart: the Bush Hyrax has a white eyebrow, whereas the Rock Hyrax is more uniformly colored. Tree Hyraxes (five species) are typically much darker with distinct facial markings, denser fur and a pale dorsal crest. All hyraxes can be noisy, but the nocturnal Tree Hyrax is easily the most vociferous - its bizarre ratchet-like croaks and tormented screams wake or disturb many a person out on safari!

Hyraxes have many predators including Verreaux's Eagle, Leopard, Caracal and African Rock Python. It is thought that hyrax and elephant may have evolved from a common ancestor in some distant era; the species share some interesting features including the arrangement of their toes – four front and three rear – which are equipped with hoof-like nails, and internal testicles. For such a small mammal, hyrax have an extraordinarily long gestation period of seven months.

ROCK HYRAX
Procavia capensis
L:16-22 in. (40-56 cm)
W:4-12 lb (1.8-5 kg)

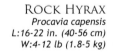

TREE HYRAX
Dendrohyrax dorsalis
L:16-22 in. (40-56 cm)
W:4-12 lb (1.8-5 kg)

AFRICAN ELEPHANT

African Elephants are the largest land mammals but it was only in 2010 that genetic studies concluded that the Savannah Elephant and Forest Elephant were distinct species. The Forest Elephant differs from its larger relative not only in its smaller size, but also in the shape of its ears (rounded) and its tusks (straighter); and while the Savannah Elephant has four toes on the front and three on the rear, the Forest Elephant has five toes on the front and four on the hind feet.

Savannah Elephants may consume over 600 lbs (270 kg) of leaves, grass, pods, bark and roots each day. Over half of the food eaten is poorly digested and deposited as fibrous dung within 24 hours. In this way, elephants break down plant material but also promote regeneration through seed dispersal, soil fertilisation and the opening up of previously shaded areas to light. Along with the minuscule but equally impactful termites, elephants are the "landscape gardeners" of Africa. In fenced reserves, however, elephant populations may threaten biodiversity due to radical habitat modification.

Elephants live in family groups led by a dominant female (the matriarch) which comprise related "sisters", "aunts" and their offspring and have an intimate knowledge of a home range. Adult males and "teenagers" of 12 and older, typically range in pairs, threesomes or groups of a dozen or more. Cows typically give birth to a single baby once every four or five years, and may live for up to 60 years. Mature males periodically enter a period of "musth" – a condition of high testosterone levels characterized by leaking temporal glands and dribbling urine – and then intimidate or fight with other bulls. Elephants in this condition should be treated with caution by safari guides!

SAVANNAH ELEPHANT
Loxodonta africana
L:15 ft (4.5m); H:8-12 ft (2.5-4 m)
Wm: up to 13,000 lb (6,000 kg)
Wf: up to 7,000 lb (3,200 kg)

Rear foot of
Savannah Elephant

FOREST ELEPHANT
Loxodonta cyclotis
L:10 ft (3 m); H:up to 8 ft (2.5 m)
W: up to 6,000 lb (2,700 kg)

HIPPOPOTAMUS

Hippos once occupied almost every river system in Africa, from the southern Cape wetlands to the Nile Delta in Egypt, but due to hunting pressure it is now largely restricted to protected areas south of the Sahara. Hippos require deep water in which to submerge their bulky bodes and a supply of short grass on which to feed. Their skin lacks sweat glands, so hippo are prone to dehydration and must spend most of the day in water or mud, although they may bask in the sun for short periods. Hippos are extremely vocal when in water (but silent on land), as individuals grunt, honk and blow air from their nostrils. Calling seems to be contagious, and noisy bouts of honking and wheezing are made in response to disturbances, or when returning to the water after a night of feeding.

Hippos leave their aquatic refuge at sunset to wander down well-trodden pathways to favored feeding grounds. Flat areas colonized by creeping grasses are preferred, and a resident population maintains a lawn-like landscape. Individuals consume up to 130 lbs (60 kg) of grass per night.

Hippos live in a hierarchical society in which individuals constantly display their status to one another. Adult females with their successive offspring form the foundation of social units called pods, and occupy a home range on a stretch of river or lake. Mature males hold dominance in a restricted range and fierce, bloody clashes between rivals are commonplace. Hippo pods tend to be sedentary during the dry season but move far and wide when rain fills seasonal waterbodies.

Babies are born in shallow water but are able to swim immediately and suckle while completely submerged. Youngsters are playful for the first year of life and weaned at around eight months.

HIPPOPOTAMUS
Hippopotamus amphibius
L:12 ft (3.5 m); H:4 ft (1.2 m)
Wm:7,000 lb (3,200 kg)

WHITE RHINOCEROS

Second in size only to the African Elephant, the White Rhino is an animal of open country. In spite of its name, it does not differ from the Black Rhino in its skin color, and the names are misleading. Like its smaller cousin, the color of the its skin is determined by the soil of a particular region, as the animals roll in mud and dust. It is in the shape of the mouth that the two differ so markedly, and this also determines their diet. The broad, flat mouth of the White Rhino is designed to crop large mouthfuls of grass.

Adult females live in overlapping home ranges and are often accompanied by their most recent offspring. They also tend to associate with other females and groups of a dozen or more may gather. Males are much less sociable and occupy well-patrolled territories with numerous conspicuous dung middens. Females and young add their own dung to a male's midden, but do not engage in the male's ritual of spreading and urine spraying. Rhino calves remain with their mother for two to three years, by which time she may be ready to deliver another calf. Interestingly, the juvenile White Rhino always runs ahead of its mother, whereas the Black Rhino youngster typically runs behind. Adult rhinos have no enemies other than man, but Lion and Spotted Hyena may prey on calves.

White Rhinoceros were close to extinction at the start of the 20th century due to excessive hunting. Only 30 or so individuals survived when South Africa's Umfolozi Game Reserve was created in 1897, but effective conservation allowed their population to recover strongly, especially since the 1960s when translocations to other protected areas were perfected. Poaching has increased sharply in the past few years, however, as the demand for horn in the Far East has increased; the supposed medicinal properties of the horn are a complete fallacy but tradition persists.

SOUTHERN WHITE RHINOCEROS
Ceratotherium simum
L:12 ft (4 m); H:6 ft (1.7 m)
Wm:5,000 lb (2,300 kg)

BLACK RHINOCEROS

The Black Rhino has a hooked, prehensile upper lip, and carries its head high, in contrast to the drooping head of its grass-eating relative, the White Rhino. A browser of herbs, low woody shrubs, and tree foliage, the Black Rhino uses its pointed lip to grasp leaves and twigs, sometimes employing its horns to snap branches which are out of reach. Its wrinkled skin varies in color depending upon the tone of the mud in which it wallows to cool down or the dust it rolls in to combat ectoparasites. So it is, that Black Rhinos may be gray, rusty-red or even white!

Black Rhino are reputed to be short-tempered and readily charge as a first means of defense. Trackers require great skill and patience to approach these animals.

The preferred habitat of Black Rhino is the fringe of thickets and areas of dense woody growth, although individuals in Tanzania and Kenya may occupy more open habitats (such as the bowl of Ngorongoro Crater). They live in established territories but may share overlapping ranges and water holes without serious confrontation. Home ranges never extend more than 15 miles (24 km) from a permanent supply of water and are criss-crossed by frequently used trails, marked by both sexes with dung middens. "Dunging" is a social behavior and serves as a form of communication, such that a female on heat can be picked up by males.

Poaching has devastated the Black Rhino population, from an estimated 60,000 individuals in 1970 to less than 2,000 today, with just small, fragmented populations surviving in Tanzania, Kenya, Zimbabwe and Namibia. The situation is better in South Africa where conservation action and relocations has resulted in a secure population but this is now under increasing pressure from poachers.

BLACK RHINOCEROS
Diceros bicornis
L:10 ft (3 m); H:5 ft (1.5 m)
Wm:2,500 lb (1,200 kg)

PIGS

The Common Warthog is the most frequently seen of Africa's pigs, being widespread in savannah and open woodland, and active by day. Its close relative, the Desert Warthog, occurs in arid northern Kenya, Somalia and Ethiopia. The other three pig species inhabit forest and are primarily nocturnal.

Due to their bizarre, warty faces and habit of running with tails erect, warthogs are entertaining animals to watch as well as being important members of the herbivore community in savannah and open woodland. They feed on short green grass in the wet season and on succulent tubers and bulbs, which they uproot with their snouts, in the dry season. Warthogs give birth to two or three piglets which remain in the underground burrow for six weeks. It is common for two or more sows to stick together and for their piglets to assemble in 'nursery groups'. Despite being tenaciously defended by their mothers, many piglets do not survive their first year as large cats, hyenas, jackals and large eagles relish them as prey.

The Bushpig is widespread throughout densely-wooded habitats while the Red Forest Hog occurs only in equatorial rainforest of central Africa. The three species of Giant Forest Hog occur in montane forest as well as lowland rainforest.

COMMON WARTHOG
Phacochoerus africanus
L:4 ft (1.2 m); H:25 in. (66 cm)
W:100-220 lb (45-100 kg)

BUSHPIG
Potamochoerus larvatus
L:4 ft (1.2 m); H: 32 in. (80 cm)
W:120-250 lb (54-115 kg)

GIANT FOREST HOG
Hylochoerus meinertzhageni
L:8 ft (2.5 m); H:3 ft 2 in. (1 m)
Wm:330-600 lb (150-275 kg)

RED RIVER HOG
Potamochoerus porcus
L:4 ft (1.2 m); H: 32 in.(80 cm)
W:120-250 lb (54-115 kg)

ZEBRAS

Few animals are as strongly synonymous with the African continent as zebras - the only wild members of the horse family south of the Sahara. The Plains Zebra is widespread in savannah and open woodland with several races distinguished by the coat pattern (southern races have distinct "shadow stripes"). The Mountain Zebra occurs in rocky terrain of Namibia and the Cape mountains, while Grevy's Zebra occurs in arid north Kenya, Somalia and Ethiopia.

Zebras are exclusive grazers, favoring short coarse grasses. They are particularly fond of freshly sprouted grass on recently burnt ground and will move large distances in search of this fodder; they are dependent on drinking water.

Zebras live in small family groups, usually consisting of between four and eight, led by a single dominant stallion. The adult mares in a group are usually related. Once they are able to fend for themselves, male offspring are evicted from the herd by their father - the stallion. Once the mares reach sexually maturity, they too leave the harem, being lured away by other stallions. Zebras frequently associate with antelopes, gazelles, giraffe and even ostrich, benefiting from the different anti-predator senses and reactions of these animals. Zebras feature commonly in the diet of Lion and Spotted Hyena, however, with youngsters being particularly susceptible. Stallions are vigorous in defense of their harem, and capable of inflicting life-threatening kicks to Lion.

PLAINS ZEBRA
Equus burchellii
L:7 ft 8 in.(2.3 m)
H:4 ft 5 in. (1.3 m)
Wm:550 lb (250 kg)

MOUNTAIN ZEBRA
Equus zebra
L:8 ft (2.4 m)
H:5 ft (1.5 m)
Wm:750 lb (320 kg)

'Shadow stripes'
of southern races
of Plains Zebra

GREVY'S ZEBRA
Equus grevyi
L:8 ft 8 in (2.6 m)
H:5 ft (1.5 m)
Wm:800 lb (390 kg)

GIRAFFE

Giraffe are the tallest members of the animal kingdom, with adults averaging a height of around 18 feet (5 meters). Males can be told from females by the bald tops to their horns. The giraffe's unique form is the result of some remarkable adaptations and has enabled it to exploit a food niche not utilized by other herbivores – the foliage on the uppermost branches of trees.

Giraffe have an unusual social system in which females live apart from males in large home ranges. The males may be solitary, but may congregate in bachelor herds. Their large size is a deterrent to most predators, but Lions are capable of toppling fully-grown adults and some prides actually select them as prey. A single calf is born and although mothers put up a stern defense against predators, less than a quarter of young survive their first year.

Giraffe are selective browsers, favoring various species of *Acacia*, *Balanites*, *Commiphora* and *Ziziphus*, some of which have evolved chemical defenses and release unpalatable tannins when over-browsed. The thick blue tongue is able to wrap around even the thorniest of twigs to remove nutritious foliage.

There are seven species of giraffe, each with a distinctive coat pattern. The Southern Giraffe occupies the area south of the Zambezi, while the Maasai Giraffe occurs in Tanzania and southern Kenya. Most distinctive of all, is the beautifully-patterned Reticulated Giraffe of the semi-arid savannah of central and northern Kenya.

SOUTHERN GIRAFFE
Giraffa camelopardalis
H:18 ft (5.5 m)
Wm: 3,000 lb (1 300 kg)
Wf: 2,000 lb (950 kg)

Reticulated Giraffe   Maasai Giraffe

Buffalo

The Cape Buffalo - a massive relative of the domestic cow - is regarded as one of Africa's "Big Five" due to its appeal as a trophy animal among hunters. Buffalo are completely dependent upon surface water, so are absent from arid and semi-arid regions but are widespread and common in savannah, woodland and forest environments, although few now survive beyond the borders of protected areas. Buffalo are host to several diseases which may be lethal to domestic cattle and have therefore been eliminated from areas suitable for ranching.

Cape Buffalo are gregarious animals with herds typically numbering several hundred, but sometimes over 1,000. Several adult bulls, in prime breeding condition, accompany the herd which otherwise consists of cows, their calves and juveniles of both sexes. Old bulls, past their prime, keep each other company in bachelor groups. Their large size and gregarious nature make buffalo difficult quarry for predators but some lion prides actually specialize in hunting these big bovines. Older bulls are typically targeted by Lions although it may take a pride several hours to corner, pin down and dispatch a belligerent buffalo. Calves may be preyed upon by clans of Spotted Hyena which will disturb a herd after dark to cause confusion and separate young from their mothers.

Cape Buffalo are non-selective "bulk grazers" which favor taller grasses. By munching on these grasses and trampling rank grass underfoot, they open up areas for other more selective herbivores such as wildebeest and zebra. In common with many herbivores, buffalo herds move in response to rainfall and the resultant onset of nutritious grass growth. Herds often break up into smaller units during the wet season, but gather in large numbers again when seasonal rains come to an end.

The Forest Buffalo of equatorial rainforests is smaller than its savannah cousin, with shorter horns, tufted ears and a rich sepia-orange coat.

CAPE BUFFALO
Syncerus caffer
L:10 ft (3 m); H: 5 ft (1.5 m)
Wm: 1,000-1,500 lb (450-680 kg)

FOREST BUFFALO
Syncerus nanus
L:8 ft (2.4 m); H: 4 ft 3 in. (1.2 m)
Wm: 800 lb (360 kg)

Wildebeest (Gnu)

There are four species of wildebeest, with the famous migrant of the Serengeti-Mara known as the White-bearded Wildebeest. The Blue Wildebeest ranges from eastern South Africa, into the Kalahari and the Okavango. Heck's and Johnstone's Wildebeest have smaller ranges.

Wildebeest are gregarious, forming herds of between ten and many thousands. The spectacular annual migration of wildebeest across the Serengeti is a well-known phenomenon and this seasonal movement in response to rainfall and resultant grass growth was probably shared by all populations of this unusual herbivore in the past. Today, wildebeest over much of Africa have been hemmed into protected areas and are no longer able to follow traditional migration routes due to agricultural expansion, human settlements and fences. Short, nutritious grass is the required food of wildebeest. Optimum grazing conditions are created by a variety of factors including rain, fire, soil chemistry and grazing pressure from other herbivores such as buffalo. In higher rainfall areas, small herds may be sedentary, but the majority must move to rotate pasture. During the breeding season, male wildebeest occupy territories which - in extreme cases - may be no greater than the size an average suburban yard; the site is distinguished by the accumulation of droppings in a bare depression where the bull scrapes and rolls. Females synchronize the birth of their single calves at optimal grazing times and this also reduces the toll taken by Lion, Spotted Hyena, Cheetah and Wild Dog.

The distinctive Black Wildebeest is restricted to the temperate highveld plateau of South Africa where it was hunted almost to extinction in the late 1800s. Today, all surviving animals are derived from captive-bred stock (a story similar to that of the North American Bison, to which it bears a slight resemblance).

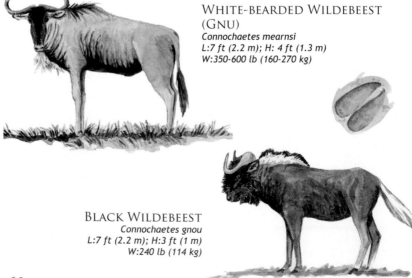

White-bearded Wildebeest (Gnu)
Connochaetes mearnsi
L:7 ft (2.2 m); H: 4 ft (1.3 m)
W:350-600 lb (160-270 kg)

Black Wildebeest
Connochaetes gnou
L:7 ft (2.2 m); H:3 ft (1 m)
W:240 lb (114 kg)

HARTEBEEST, TOPI AND TSESSEBE

This group of antelope are characterized by high shoulders and a long-snouted face. This gives them a rather ungainly appearance, but this is deceptive for they are regarded as the fastest runners among antelope.

Hartebeest are exclusive grazers favoring narrow-bladed grasses. Open habitats on the fringe between grassy glades and wooded drainage lines seem to be preferred by all hartebeest. There are five species in eastern and southern Africa, with horn shape being the most variable and distinguishable trait. Female hartebeest live in small herds although large aggregations may occur in some seasons. Adult males hold territories which are marked with extensive dung middens, and females which feed in these areas when they are on heat, will be mated with by the territory holder. Fierce fights may ensue between rival bulls at this time. The Hirola is a strange and critically endangered hartebeest restricted to northeastern Kenya and possibly Somalia.

The Southern Tsessebe of southern Africa and the Serengeti Topi of East Africa were until recently regarded as two races of the same species, but the former is a more slender animal in both its body and horn shape. Topi males typically stand on termite mounds within their territories, while the females roam a home range in small herds.

In South Africa, two closely-related members of the hartebeest tribe - the Blesbok and Bontebok - differ only in the amount of white on their face, but wild populations were slaughtered to the point of extinction by Boer settlers and survive today only as commercially ranched "livestock" (although many have been introduced to protected areas).

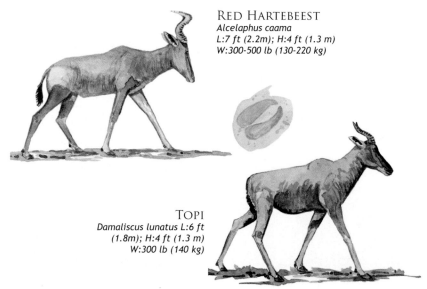

RED HARTEBEEST
Alcelaphus caama
L:7 ft (2.2m); H:4 ft (1.3 m)
W:300-500 lb (130-220 kg)

TOPI
Damaliscus lunatus L:6 ft
(1.8m); H:4 ft (1.3 m)
W:300 lb (140 kg)

67

KUDU AND NYALA

These are spiral-horned antelope that occupy woodland and forest over much of Africa. They are alert and agile, and all have striped flanks to aid camouflage by breaking up their body outline in dense vegetation.

The Greater Kudu is a browser which favors dry woodland. Only males carry the spectacular corkscrew horns. Females and immatures live in small herds with mature males in tow during the dry season rut. Greater Kudu are prodigious jumpers able to clear most fences with ease. The Lesser Kudu is a smaller, more slender antelope, favoring dryer semi-arid savannah from northern Tanzania into the Horn of Africa.

Common Nyala occur in a limited range south of the Zambezi along Africa's eastern shore, but are abundant in many South African reserves. The impressive horned males have dark shaggy coats, while the slender ewes are rusty red with distinctive white striping. The Mountain Nyala is an impressive antelope confined to the highlands of Ethiopia where it is common only in Bale National Park.

GREATER KUDU
Strepsiceros strepsiceros
L:8 ft (2.5 m); H:5 ft (1.4 m)
W:265-690 lb (120-315 kg)

LESSER KUDU
Ammelaphus imberbis
L:5 ft 2 in. (1.6 m)
H:3 ft 2 in. (1 m)
W:120-230 lb (56-108 kg)

COMMON NYALA
Nyala angasii
L:6 ft (1.8 m)
H:3 ft 8 in. (1.2 m)
W:130-308 lb (62-140 kg)

MOUNTAIN NYALA
Tragelaphus buxtoni
L:6 ft (1.8 m)
H:4 ft 2 in. (1.3 m)
W:330-660 lb (150-300 kg)

BUSHBUCK, SITATUNGA AND BONGO

Bushbuck are perhaps the most successful and widespread of all African antelope, occurring in wooded habitats from the coastal forests of the southern Cape, the highlands of East Africa, the equatorial forests of the Congo Basin and streamside thickets in dry savannah. Several distinct subspecies are recognized including the Common Bushbuck, Chobe Bushbuck and Harnessed Bushbuck.

Adapted for life in reedbeds and other aquatic habitats, the Sitatunga has specialized elongated hooves. It is at home in Botswana's Okavango Delta, the western shores of Lake Victoria, northern Zambia and swampy clearings of the Congo Basin.

The Bongo is a majestic, heavy-bodied antelope of equatorial lowland rainforest and montane forest, encountered most often in the Kenyan highlands and forest clearings of the Congo Basin. Interestingly, the Bongo favors disturbed habitats where regrowth of fresh leaves occurs in the wake of tree falls, landslides, elephant browsing and even logging. It usually occurs singly but several may gather at water.

COMMON BUSHBUCK
Tragelaphus scriptus
L:4 ft (1.2 m); H:30 in. (85 cm)
W:55-176 lb (25-80 kg)

SITATUNGA
Tragelaphus spekei
L:6 ft (1.7 m)
H:3 ft 2 in. (1 m)
W:130-265 lb (60-120 kg)

BONGO
Tragelaphus euryceros
L:8 ft (2.5 m)
H:4 ft 2 in. (1.3 m)
W:440-880 lb (200-400 kg)

ELAND

Largest of all antelope, Eland occur in a variety of habitats from semi-desert and savannah to sub-alpine grasslands of high mountain slopes. Males and females are alike and both have straight, spiral horns. The males are significantly larger.

Small groups are the typical social units, but herds of over 100 may gather seasonally. Males often live alone. Eland are mainly browsers but they will graze on grass occasionally. An interesting feature of their feeding is to hook branches down with their horns in order to reach foliage that is otherwise out of reach. Eland also eat wild cucumber and other fruit. Lion are the only predators of adults, but Spotted Hyena may take calves.

The Eland is the most frequently depicted animal in San-bushmen rock art. The large antelope was not only the most desired species to hunt and eat, but was also integral to San culture and mythology.

COMMON ELAND
Taurotragus oryx
L:10 ft (3 m); H:5 ft (1.6 m)
W:700-2,000 lb (320-940 kg)

Eland rock art
at Tsodilo Hills,
Botswana

Impala and Oribi

The Common Impala is probably the most abundant and adaptable of the African antelope, being both a grazer and a browser. It occurs at very high densities in ideal habitat. Fringes or 'ecotones' which provide a variety of grazing and browsing are favored, typically at the junction of savannah and woodland.

The Black-faced Impala is confined to Namibia where it is common in the Etosha National Park, and in southeastern Angola.

Impala live in small to large herds which may be comprised of females and immature males. Dominant males hold territories in which they attempt to keep a breeding herd, but the task of rounding up, mating and chasing challengers is exhausting and males seldom stay in command for more than two months. Non-territorial males live in 'bachelor' herds. Only the males carry the graceful, lyre-shaped horns.

Oribi have similar slender proportions to Impala but they are smaller with straight horns and conspicuous black gland spots below each ear. Open grassland is the favored habitat of Oribi which is primarily a grazer of fresh grass but also feeds on leafy herbs.

COMMON IMPALA
Aepyceros melampus
L:4 ft 5 in. (1.3 m)
H:35 in. (90 cm)
W:88-165 lb (40-75 kg)

ORIBI
Ourebia ourebi
L:4 ft (110 cm)
H:25 in. (62 cm)
W:23-36 lb (10-16 kg)

ORYX

Oryx are regal, horse-like antelope with lance-shaped horns. They are powerfully built and both sexes possess horns although those of females are more slender.

These antelope can survive without drinking water as they are able to extract sufficient moisture from their diet (although they will drink readily when water is available) and have various morphological adaptations. In order to survive extreme ambient temperatures of up to 113°F (45°C), oryx allow their own body temperature to rise accordingly and thus prevent the loss of moisture through perspiration. The antelope's hot blood is passed through a network of veins along its nasal passage before entering the brain in a system not unlike that of a car radiator.

Oryx are gregarious and typically form herds of up to 30 individuals. The herds comprise adult females and their young, as well as subadult males. Mature males occupy fixed territories through which female herds pass and provide mating opportunities. Rivalry between neighboring males, or wandering challengers, often leads to intense clashes which may result in broken horns, serious injuries or even death. Oryx feed primarily on grass, but will browse on shrubs and regularly eat succulent wild cucumbers and underground tubers, as well as acacia seed pods.

The Southern Oryx of the Namib and Kalahari is better known as the Gemsbok. The Beisa Oryx and Fringe-eared Oryx occur in semi-arid East Africa, their ranges being separated by the Tana River.

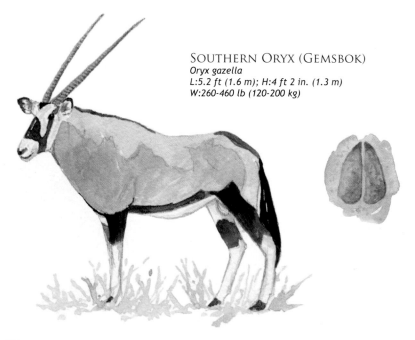

SOUTHERN ORYX (GEMSBOK)
Oryx gazella
L:5.2 ft (1.6 m); H:4 ft 2 in. (1.3 m)
W:260-460 lb (120-200 kg)

SABLE AND ROAN

Sable and Roan are large, horse-like antelope with long manes. They are closely related and favor areas of taller grassland on the fringes of broad-leaved woodland. Both live in small herds consisting of numerous adult females, which have a hierarchy according to seniority, as well as subadults of both sexes. A single dominant bull accompanies the herd, and although he may wander off to feed alone he is never far from his harem. At the end of their nine month pregnancy, females temporarily leave the herd to give birth to a single calf. The infant remains hidden in tall grass for its first week.

Sable Antelope are among the most strikingly colored of all antelope. The bulls are jet-black, while females and subadults have rich chestnut coats. The long curved horns are formidable weapons and bulls will ward off all predators except Lion (although even these powerful cats treat adult sable with caution). The "Giant Sable" of Angola is considered to be a geographical race.

Roan Antelope are widespread in woodland south of the Sahara but are nowhere common. They are selective grazers of particular species of medium-length grasses and appear more susceptible to drought and disease than most other antelope. With their long, tufted ears and robust corrugated horns, they are among the most distinctive and attractive of antelope.

ROAN ANTELOPE
Hippotragus equinus
L:7 ft 8 in. (2.4 m)
H:5 ft (1.4 m)
W:480-650 lb (220-280 kg)

SABLE ANTELOPE
Hippotragus niger
L:6 ft 8 in. (2.1 m)
H:5 ft (1.4 m)
W:450-580 lb (204-260 kg)

73

GAZELLES

Gazelles are the most widespread of all antelope, occurring not only throughout the drier parts of Africa, but also in the Middle East and across Asia to Siberia and China. All gazelles are gracefully built and characterized by pale, sandy-colored coats and corrugated, S-shaped horns.

The most remarkable aspect of gazelle biology is the ability of most species to flourish in arid areas devoid of surface water. Gazelles are able to extract the moisture they need from their food and reduce moisture loss by absorption of feces and urine fluid. Most amazing, however, is the gazelle's ability to allow its body temperature to rise – by as much as 50°F (10°C) - with the ambient temperature. This strategy is also employed by oryx and camel which, like gazelles, draw air through convoluted nasal passages in order to cool down.

Gazelles are browsers of herbs, shrub foliage and seedpods, but also feed on fresh grass, so can switch diet according to environmental conditions. They are gregarious and exceptionally alert, relying on speed – as well as their choice of open country - to avoid predation. Cheetah are up to this challenge, however, and often target gazelles ahead of other prey.

The small, compact Thomson's Gazelle is widespread in eastern Africa where it is often the most abundant herbivore in open habitats. The larger Grant's Gazelle prefers drier conditions although the two species may be seen side-by-side.

A number of rare gazelle species that occur in and north of the Sahara are severely endangered and survive only in small pockets of suitable habitat.

THOMSON'S GAZELLE
Eudorcas nasalis
L:4 ft (1.2m); H:25 in. (65cm)
W:30-60 lb (15-28kg)

GRANT'S GAZELLE
Nanger granti
L:5 ft (1.5m); H:36 in. (90cm)
W:84-175 lb (38-80kg)

SPRINGBOK AND GERENUK

The Springbok is the only gazelle which occurs in the dry southwestern corner of Africa, isolated from its relatives by the moist woodland belt of central Africa. It shares much in common with other gazelles although it has some strange anatomical differences such as hollow horn bases like those of goats.

Springbok are mixed feeders, taking mostly grass in summer and herb and shrub foliage in the dry winter months. The large velvety pods of the camelthorn acacia are a much favored food source in the Kalahari. The Springbok's most remarkable behavior is "pronking" – its habit of springing up on its hooves. This begins as a rocking gait, progresses to a 'stot' and then to full scale bouncing on stiff legs with the back arched. Once one animal in a herd begins to pronk the rest join in and create quite a spectacle; this behavior is thought to display fitness to potential predators. Less than 200 years ago there were estimated to be many millions of springbok in the Karoo region of South Africa, but these herds were slaughtered by settlers. Good numbers still survive in the Kalahari and over much of Namibia.

The Gerenuk is a gazelle with an elongated neck which allows it to reach foliage in the canopy of small trees out of reach to most other browsers. As if this physical advantage were not enough, the Gerenuk also stands upright on its slender hind legs to give it even greater reach. By these means, this unique gazelle is able to occupy a distinctive niche. Gerenuk live in harem groups of 8 to 12, with one dominant male. They are distributed in semi-arid acacia scrubland from northeastern Tanzania, through Kenya into the Horn of Africa.

SPRINGBOK
Antidorcas marsupialis
L:4 ft (1.2 m); H:30 in. (80 cm)
W:100 lb (46 kg)

GERENUK
Litocranius walleri
L: 5 ft (1.5 m); H:4 ft (1.2 m)
W: 64-110 lb (29-50 kg)

75

Waterbuck and Reedbuck

Waterbuck are large, heavy-bodied antelope with long, shaggy coats. The males have magnificent long sweeping horns, while the females are hornless. Two species are recognized: the Common Waterbuck of southeastern Africa which has a broad white ring on its rump, and the darker-coated Defassa Waterbuck of eastern and western Africa, which has a large white patch under the tail. Unusual among antelope, waterbuck have a strong body scent and are good swimmers.

Waterbuck are grazers and favor the wooded margins of rivers and wetlands, where family groups typically occupy the same home range for many years, sometimes for several generations. Waterbuck drink daily and are never found more than a few miles from water. They are commonly seen out in the open, either on floodplains or sandy riverbeds.

The Southern Reedbuck and Bohor Reedbuck occur in small groups of ewes and solitary rams which attempt to keep the females under their influence, as their marshy home ranges shift with fluctuating conditions. A sharp whistle is the alarm call of reedbuck which have Cheetah and Leopard among their chief predators. The Mountain Reedbuck is adapted for life on grassy hillsides.

Common Waterbuck
Kobus ellipsiprymnus
L:6 ft 5 in. (2 m); H:4 ft (1.2 m)
W:350-570 lb (160-260 kg)

Southern Reedbuck
Redunca arundinum
L:5 ft 7 in, (1.6m);
H:38 in. (96cm)
W:86-170 lb (39-80kg)

KOB AND LECHWE

These antelope favor seasonal marshlands which are productive but fluctuating habitats. For much of the year, the marshlands are fertile lawns of high quality grazing, but at other times they are flooded or burnt so the antelope must move into fringing woodlands. The social organization and behavior of these interesting antelope is adapted accordingly.

The Uganda Kob is a robust antelope that lives in large aggregations on floodplains with distinct grazing and drinking areas. Adult males compete intensely for receptive females, with dozens converging in small "hubs" of just one acre (0.4 hectares) which are littered with droppings and reek of urine soaked soil.

Red Lechwe are similar in appearance to kob but are more slender with longer horns in the males. They possess elongated hooves adapted for life in permanent wetlands with clay soils. Lechwe occur in traditional herds, avoiding the intense social limitations of the kob in their seasonally shrinking habitats. The distinctive Black Lechwe occurs only in Zambia's Bangweulu Swamps, while the Kafue Lechwe is restricted to the Kafue floodplain in Zambia.

Puku are smaller than kob or lechwe and tolerant of seasonal fluctuations in habitat, being able to live in woodlands during the rainy season. They are common only in Zambia's Luangwa Valley but small numbers occur along the Chobe River.

RED LECHWE
Kobus leche
L:6 ft (1.8 m); H:4 ft (1.2 m)
W:136-280 lb (62-128 kg)

UGANDA KOB
Kobus thomasi
L:6 ft (1.8 m); H:4 ft (1.2 m)
W:130-260 lb (60-120 kg)

DUIKERS

All but one of Africa's 16 duiker species are denizens of temperate or tropical forest. This exception is the Gray Duiker which favors savannah and open woodland. Duikers range in size from the tiny 9 lb (4 kg) Blue Duiker to the 176 lb (80 kg) Yellow-backed Duiker of equatorial rainforests.

The nature of their dense habitat, combined with the small size and secretive ways, make duiker among the least-known of African mammals. To a greater or lesser extent duikers feed on fallen fruit, as well as leaves, flowers, bark, gum and roots. Duikers are the only antelope to exhibit omnivorous tendencies and regularly feed upon insects, small vertebrates, eggs and even bird nestlings. Duikers are territorial and most species live in monogamous pairs. Both sexes are equipped with slit-shaped pre-orbital glands from which they excrete a strong scented paste that is rubbed onto twigs and branches to demarcate its home range.

Most duikers snort and whistle, and traditional hunters frequently imitate the bleating call to lure them towards their nets, guns or clubs. Apart from man and his dogs, Leopards and African Crowned Eagles are their most significant predators.

GRAY DUIKER
Sylvicapra grimmia
L:45 in. (110 cm); H:28 in. (70 cm)
W:33-50 lb (15-25 kg)

RED DUIKER
Cephalophus natalensis
L:30-40 in. (76-100 cm); H: 15 in. (40 cm)
W:25-30 lb (11-14 kg)

YELLOW-BACKED DUIKER
Cephalophus silvicultor
L:5-6 ft (1.4-2 m); H: 32 in. (80 cm)
W:100-176 lb (45-80 kg)

BLUE DUIKER
Philantomba monticola
L:25 in.(70cm); H:14 in.(36cm)
W:9 lb (4.2 kg)

KLIPSPRINGERS AND MINI ANTELOPE

Klipspringers are remarkable little antelope with several physical adaptations to their preferred habitat of rocky outcrops and mountain sides. Most unusually, the Klipspringer (this name means "rock jumper" in Afrikaans) has rubbery, cone-like hooves that cushion the stocky little antelope as it bounds among boulders. These small antelope are browsers of herbs and low shrubs. Several subspecies are recognized including the Maasai Klipspringer and the Kaokoveld Klipspringer.

Steenbok are small, brick-red antelope of open savannah habitats. Their large rounded ears with white linings are their most distinguishing feature, along with a black nose bridge and slender, upright horns. Grass, leaves, seedpods and berries make up its diet.

Dikdik are tiny, slender antelope with huge eyes and a distinctive trunk-like snout. They occur in semi-arid savannah habitats dominated by acacia scrub and bush clumps, and have adaptations to allow them to survive in areas with no drinking water. In common with other miniature antelope, it is a browser rather than a grazer, and lives in monogamous pairs in a clearly defined home range. Eight species occur in East Africa, with another – the Damara Dikdik – in Namibia.

Suni are tiny, secretive antelope of forests and thickets at the base of mountain ranges, and along the coast from Zululand to Kenya. They are extremely shy and seldom encountered. Other rarely-encountered miniature antelope not illustrated here are the Cape Grysbok (which lives in fynbos heathland of the Cape), and the Sharpe's Grysbok (which favors *Brachystegia* woodland).

KLIPSPRINGER
Oreotragus oreotragus
L:35 in. (88cm); H:22 in. (55 cm)
W:20-35 lb (9-16 kg)

STEENBOK
Raphicerus campestris
L:35 in. (90cm); H:24 in. (60 cm)
W:20-25 lb (9-12 kg)

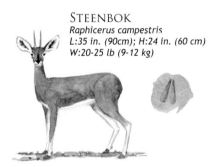

KIRK'S DIKDIK
Madoqua kirkii
L:25 in. (70 cm); H:15 in. (38 cm)
W:9-16 lb (5-7 kg)

SUNI
Neotragus moschatus
L:22 in. (58 cm); H:12 in. (35 cm)
W:8-13 lb (4-6 kg)

79

SQUIRRELS

Squirrels are rodents and, like their mouse and rat relatives, have prominent incisor teeth for gnawing at seeds, nuts and other plant material. All squirrels have long bushy tails and some are quite boldly patterned. They are active by day and are frequently encountered in savannah, forest and even in semi-deserts.

Tree squirrels forage on trunks and branches in savannah and woodland, and also spend time on the ground among fallen leaves and twigs. They often draw attention to themselves with their chirping alarm calls, accompanied by rapid flicking of their bushy tails. A variety of red squirrels occur in coastal forest from Zululand north to Kenya, and in montane forest patches where sun squirrels are also resident.

Ground Squirrels occur in the Kalahari and arid parts of Namibia, as well as the dry savannah of Tanzania, Kenya and Ethiopia. These are the largest of African squirrels and have the habit of using their raised tail as a shade umbrella in hot weather.

STRIPED
GROUND SQUIRREL
Geosciurus inauris
L:20 in. (50 cm)
W:2.2 lb (1 kg)

TREE SQUIRREL
Paraxerus cepapi
L:14 in. (35 cm)
W:7 oz (190 g)

SCRUB HARE
Lepus saxatilis
L:18 in. (45 cm)
W:2.2-6 lb (1-3 kg)

HARES AND RABBITS

Hares and rabbits are closely related and there is often no clear distinction between the various species. In general, rabbits are shorter-eared and burrow-living while hares have longer ears and find shelter above ground. African hares are primarily nocturnal and spend most of the day resting in tall grass or thickets. Hares are among the most frequently encountered mammals on safari night drives as they skip on and off vehicle tracks, confused - no doubt - by the lights. Cheetah sometimes flush and capture hares as they pace through grasslands, while eagle-owls and small carnivores hunt them after dark. Rock Hares (also known as rock rabbits) are attractive reddish-gray animals which live in hilly or mountainous habitats.

PORCUPINE AND OTHER RODENTS

The African Porcupine is the largest of the continent's diverse array of rodents. This highly adaptable creature occurs in virtually every habitat type south of the Sahara, from the harsh Namib and Kalahari to lush montane forests. Family groups live in caves or burrows emerging after dark to feed on bark, roots and fallen berries, as well as in *shambas* (vegetable plots). Porcupines are also known to gnaw on bones for their high calcium content. When threatened, porcupines turn their back on their adversary and rattle their long quills. Lions or Leopards may come away from a confrontation with a face full of quills.

The Springhare is a rather bizarre kangaroo-like rodent of semi-arid scrubland and dry savannah where it lives in colonies of ten individuals or more. A network of burrows is established by the colony in sandy terrain and the rodents emerge at dusk to feed on grass shoots and stems, as well as other herbage of low nutrient value. When seen after dark in the light of a beam, the reflective eyes bob up and down as the animals hop and spring about.

A great variety of mice, rats, gerbils, dormice, molerats and other rodents occur throughout Africa's varied habitats but most are nocturnal, shy and seldom seen. It is beyond the scope of this book to describe or illustrate these little creatures but it should not be forgotten that they play a vital role in ecosystems, as herbivores, seed dispersers and prey for a wide variety of small carnivores, owls, hawks and snakes.

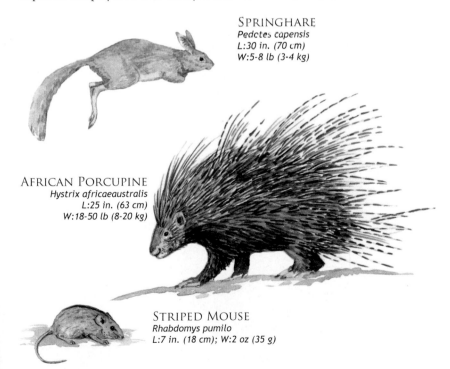

SPRINGHARE
Pedetes capensis
L:30 in. (70 cm)
W:5-8 lb (3-4 kg)

AFRICAN PORCUPINE
Hystrix africaeaustralis
L:25 in. (63 cm)
W:18-50 lb (8-20 kg)

STRIPED MOUSE
Rhabdomys pumilo
L:7 in. (18 cm); W:2 oz (35 g)

ELEPHANT-SHREWS AND HEDGEHOG

With so many large and spectacular mammals to be seen in Africa, it is hardly surprising that many smaller creatures go largely unnoticed.

The elephant-shrews (or sengis) are mouse-like animals with a long trunk-like snout which gives them a slightly elephantine appearance. Most species are active by day when they forage among rocks or along shaded pathways in a home range which has numerous shelters or burrows. They avoid exposed situations where they would be vulnerable to birds of prey. Ants, termites, earthworms and crickets are among the favored food items. For such tiny creatures, elephant-shrews have a comparatively long gestation period and the newborn infants are well-developed to minimize impacts of predation. There are three species of giant elephant-shrew in East Africa. These much larger creatures are about the size of a domestic rabbit although slender with long legs, tail and snout. Terrestrial invertebrates are foraged for in the leaf litter of forests.

Hedgehogs are nocturnal insect-eaters well known to many Europeans who see them in their gardens, woods and - all too often - as road casualties. The African species favor dry savannah or grassland habitats, feeding on worms, termites, beetles, fungi and fallen fruits. Hedgehogs characteristically roll themselves up into a ball when threatened, leaving would-be predators with nothing to attack but a spiny sphere of prickles.

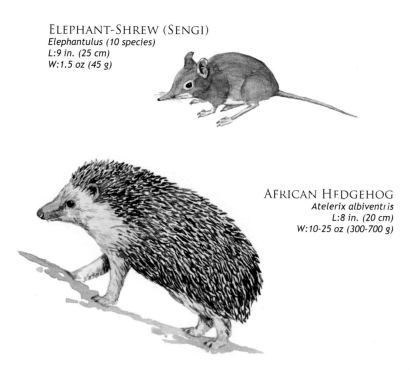

ELEPHANT-SHREW (SENGI)
Elephantulus (10 species)
L:9 in. (25 cm)
W:1.5 oz (45 g)

AFRICAN HEDGEHOG
Atelerix albiventris
L:8 in. (20 cm)
W:10-25 oz (300-700 g)

BATS

Bats are among the most misunderstood of all animals, with irrational fears pervading human folklore in many cultures, and an almost complete ignorance of the vital role that different species play in the control of insects and the life cycles of fruiting plants. Bats are divided into two distinct groups - the insectivorous (micro) bats and fruit-eating (macro) bats.

Fruit bats are sometimes known as 'flying foxes' on account of their dog-like snout, and the largest species may have a wingspan of one meter. Males have repetitive bell-like calls, and all chatter and squeak when feeding. In addition to feeding on figs and other fruit (and then dispersing the seeds), fruit bats relish nectar and pollinate the ornate flowers of sausage trees and baobabs.

Insect-eating bats are characterised by tiny eyes, sharply pointed teeth, strangely shaped ears, and many also have bizarre nose structures. Seen up close, they appear rather frightening and this has no doubt contributed to their unpopularity. Vampire bats are confined to Tropical America where they suck the blood from sleeping mammals and may spread disease among livestock, but no African bats behave in this way. Indiscriminate persecution of bats makes victims out of many harmless and ecologically useful species. Micro bats are among the most important predators of mosquitoes.

Able to find their way and hunt in complete darkness, micro bats use ultrasound (inaudible to the human ear) to navigate by echo-location. A call or chirp is made and 'read' as it bounces back to the bat's sensitive ear receptors. This enables the bat to determine the precise distance between itself and a tree, rock, or other object so as to avoid collision. Every species of bat has its own distinct call, and researchers determine their identity in this way. Small insectivorous bats are often seen hunting or skimming rivers and pools, at dusk.

EPAULETTED
FRUIT-BAT
Epomophorus (6 species)
L:6 in. (14 cm)
W:8 oz (200 g)

YELLOW-WINGED BAT
Lavia frons
L:4 in. (10 cm); W:1.2 oz (36 g)

WHALES AND DOLPHINS

Whales and dolphins live their lives largely unseen to humans but whale-watching has become a popular activity around the world, and dolphins have long captured the human imagination. Africa has a diverse assemblage of whales and dolphins in its coastal waters. Collectively, whales, dolphins and porpoises are known as cetaceans.

The Southern Right-Whale is the most commonly observed species in South African waters, with popular viewing sites on the southern Cape coast. Females come close to shore from June to September when they give birth to their calves in sheltered bays. This whale is distinguished by the absence of a fin on its back, lack of throat grooves, and typically has crusty white barnacle growths on its head and body. Tiny crustaceans are the principal food. Humpback Whales visit the east coast of Africa between May and September, when Antarctic waters are at their coldest. This whale is best known for its extraordinary repertoire of underwater calls which are often recorded as "whale song".

Bottle-nosed Dolphins are highly intelligent cooperative hunters which follow the annual "Sardine Run" – when huge shoals of these small fish move between the Cape and Durban on the South African coast, from June to August. These dolphins, along with sharks, seabirds and fishermen, feast on the bounty of sardines. Common Dolphins can be seen just beyond the continental shelf on boat trips around the Cape Peninsula and all the way along the southern and eastern coast of Africa.

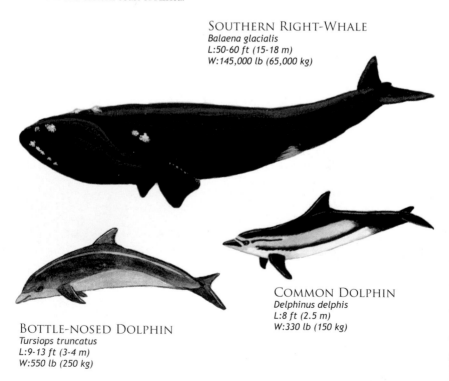

SOUTHERN RIGHT-WHALE
Balaena glacialis
L:50-60 ft (15-18 m)
W:145,000 lb (65,000 kg)

COMMON DOLPHIN
Delphinus delphis
L:8 ft (2.5 m)
W:330 lb (150 kg)

BOTTLE-NOSED DOLPHIN
Tursiops truncatus
L:9-13 ft (3-4 m)
W:550 lb (250 kg)

AFRICAN BIRDS

Over 2,300 species of birds have been recorded in Africa south of the Sahara, almost 25% of the world's nearly 10,000 species. There are 108 families of birds in Africa, and 17 of these are unique to the continent. Among the endemic families are turacos, mousebirds, sugarbirds and guineafowl, as well as the Secretarybird, Shoebill and Hamerkop which are the sole representatives of their families.

Africa's birds, like those elsewhere, fall into three categories: residents, migrants and nomads (wanderers). Eurasian migrants visit Africa between September and April, while intra-African migrants move from the tropics to the sub-tropics.

Birds are most conspicuous in savannah habitats, and all of the large national parks and other protected areas support a diverse avifauna including eagles, storks, bee-eaters, hornbills, rollers and starlings. Forests are home to some spectacular birds but trogons and others are typically elusive and shy. Deserts, grasslands and heathlands are home to a lower diversity of birds but many interesting species live in these environments. Birds abound wherever there is water, so lakes, wetlands, rivers, estuaries and coastlines are excellent birdwatching habitats.

BIRD WATCHING

Featured in this section is a selection of the larger, more colorful and conspicuous birds likely to be seen on safari in eastern and southern Africa, as well as some species from equatorial rainforest, coasts and ocean, and the island of Madagascar.

By going through these pages, you will become familiar with the main bird families, while being able to identify a large proportion of the species you encounter.

Knowing which family a bird belongs to is the first step of identification, with overall size, length of legs, and bill shape being vital factors. Your confidence as a birder will grow as you become familiar with the species illustrated here, and are able to categorize the other birds you see to their appropriate family or group.

Of particular importance when identifying birds beyond the family level, is noting plumage details, tail shape and the color of bill, legs and toes. The diagram below illustrates the important body parts. Another crucial factor in identifying many birds is voice, as many similar species have completely different calls or songs.

More comprehensive guide books are available for all the countries and regions within the scope of this book.

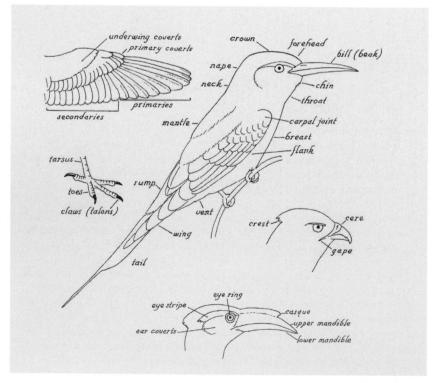

PELICANS, CORMORANTS AND DARTER

With their huge bills and flexible pouches, pelicans are unmistakable. They spend much of their time in the water, paddling with their big webbed feet, but also soar to great heights in thermals. The two species of African pelicans are gregarious and often fish in small flocks which cooperate to drive fish into shallow areas where they are scooped up. They are opportunistic and may scavenge fish from anglers.

Cormorants and darters are predominantly black or dark brown in color, with bills suitable for catching fish underwater. They are terrific divers but do not have waterproof plumage like ducks and grebes, so perch with wings outstretched to dry their oily feathers. Several African species frequent seashores, but the large White-breasted Cormorant and slender Reed Cormorant can be seen in rivers and freshwater lakes. The African Darter has long tail feathers and a dagger-shaped bill with which it spears fish. Darters swim low in the water with only their slender necks and heads protruding, so have the nickname "snake birds".

GREAT WHITE
PELICAN
Pelecanus onocrotalus
5 ft 2 in. (1.6 m)

WHITE-BREASTED
CORMORANT
Phalacrocorax lucidus
3 ft (90 cm)

REED
CORMORANT
Microcarbo africanus
20 in. (52 cm)

AFRICAN DARTER
Anhinga rufa
32 in. (80 cm)

HERONS, EGRETS AND BITTERNS

These are medium-sized to large birds with long slender necks and legs, and dagger-like bills. All have a distinctive S-shaped neck which is tucked in when flying. Herons are generally larger than egrets, while the bitterns tend to be shorter- legged than either. While herons and egrets forage openly on lakeshores, pools and floodplains, bitterns are much more secretive and keep largely to reedbeds. The nocturnal night-herons roost in thickets or reeds during the day, emerging after dark to patrol the fringes of rivers and ponds. The Goliath Heron is the largest member of the family and occurs singly or in pairs; frogs, fish and even baby crocodiles feature in its diet. The Gray Heron is the most widespread of the larger herons, while the small Green-backed Heron is often encountered along quiet rivers and lake fringes. Egrets are often gregarious, particularly the Cattle Egret which often forages away from water in farmlands. In the past, many thousands of egrets were slaughtered for the plume trade, but most African species are common and many may have expanded in range and numbers due to the creation of artificial dams. Several heron species may join storks, ibises and cormorants to nest communally in "heronries".

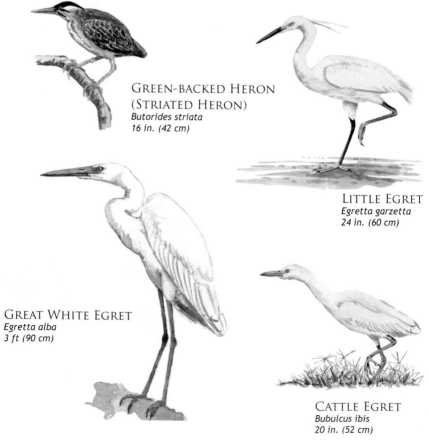

GREEN-BACKED HERON
(STRIATED HERON)
Butorides striata
16 in. (42 cm)

LITTLE EGRET
Egretta garzetta
24 in. (60 cm)

GREAT WHITE EGRET
Egretta alba
3 ft (90 cm)

CATTLE EGRET
Bubulcus ibis
20 in. (52 cm)

BLACK-HEADED HERON
Ardea melanocephala
3 ft (95 cm)

GRAY HERON
Ardea cinerea
3 ft (95 cm)

GOLIATH HERON
Ardea goliath
4 ft 8 in. (1.4 m)

Hamerkop, Shoebill and Grebes

The Hamerkop and Shoebill resemble aberrant storks or herons, and share similar habits. They are the sole representatives of their families, and occur only in Africa. The Hamerkop (named for its hammer-shaped head) is widespread throughout the continent where it frequents riversides and pools in search of frogs and toads. Pairs build a gigantic dome-shaped nest in the fork of a large tree, usually adding to the structure throughout the year. The enormous and rather bizarre Shoebill is restricted to large papyrus swamps and reedbeds in Uganda and Zambia where it feeds mostly on lungfish and catfish. A sighting of the rare Shoebill is a major highlight for many serious birders visiting Africa.

Grebes are small to medium-sized waterbirds, superficially similar to ducks and loons. Many have colorful head plumes and engage in elaborate courtship displays. They have pointed bills, fairly long necks and very short tails. The feet of grebes are set far back on the body which makes walking on land virtually impossible. The entirely aquatic grebes feed largely on fish captured by diving or "up-ending". They fly only after dark, moving from one water body to another. The Little Grebe is the most common and widely distributed.

HAMERKOP
Scopus umbretta
20 in. (52 cm)

SHOEBILL
Balaeniceps rex
4' ft (120 cm)

LITTLE GREBE
(DABCHICK)
Tachybaptus ruficollis
11" (28 cm)

Ibises and Spoonbill

Ibises and spoonbills are large wading birds with long necks and legs. Most favor shallow water and muddy shore habitats, but some ibises forage in grasslands or forest clearings. Ibises and spoonbills are gregarious, often feeding, nesting or roosting in flocks, sometimes alongside herons, egrets and other birds.

The widespread Hadeda Ibis often announces itself with a raucous call and this bird now occupies wooded suburbs of many African cities. The African Sacred Ibis has adapted to scavenge from garbage dumps, while the Glossy Ibis is a bird of wetlands. The distinctive Southern Bald Ibis is found only in the montane grasslands of southern Africa. The African Spoonbill uses its flattened bill to sweep small crustaceans off the substrate so they can be easily grasped.

AFRICAN
SPOONBILL
Platalea alba
3 ft (90 cm)

HADEDA IBIS
Bostrychia hagedash
2 ft 6 in. (76 cm)

AFRICAN
SACRED IBIS
Threskiornis aethiopicus
2 ft 8 in. (80 cm)

SOUTHERN
BALD IBIS
Geronticus calvus
2 ft 6 in. (76 cm)

91

STORKS

Storks are large, long-billed and long-legged birds with supreme soaring abilities. Although lacking talons and hooked bills of true raptors, storks are formidable predators which feed on a variety of living and dead animals. Some storks are specialized fish eaters and possess a unique trigger mechanism which allows them to snap their bill shut instantly.

Of 19 stork species around the world, eight occur in Africa. The fabled European White Stork is a non-breeding migrant, although a small number are resident on the southwestern Cape of South Africa. Like several other storks, they gather in large flocks, often wheeling above in thermals as they move from one feeding area to another. The bald-headed Marabou frequently attends carcasses with vultures and scavenges in and around cities such as Nairobi. The elegant Saddle-billed Stork is usually seen in pairs which forage along rivers and in wetlands. The African Openbill and Yellow-billed Stork are gregarious and nest in large colonies. All storks lay two to four eggs in a large platform of sticks.

YELLOW-BILLED STORK
Mycteria ibis
3 ft 2 in. (1 m)

SADDLE-BILLED STORK
Ephippiorhynchus senegalensis
5 ft (1.5 m)

African Openbill
Anastomus lamelligerus
3 ft (90 cm)

Marabou Stork
Leptoptilos crumeniferus
5 ft (1.5 m)

White Stork
Ciconia ciconia
3 ft 6 in. (1.1 m)

Wooly-necked Stork
Ciconia episcopus
2 ft 8 in. (85 cm)

FLAMINGOS

Flamingos are unmistakable birds of shallow lakes and coastal lagoons. Their extraordinarily long neck and legs, and predominantly pink plumage prevent confusion with any other group of birds. The call of a flamingo is a goose-like 'honk'.

Two of the world's five flamingo species occur in Africa, with the Lesser Flamingo numbering in the millions. Despite this large population size, this flamingo has highly specific habitat requirements and is therefore vulnerable to population crashes. Large breeding colonies occur in East Africa's Rift Valley lakes (particularly Lake Natron) and at the Makgadikgadi Pans in northern Botswana.

The more widespread Greater Flamingo has less specific habitat requirements and feeds in deeper water than its smaller relative. All flamingos have a uniquely-shaped bill designed for filtering small organisms from the water. The Greater Flamingo feeds predominantly on tiny aquatic creatures while Lesser Flamingos favor blue-green algae.

Flamingo breeding activity is synchronized with rainfall. Huge flocks that are resident at a particular locality on one day may suddenly depart overnight to a favored breeding site which is usually a hot and inhospitable rain-filled lake. A single chalky-white egg is laid in a cone-shaped mud nest manufactured by the adults with their feet and bills.

Known predators of flamingos include the African Fish-Eagle and Golden Jackal, while the Marabou Stork may raid nests for eggs and young.

GREATER FLAMINGO
Phoenicopterus roseus
4 ft 6 in. (1.4 m)

LESSER FLAMINGO
Phoeniconaias minor
3 ft (90 cm)

CRANES

Cranes are long-legged birds of grasslands and wetlands, famous for the elaborate courtship 'dances' performed by pairs. These graceful birds have inspired artists and conservationists around the world, but several species are now threatened due to habitat loss.

There are four crane species in Africa, with the Gray Crowned Crane being the most widespread in savannah habitats of eastern and southern Africa. The large Wattled Crane is confined to permanent wetlands such as the Okavango Delta, while the Blue Crane is largely restricted to South Africa.

Cranes have a varied diet and feed by pecking on the ground or probing mud. Invertebrates, frogs, lizards, seeds and agricultural grain are all eaten. The famous "dances" of cranes involve synchronized bows, wing spreads and leaps, and pairs bond for life. Cranes have a bugle-like call often uttered in flight. The nest is a platform of grass or reeds, often surrounded by a moat of water. Two young are usually raised.

WATTLED CRANE
Bugeranus carunculatus
4 ft (1.2 m)

BLUE CRANE
Anthropoides paradiseus
3 ft 2 in. (1 m)

GRAY CROWNED CRANE
Balearica regulorum
3 ft 6 in. (1.1 m)

95

DUCKS AND GEESE

Across the world, ducks and geese are symbolic of wild places, even though a good number have adapted to man-made environments. Together with swans (of which there are no species in sub-Saharan Africa) ducks and geese are often referred to as "waterfowl" or "wildfowl" which indicates their age-old significance as a source of food and sport. There are over 150 species around the world, of which about 30 occur in Africa. All live in aquatic habitats where they feed on plant matter and invertebrates. Large clutches (up to 14 eggs in some species) are laid in a bowl among vegetation or in a tree cavity.

The Egyptian Goose is perhaps the most widespread of African waterfowl, and these noisy birds are aggressive in defense of their territories and young. The White-faced Whistling-Duck is one of two similar species that call with a sweet, high-pitched whistle when coming and going from feeding grounds or roost sites. The Red-billed Teal is one of several "typical" ducks which feed by dabbling at the water's edge or "up-ending" in deep water. The toy-like African Pygmy-Goose favors quiet inlets where water lilies abound.

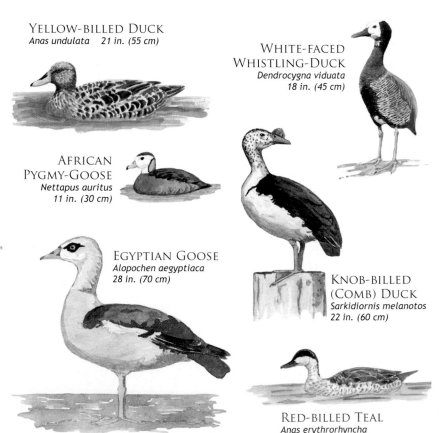

YELLOW-BILLED DUCK
Anas undulata   21 in. (55 cm)

WHITE-FACED
WHISTLING-DUCK
Dendrocygna viduata
18 in. (45 cm)

AFRICAN
PYGMY-GOOSE
Nettapus auritus
11 in. (30 cm)

EGYPTIAN GOOSE
Alopochen aegyptiaca
28 in. (70 cm)

KNOB-BILLED
(COMB) DUCK
Sarkidiornis melanotos
22 in. (60 cm)

RED-BILLED TEAL
Anas erythrorhyncha
18 in. (45 cm)

CRAKES, RAILS, GALLINULES, MOORHENS, COOTS AND FINFOOT

Collectively known as rallids, these are small to medium-sized birds with stubby tails and short rounded wings. Most are incredibly shy and typically solitary, although the gregarious coots do not follow this trend. All are omnivorous, feeding on insects, amphibians and a variety of plant material. Because they live in reedbeds and other dense habitats, rallids are vocal in advertisement of their territories. Among the species which are most often encountered are the Red-knobbed Coot and Common Moorhen which may be abundant around dams, lakes and estuaries. The skittish Black Crake resides along rivers and pools. With its bright red bill and frontal shield, the African Purple Swamphen (gallinule) is a spectacular bird. The tiny flufftails are the most elusive of all rallids. The African Finfoot is a shy and peculiar waterbird belonging to a separate family.

BLACK CRAKE
Amaurornis flavirostra
7 in. (18 cm)

AFRICAN PURPLE SWAMPHEN
Porphyrio madagascariensis
18 in. (46 cm)

RED-KNOBBED COOT
Fulica cristata
16 in. (40 cm)

AFRICAN FINFOOT
Podica senegalensis
22 in. (60 cm)

COMMON MOORHEN
Gallinula chloropus
13 in. (33 cm)

OSTRICH

Ostrich are the world's largest birds, weighing up to 250 lbs (120 kg) and being unable to fly. A single egg is the size of 24 chicken eggs.

The Common Ostrich occurs in savannah and desert where it lives in pairs or larger family groups. The eggs are laid in a scrape on the ground, with several females laying in one "nest"; each hen lays 3 to 8 eggs, with a record of 43 in one. Leaves, succulent plants, seeds, pods and flowers are the main food. Cheetah are among the predators of adults, while eagles may attack the youngsters.

The Somali Ostrich is restricted to the Horn of Africa (western Ethiopia, Somalia and northwestern Kenya).

Ostrich have been domesticated in South Africa and Namibia (as well as in Texas and Australia). Wild ostriches are limited to large reserves and wilderness areas.

The East African race *massaicus* has a pink neck

COMMON OSTRICH
Struthio camelus
7 ft. (2.2 m)

BUSTARDS AND KORHAANS

Bustards are medium-sized to large birds of open landscapes, including deserts. All species have distinctive calls and territorial displays. Plumage is usually in various shades of brown or gray, and sometimes with black and white. Males are usually larger than females, often with bold facial markings. Seeds, succulent plants and insects feature in the diet. The camouflaged eggs are laid in scrapes on bare ground. The 40 lb (18kg) Kori Bustard is the world's heaviest flying bird.

Korhaan is an Afrikaans word used for the smaller bustards that occur in South Africa.

KORI BUSTARD
Ardeotis kori
4 ft 2 in. (130 cm)

RED-CRESTED KORHAAN
Lophotis ruficrista
20 in. (50 cm)

NORTHERN
BLACK KORHAAN
Afrotis afraoides
20 in. (50 cm)

BLACK-BELLIED BUSTARD
Lissotis melanogaster
24 in. (60 cm)

GUINEAFOWL, SPURFOWL AND FRANCOLINS

These ground-dwelling birds are close relatives of partridges, pheasants and turkeys. They are collectively known as "game birds" due to their popularity in human cuisine and sport hunting. Most African species are drably colored to blend in with their savannah and grassland habitats, but all are highly vocal. They have short, rounded wings which allow for rapid but brief flight, and they often burst from cover in a flurry. All have strong legs, well-developed for scraping for seeds and bulbs in hard soil. In several species the adult males have sharp rear-facing spurs above the hind toe (as in the domestic chicken) which are used in territorial fights. Most francolins and spurfowl live in pairs or small coveys, but the guineafowl are gregarious and may live in flocks of 100 or more. The Helmeted Guineafowl is widespread and often abundant in savannah and grassland, while the spectacular Vulturine Guineafowl lives in semi-arid scrublands of eastern Africa.

Quails (of which there are three African species) are miniature partridges, while the superficially similar buttonquails are thought to be more closely related to coursers.

CRESTED GUINEAFOWL
Guttera pucherani
20 in. (50 cm)

VULTURINE GUINEAFOWL
Acryllium vulturinum
2 ft. 3 in. in. (68 cm)

HELMETED GUINEAFOWL
Numida meleagris
24 in. (60 cm)

CRESTED FRANCOLIN
Dendroperdix sephaena
13 in. (34 cm)

SWAINSON'S SPURFOWL
Pternistes swainsonii
20 in. (50 cm)

NATAL SPURFOWL
Pternistes natalensis
20 in. (50 cm)

RED-BILLED SPURFOWL
Pternistes adspersus
20 in. (50 cm)

YELLOW-NECKED SPURFOWL
Pternistes leucoscepus
20 in. (50 cm)

VULTURES

Vultures are the undertakers of the African savannah, feeding primarily on the carcasses of large mammals, including the remains of carnivore kills. These big birds are superbly equipped for a scavenging lifestyle, as they soar to great heights in order to scan the countryside below. When one beady-eyed vulture spots a meal, it attracts many others as it descends rapidly to the scene. A squabble invariably ensues among feeding vultures as individuals feed voraciously. The White-backed Vulture is usually the most numerous species, while the massive Lappet-faced Vulture is the most dominant. The uncommon White-headed Vulture is often the first to locate a carcass, but it just as often pirates a smaller meal from an eagle or stork. The Hooded Vulture has a varied diet which includes termites and carnivore droppings, while the Egyptian Vulture is known to throw small rocks at ostrich eggs in order to open and eat them.

RÜPPELL'S VULTURE (GRIFFON)
Gyps rueppellii
3 ft 5 in. (105 cm)

WHITE-HEADED
VULTURE
Trigonoceps occipitalis
3 ft 1 in. (94 cm)

LAPPET-FACED VULTURE
Torgos tracheliotus
4 ft (120 cm)

HOODED VULTURE
Necrosyrtes monachus
2 ft 3 in. (70 cm)

PALM-NUT VULTURE
Gypohierax angolensis
2 ft. (60 cm)

WHITE-BACKED VULTURE
Gyps africanus
3 ft 2 in. (95 cm)

EGYPTIAN VULTURE
Neophron percnopterus
2 ft 1 in. (65 cm)

BEARDED VULTURE
Gypaetus barbatus
3 ft 6 in. (110 cm)

Eagles

Africa is home to a variety of impressive eagles, some no bigger than a hawk, others massive. All are equipped with powerful talons and a strong, hooked bill for grasping and tearing their prey. Eagles are masters of flight, soaring effortlessly on thermals or swooping at great speed. Pairs typically mate for life, nesting on or below a tree canopy, or on a precipitous cliff. Several similarly-plumaged "brown eagles" pose identification problems for beginners, while the immature plumages of many are similarly confusing.

The African Fish-Eagle is a conspicuous resident of waterways and lakes, where its piercing cry is an evocative sound. The short-tailed Bateleur soars with hardly a wing beat above the savannah tree tops, while powerful Martial and African Crowned Eagles prey upon monitors, hyrax and even small antelope. As their name suggests, the snake-eagles prey primarily on snakes including venomous cobras and adders.

MARTIAL EAGLE
Polemaetus bellicosus
2 ft 8 in. (85 cm)

BATELEUR
Terathopius ecaudatus
2 ft 1 in. (62 cm)

AFRICAN
HAWK-EAGLE
Aquila spilogaster
2 ft. (64 cm)

VERREAUX'S
(BLACK) EAGLE
Aquila verreauxii
2 ft 8 in. (88 cm)

BROWN SNAKE-EAGLE
Circaetus cinereus
2 ft 4 in. (70 cm)

AFRICAN FISH-EAGLE
Haliaeetus vocifer
2 ft 4 in. (70 cm)

LONG-CRESTED EAGLE
Lophaetus occipitalis
1 ft 8 in. (56 cm)

WAHLBERG'S EAGLE
Hieraaetus wahlbergi
1 ft 9 in. (58 cm)

AFRICAN CROWNED EAGLE
Stephanoaetus coronatus
2 ft 8 in. (86 cm)

TAWNY EAGLE
Aquila rapax
2 ft 4 in. (70 cm)

Hawks, Buzzards and Harriers

A variety of sparrowhawks and goshawks (collectively known as accipiters) and buzzards (mostly of the genus *Buteo*) can be found in most African habitats, although many are unobtrusive or even secretive. The Little Sparrowhawk and African Goshawk are predators of birds, while the Dark Chanting-Goshawk and Lizard Buzzard prefer reptiles. The Gabar Goshawk takes birds, lizards and squirrels. The specialized Bat Hawk preys almost exclusively on these winged mammals and is active only at dusk and dawn. The Jackal and Augur Buzzards are birds of grassy hills and mountains, where they may be joined by migratory Common and Steppe Buzzards.

Augur
Buzzard
Buteo augur
22 in. (58 cm)

Montagu's Harrier
Circus pygargus
18 in. (48 cm)

Dark
Chanting-Goshawk
Melierax metabates
20 in. (52 cm)

Gabar Goshawk
Micronisus gabar
13 in. (34 cm)

African
Goshawk
Accipiter tachiro
14-17 in. (36-44 cm)

SECRETARYBIRD, HARRIER-HAWK AND KITES

The unique Secretarybird is a specialized bird of prey which hunts snakes, lizards and rodents in open savannah or grassland. Pairs of these elegant birds construct a large platform nest of sticks, usually on a flat-crowned tree. The fish-eating Osprey is a non-breeding migrant to Africa, where it takes up residence on lake shores and coastal estuaries. The African Harrier-hawk is a strange raptor, with bare facial skin and double-jointed legs that allow it to raid cavities for nestlings and roosting bats. Harriers are narrow-winged, long-tailed raptors of grasslands and wetlands where they glide in buoyant flight in search of their rodent and bird prey. The rather gull-like Black-shouldered Kite is a common roadside bird, while the scavenging Yellow-billed and Black Kites may be numerous around towns and villages.

SECRETARYBIRD
Sagittarius serpentarius
4 ft 5 in. (1.4 m)

BLACK-SHOULDERED
KITE
Elanus caeruleus
13 in. (32 cm)

YELLOW-BILLED KITE
Milvus parasitus
13 in. (55 cm)

AFRICAN HARRIER-HAWK
(GYMNOGENE)
Polyboroides typus
2 ft 1 in. (65 cm)

107

Falcons and Kestrels

These small to mid-size birds of prey are characterized by long pointed wings. They are further distinguished from other raptors by the notch, or "tooth" on the cutting edge of the upper bill. Most have dark moustacial stripes from the base of the eye to the throat. The Lanner and Peregrine Falcons are bird hunters, stooping at great speed to knock down their prey in flight. The Peregrine has been clocked at more than 100 mph (160 km/h) which makes it the fastest of all birds. Kestrels feed primarily on rodents or insects such as winged termites and locusts, and they often gather in large numbers when food is abundant. The Lesser Kestrel is one of several Eurasian species that are non-breeding migrants to Africa. The Pygmy Falcon is hardly bigger than a shrike and feeds mostly on sand lizards. All falcons and kestrels nest either on a rocky ledge or in a cavity.

Lanner Falcon
Falco biarmicus
16 in. (42 cm)

Pygmy Falcon
Polihierax semitorquatus
7 in. (18 cm)

Lesser Kestrel
Falco naumanni
12 in. (30 cm)

Amur Falcon
Falco amurensis
12 in. (30 cm)

Lapwings and Plovers

These are medium-sized to small birds with slender legs, of open habitats such as short grasslands, farmlands and the shores of lakes, rivers and sea. Africa has 18 resident species and several seasonal migrants from Eurasia. The plumage of most species is brown, gray or black, with paler underparts and variable amounts of white on the wings; some have bold head or chest patterns. They are usually seen in pairs or small groups, quietly running off when approached or - if nesting - putting on a noisy distraction display. Two to four camouflaged eggs are laid on the ground in a shallow scrape. Pairs of Blacksmith Lapwings have been observed to defend their eggs or nestlings from trampling by elephant and buffalo, by calling raucously and constantly flying into the face of the large mammals! Invertebrates such as worms, insects and crustaceans are the main food of lapwings and plovers.

AFRICAN WATTLED LAPWING
Vanellus senegalensis
12 in. (30 cm)

THREE-BANDED PLOVER
Charadrius tricollaris
7 in. (18 cm)

CROWNED LAPWING
Vanellus coronatus
12 in. (30 cm)

BLACKSMITH LAPWING
Vanellus armatus
12 in. (30 cm)

WHITE-CROWNED LAPWING
Vanellus albiceps
12 in. (30 cm)

Waders (shorebirds)

This is a group of small to mid-sized birds which includes sandpipers, godwits, snipes and curlews.

These waders have sensitive bill tips and probe mud or sand for their invertebrate prey. The length of neck, bill and legs is extremely variable as each species exploits a particular food source in a particular niche. With the exception of the African Snipe, all species seen in Africa are non-breeding migrants from the Arctic circle or temperate parts of Eurasia. They are present in greatest numbers between September and March, but some individuals remain in Africa throughout the year. Waders typically gather in mixed species flocks on tidal mudflats, along beaches and on lake shores. Seeing large flocks of sandpipers rise, circle and land on a lake shore can be a truly spectacular sight.

Oystercatchers are birds of rocky coastlines where they pry open mussels, oysters and other bivalves with their chisel-shaped bills.

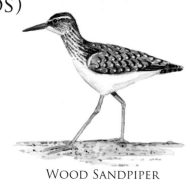

Wood Sandpiper
Tringa glareola
9 in. (21 cm)

Common Greenshank
Tringa nebularia
13 in. (32 cm)

Sanderling
Calidris alba
8 in. (19cm)

African Black Oystercatcher
Haematopus moquini
12 in. (30 cm)

Common Sandpiper
Actitis hypoleucos
8 in. (19 cm)

BIRD MIGRATION

Each year, millions of birds move into Africa from Europe and Asia to escape the shorter days, reduced food supplies and harsh weather of the northern winter.

From late August to April the continent is visited by storks, eagles, falcons, kestrels, buzzards, harriers, sandpipers, bee-eaters, swallows, shrikes, warblers and many others that breed in the Palearctic region but find abundant food supplies in the savannahs and grasslands of sub-Saharan Africa. All of them feed on live prey such as termites, locusts and other insects that multiply during the productive southern summer or in the ever-warm tropics.

Modern satellite and computer technology is helping to unravel the triggers, timing and routes of migratory birds. The most intriguing aspect of migration is navigation: just how do birds find their way? Individual birds have been shown to return time-and-again to the same patch of woodland, from their breeding grounds thousands of miles away. An internal magnetic-compass combined with recognition of external markers such as rivers, mountains and coastlines (for repeat flyers) and the position of the sun, are regarded as the primary orientation and navigation tools, while the many species that fly at night use the stars to provide guidance.

Birds that travel over land can feed as they go, but for those that must cross oceans or barren deserts, they must prepare themselves by feeding as much as possible to deposit fat as fuel; remarkably, the small warblers can double their weight prior to migration!

Migratory birds face many threats of which exhaustion and hunger are paramount. A spell of bad weather can have catastrophic results for millions of birds that depend on refuelling with food or water. Habitat destruction - particularly along fragile coastlines and estuaries - can eliminate crucial stop-over sites. In southern Europe, 'sportsmen' kill millions of small and large birds each year, with island countries such as Malta and Cyprus exacting a huge toll. There is no doubt that climate change is modifying the timing of migration, with certain species leaving later or arriving sooner.

In addition to the long-distance Palearctic migrants, there are many intra-African migrants; birds such as Wahlberg's Eagle, Yellow-billed Kite, Woodland Kingfisher, Broad-billed Roller, Red-chested Cuckoo and Lesser Striped Swallow move into southern Africa from the tropics to breed between October and March.

And on an even more local level, some birds are altitudinal migrants; moving from the high plateaus and mountains to the warmer coastal lowlands during the southern winter.

The Barn Swallow is one of the most abundant migrants and typically takes about three weeks to travel a distance of some 6,000 miles (10,000 km) from Europe to southern Africa.

JACANAS, STILT, AVOCET, COURSERS, THICK-KNEES AND PRATINCOLES

This diverse group of birds are related to lapwings and waders, but several species have a specialized anatomy. The African Jacana has extraordinary long toes and claws which allows it to spread its body weight and walk on floating plants. These jacanas are also remarkable in having a polyandrous mating system in which females mate with several males which then attend to all parental duties. The Black-winged Stilt is aptly named with its very thin legs and bill, while the equally skinny Pied Avocet has a sharply up-curved bill. Thick-knees are nocturnal, large-eyed birds of open country and shorelines where their drab plumage affords superb camouflage. Many coursers are also birds of the night with camouflaged plumage, and most species are attracted to recently burned or over-grazed grasslands where they feed and raise young. The short-legged pratincoles have pointed wings and forked tails. These gregarious birds are conspicuous in flight above grasslands, croplands and marshes.

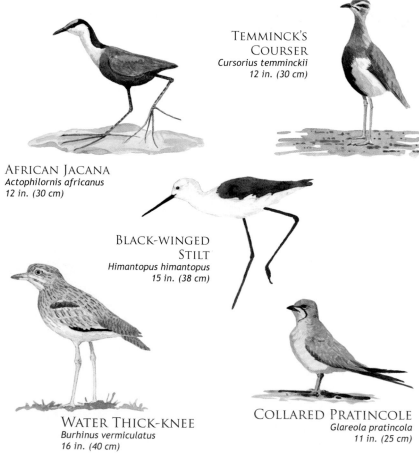

TEMMINCK'S
COURSER
Cursorius temminckii
12 in. (30 cm)

AFRICAN JACANA
Actophilornis africanus
12 in. (30 cm)

BLACK-WINGED
STILT
Himantopus himantopus
15 in. (38 cm)

WATER THICK-KNEE
Burhinus vermiculatus
16 in. (40 cm)

COLLARED PRATINCOLE
Glareola pratincola
11 in. (25 cm)

Gulls, Terns and Skimmer

These are predominantly white and pale gray birds when adult, although most have a different non-breeding plumage which can make identification difficult. Immatures have plumage in shades of brown and gray. Gulls and terns are agile in flight with long wings that extend beyond the tail when the bird is at rest. The greatest diversity occurs along seashores, but some species favor inland lakes of fresh water. The Gray-headed Gull is resident around many of Africa's lakes and, as a scavenger, also frequents garbage dumps. Terns are more slender than gulls and have longer pointed bills ideal for snapping up small fish from the surface of water. The Whiskered, White-winged and Caspian Terns frequent freshwater lakes, while the migratory Gull-billed Tern regularly visits Rift Valley lakes. The Arctic Tern undergoes an extraordinary migration each year from its breeding grounds close to the north pole to the fringe of Antarctica, and numbers can be seen along the African coast. It is usual for several species of tern to mingle and roost together on isolated beaches. The African Skimmer resides on larger rivers where it "skims" the water surface to capture small fish. This black and white bird has a unique bill with the lower mandible being longer than the upper. Like terns, skimmers lay their eggs in a shallow scrape on an exposed bed of sand.

WHISKERED TERN
Chlidonias hybrida
11 in. (26 cm)

GRAY-HEADED GULL
Chroicocephalus cirrocephalus
17 in. (42 cm)

SOOTY TERN
Onychoprion fuscata
17 in. (42 cm)

AFRICAN SKIMMER
Rynchops flavirostris
15 in. (38 cm)

COMMON TERN
Sterna hirunda
12 in. (32 cm)

DOVES AND PIGEONS

Doves and pigeons are familiar birds across the world, for the Rock Dove is resident in many large cities and domesticated hybrids are kept as 'racing pigeons'. Doves are generally smaller than pigeons, but there are no distinct physical differences. There are over 30 species of pigeon and dove in Africa where they occur in all habitats from semi-desert to tropical rainforest. The African Mourning-Dove is one of several similar "ring-necked" doves, while the Emerald-spotted Wood-Dove is a common but inconspicuous bird of savannah where its mournful call is repeated throughout the day. Most doves feed exclusively on seeds but some larger pigeons favor berries. The African Green-Pigeon relishes ripe figs and may spend hours gorging itself in a single tree.

AFRICAN
GREEN-PIGEON
Treron calvus
11 in. (28 cm)

LAUGHING DOVE
Spilopelia senegalensis
7 in. (18 cm)

EMERALD-SPOTTED
WOOD-DOVE
Turtur chalcospilos
7 in. (18 cm)

RED-EYED DOVE
Streptopelia semitorquata
12 in. (30 cm)

NAMAQUA DOVE
Oena capensis
11 in. (28 cm)

CAPE TURTLE-DOVE
Streptopelia capicola
11 in. (28 cm)

SANDGROUSE

Sandgrouse are plump, pigeon-like birds which feed exclusively on the ground. Their intricately-patterned plumage affords excellent camouflage in their preferred habitats of desert, scrubland and semi-arid savannah. With a diet consisting largely of dry seeds, sandgrouse must drink daily and large numbers typically congregate at favored waterholes. Different species have particular drinking times, with the Double-banded Sandgrouse quenching their thirst at dusk or after dark, and the Yellow-throated Sandgrouse drinking only in the morning. In a unique anatomical adaptation, male sandgrouse have absorbent breast feathers which enable them to carry water droplets back to their nestlings which may be many miles away. Sandgrouse fly rapidly and call in flight, often giving their presence away from a distance. Falcons are among the chief predators of sandgrouse, often waiting at favored drinking sites to ambush their quarry.

YELLOW-THROATED
SANDGROUSE
Pterocles gutturalis
12 in. (30 cm)

DOUBLE-BANDED SANDGROUSE
Pterocles bicinctus
9 in. (21 cm)

NAMAQUA SANDGROUSE
Pterocles namaqua
10 in. (25 cm)

BLACK-FACED SANDGROUSE
Pterocles decoratus
9 in. (21 cm)

Parrots and Lovebirds

With just 20 species, half of which have very restricted distributions, Africa has a small variety of parrots in comparison to South America or Australia. Parrots are readily identified by their large head and strongly hooked bill. They are fast fliers, usually moving in a straight line and letting out a strong piercing call while on the move. African parrots are drably colored in comparison to their global relatives, although they display bright underwings and rumps in flight. The tiny lovebirds are more brightly plumaged in shades of lime green, yellow and red. Most lovebirds favor semi-arid scrubland and savannah where they may go about in large flocks. All parrots are hole nesters, often in palm or baobab trees. The Gray Parrot of equatorial forests is a popular cage bird due to its ability to mimic human voices, and large numbers are illegally trapped for the pet trade.

Gray Parrot
Psittacus erithacus
12 in. (30 cm)

Fischer's Lovebird
Agapornis fischeri
5 in. (13 cm)

Brown (Meyer's) Parrot
Poicephalus meyeri
10 in. (24 cm)

Brown-headed Parrot
Poicephalus cryptoxanthus
10 in. (24 cm)

CUCKOOS AND COUCALS

Cuckoos are slender birds with long tails and pointed wings which give some species a hawk-like appearance. They have arched bills and feed predominantly on caterpillars. Most cuckoos are elusive and seldom seen, but they are among the most vociferous of all birds. Some have monotonous calls which may go for hours, and sometimes even on moonlit nights. True cuckoos are brood parasites which lay their eggs in the nest of a particular host species, which then carries out parental duties oblivious to the fact that it is not raising its own offspring. In most cases, the host's eggs or nestlings are evicted, but in others, the cuckoo chick is raised alongside its own nestlings. The Diderick Cuckoo parasitizes weavers and bishops, and is one of three small iridescent green cuckoos in Africa. The larger Red-chested Cuckoo is a noisy but secretive bird which parasitizes various robin-chats and thrushes. Most cuckoos are migratory, including the Common Cuckoo which journeys to Africa from European woodlands. The coucals are larger and bulkier than true cuckoos, and possess a deeper more powerful bill. The Senegal Coucal is one of several species which favors the fringes of wetlands and proclaims its territory with a bubbling liquid call. Coucals raise their own young and do not parasitize the nests of other birds, but frequently include nestlings in their diet.

SENEGAL
COUCAL
Centropus senegalensis
16 in. (40 cm)

DIDERICK
CUCKOO
Chrysococcyx caprius
7 in. (18 cm)

RED-CHESTED CUCKOO
Cuculus solitarius
12 in. (30 cm)

Turacos and Go-away birds

Turacos are a uniquely African bird family of 23 species, most of which are forest dwellers. Some are extremely beautiful with green or violet plumage with crimson wing feathers, while the savannah-dwellers (known as "go-away birds") are predominantly gray in color. Turacos feed on berries and figs as well as flowers and leaf buds. Few birds have such harsh and unattractive calls, however, with croaks and barks being the most apt description for their vocal skills.

The go-away birds of open acacia savannah derive their name from the rasping "go-away" cry which is sounded both as a contact call and a warning. This call is given whenever a human is seen and game hunters are often frustrated when their quarry reacts to this alarm call by fleeing. The Gray Go-away-bird of southern Africa and the Bare-faced Go-away-bird of eastern Africa are among the most noticeable species on any safari. Much shyer are the richly-colored Ross's Turaco of Ugandan and Kenyan forests, Knysna Turaco of South Africa, and Ruspoli's Turaco of Ethiopian juniper forests. The impressive Great Blue Turaco is a bird of equatorial rainforest.

GREAT BLUE TURACO
Corythaeola cristata
30 in. (75 cm)

ROSS'S TURACO
Musophaga rossae
21 in. (52 cm)

**BARE-FACED
GO-AWAY-BIRD**
Corythaixoides personatus
19 in. (48 cm)

GRAY GO-AWAY-BIRD
Corythaixoides concolor
19 in. (48 cm)

**WHITE-BELLIED
GO-AWAY-BIRD**
Corythaixoides leucogaster
20 in. (50 cm)

**EASTERN GRAY
PLANTAIN-EATER**
Crinifer zonurus
20 in. (50 cm)

**PURPLE-CRESTED
TURACO**
Tauraco porphyreolopha
17 in. (43 cm)

**SCHALOW'S
TURACO**
Tauraco shalowi
16 in. (40 cm)

Owls and Nightjars

Owls are the nocturnal equivalent of hawks, preying upon rodents, birds, geckos, frogs and insects. Since owls rely on their own acute hearing to hunt, silent flight is essential and so they have soft plumage with unique fuzzy feather edges. African owls range in size from the two foot tall Verreaux's Eagle-Owl to the tiny Pearl-spotted Owlet and African Scops-Owl. Among dedicated birders, the rare Pel's Fishing-Owl is among Africa's most sought-after species. The Barn Owl is one of the world's mostly widely distributed birds, occurring on all continents. Nightjars are thought to be related to owls but these nocturnal insectivores have more in common with swifts. Many nightjars have melodic songs and they are most often seen resting on sandy vehicle tracks after dark.

Verreaux's Eagle-Owl
Bubo lacteus
2 ft 2 in. (66 cm)

Barn Owl
Tyto alba
14 in. (35 cm)

Pearl-spotted Owlet
Glaucidium perlatum
7 in. (18 cm)

Fiery-necked Nightjar
Caprimulgus pectoralis
10 in. (24 cm)

AFRICAN BARRED OWLET
Glaucidium capense
8.5 in. (22 cm)

AFRICAN WOOD-OWL
Strix woodfordii
14 in. (36 cm)

PEL'S
FISHING-OWL
Scotopelia peli
2 ft. (62 cm)

SPOTTED EAGLE-OWL
Bubo africanus
19 in. (48 cm)

AFRICAN SCOPS-OWL
Otus senegalensis
6.5 in. (16 cm)

MOUSEBIRDS, TROGONS AND BROADBILLS

Mousebirds are a uniquely African bird family with six species distributed in open savannah and woodland habitats. Their name comes from their predominantly gray color, long tail and habit of creeping around in bushes like mice. Mousebirds feed on small berries including those of mistletoe, as well as figs. Most are gregarious and call when in rapid flight.

Trogon diversity is greatest in south-east Asia and tropical America, and Africa has just three species. The beautiful Narina Trogon is a bird of evergreen forest where it feeds on katydids, cicadas and other large insects. Trogons have deep hooting calls and nest in holes.

Broadbills are also better represented in Asia, and all but one of the four African species is dressed in somber plumage. The dumpy African Broadbill lives in forest and thickets where it draws attention to itself with a strange whirring call and acrobatic display.

NARINA TROGON
Apaloderma narina
12 in. (30 cm)

AFRICAN BROADBILL
Smithornis capensis
5 in. (13 cm)

BLUE-NAPED MOUSEBIRD
Urocolius macrourus
14 in. (35 cm)

SPECKLED MOUSEBIRD
Colius striatus
13 in. (34 cm)

HOOPOES AND HONEYGUIDES

Hoopoes and wood-hoopoes are insectivorous birds with long, slender, curved bills. The African Hoopoe forages on the ground but flies into trees when disturbed, often raising its ornate glove-shaped crest. Typical of its kind, the Green Wood-Hoopoe is a gregarious, noisy bird which explores the bark of trees for beetle larvae and caterpillars. The Common and Abyssinian Scimitarbills go about in pairs but forage in the same manner as the larger wood-hoopoes. All hoopoes nest in tree cavities.

The unrelated honeyguides are drably colored birds, but all have distinctive calls. The Greater Honeyguide feeds on wax and bee larvae, sometimes leading humans to hives with its chattering call. Like cuckoos, honeyguides are brood parasites, laying their eggs in the nests of hoopoes, wood-hoopoes, barbets, bee-eaters and other hole nesters, which then raise the imposters as their own. All honeyguides have conspicuous white outer-tail feathers that are obvious in flight.

GREEN WOOD-HOOPOE
Phoeniculus purpureus
15 in. (36 cm)

ABYSSINIAN
SCIMITARBILL
Rhinopomastus minor
9.5 in. (24 cm)

AFRICAN HOOPOE
Upupa africana
11 in. (26 cm)

GREATER HONEYGUIDE
Indicator indicator
8 in. (20 cm)

123

HORNBILLS

With their over-sized, banana-shaped bills, hornbills are unmistakable and these charismatic birds are also among the most interesting to observe. Although not brightly colored, many species have colorful bills or bare facial skin, and the males of some have a raised section on the upper mandible known as a casque. Most hornbills are omnivores, feeding on berries, figs and insects, although small rodents, lizards and nestling birds may also be taken. The massive Southern Ground-Hornbill regularly preys on large snakes. Hornbills appear to mate for life and have a unique breeding strategy in which the female is sealed into a nest cavity while incubating, receiving food from her mate. Once nestlings begin to grow feathers, the female emerges and joins her partner in feeding the brood.

SOUTHERN GROUND-HORNBILL
Bucorvus leadbeateri
3 ft 4 in. (1.1 m)

WHITE-CRESTED
HORNBILL
Tropicranus albocristatus
28 in. (71 cm)

SILVERY-CHEEKED HORNBILL
Bycanistes brevis   *29 in. (74 cm)*

SOUTHERN YELLOW-BILLED HORNBILL
Tockus leucomelas
22 in. (55 cm)

RED-BILLED HORNBILL
Tockus erythrorhynchus
17 in. (42 cm)

AFRICAN GRAY HORNBILL
Tockus nasutus
19 in. (48 cm)

VON DER DECKEN'S HORNBILL
Tockus deckeni
19 in. (48 cm)

WOODPECKERS & BARBETS

Woodpeckers spend most of their time on the trunks of trees where they drill for beetle larvae and excavate nest holes. Several species feed mostly on ants. Most African woodpeckers are rather similar in appearance with greenish backs and barred or streaked underparts. Males often have bright red caps or mustache streaks. The strong tail feathers are used as a brace, while the two-forward, two-backward toe arrangement helps them grip branches. The Ground Woodpecker of southern Africa nests in sand banks and feeds in grasslands.

Barbets have some similarities to woodpeckers including the toe arrangement and ability to excavate their own nests in tree branches (although some favor sand banks or termite mounds). They have stout bills and feed primarily on berries and figs. Most barbets have strange trilling or rattling calls, often made in duet by a pair. The tinkerbirds are diminutive barbets with monotonous calls.

BEARDED
WOODPECKER
Dendropicos namaquus
9 in. (22 cm)

SPOT-FLANKED
BARBET
Tricholaema lacrymosa
5.5 in. (14 cm)

CRESTED BARBET
Trachyphonus vaillantii
9 in. (22 cm)

CARDINAL
WOODPECKER
Dendropicos fuscescens
5.5 in. (14 cm)

DOUBLE-TOOTHED
BARBET
Lybius bidenatus
10 in. (24 cm)

BLACK-COLLARED BARBET
Lybius torquatus
7.5 in. (19 cm)

ROLLERS AND BEE-EATERS

Rollers are brightly colored birds with rather large heads and strong curved bills. With its spectacular cobalt blue wings, the Lilac-breasted Roller is one of the first bird species to be noticed on safari, especially as it flies across roads or sits on prominent perches. Rollers feed on large insects, scorpions and small reptiles. Their name comes from a tumbling courtship display flight in which birds literally roll through the sky.

Bee-eaters are slender, brilliantly-colored birds with thin, down-curved bills. As their name suggests, they feed on bees as well as dragonflies and other winged insects. Most bee-eaters are gregarious when breeding at sandbank colonies, or when feeding, and many species are associated with water.

LILAC-BREASTED ROLLER
Coracias caudatus
12.5 in. tail (32 cm)

LITTLE BEE-EATER
Merops pusillus
6 in. (16 cm)

WHITE-FRONTED
BEE-EATER
Merops bullockoides
9 in. (23 cm)

SOUTHERN
CARMINE BEE-EATER
Merops nubicoides
12.5 in. tail (32 cm)

EUROPEAN
BEE-EATER
Merops apiaster
11 in. (28 cm)

BROAD-BILLED
ROLLER
Eurystomus glaucurus
11 in. (28 cm)

Kingfishers

Kingfishers are thickset birds with short tails, tiny feet, and large heads with long straight bills. Of 17 species in Africa, seven live up to their name and feed primarily on fish, but the others are "dry-land" kingfishers that prey upon lizards, beetles and other large insects. Kingfishers excavate nesting burrows in sandbanks, in tree cavities, or commandeer holes made by woodpeckers.

The Giant Kingfisher is the largest member of the family, while the tiny African Pygmy Kingfisher is one of the smallest. The Pied and Malachite Kingfisher are common along many African waterways, while the noisy and demonstrative Woodland Kingfisher is typical of the "dry-land" group.

The Gray-hooded, Woodland and Pygmy Kingfisher are intra-African migrants that navigate by the stars after dark. These species move away from the equator to breed in temperate savannah during the rainy season.

GRAY-HOODED KINGFISHER
Halcyon leucocephala
8 in. (21 cm)

BROWN-HOODED
KINGFISHER
Halcyon albiventris
8 in. (21 cm)

WOODLAND KINGFISHER
Halcyon senegalensis
8.5 in. (22 cm)

STRIPED KINGFISHER
Halcyon chelicuti
6.5 in. (17 cm)

128

GIANT KINGFISHER
Megaceryle maxima
17 in. (43 cm)

MALACHITE KINGFISHER
Alcedo cristata
5 in. (12 cm)

PIED KINGFISHER
Ceryle rudis
10 in. (25 cm)

AFRICAN PYGMY KINGFISHER
Ispidina picta
4.5 in. (11 cm)

HALF-COLLARED KINGFISHER
Alcedo semitorquata
7 in. (18 cm)

129

Larks, Longclaws, Pipits and Wagtails

Although larks are very similar in appearance to pipits, they are not in fact related, whereas the longclaws and wagtails belong to the same family as pipits. All are birds of open country, especially grasslands, although wagtails live along rivers and shorelines. The identification of most larks and pipits is a challenge even to experienced birders, but the longclaws have bright throat patches of yellow, orange or pink. Many larks have sweet melodious voices which aid identification, and the Rufous-naped Lark is one of the most widespread and conspicuous. Some larks feed primarily on seeds, but many are insectivorous like the pipits. All nest on the ground beneath grass tufts or among rocks.

Rufous-naped Lark
Mirafra africana
7 in. (18 cm)

African Pied Wagtail
Motacilla aguimp   *8 in. (20 cm)*

Rosy-throated Longclaw
Macronyx ameliae   *7 in. (18 cm)*

Cape Wagtail
Motacilla capensis   *7.5 in. (18 cm)*

African (Grassveld) Pipit
Anthus cinnamomeus   *7 in. (17 cm)*

SWIFTS AND SWALLOWS

Swifts and swallows are similar in appearance but are not closely related. Both families are adapted to feed in flight, taking minute winged insects. The most noticeable difference between swifts and swallows, is that the former have narrower wings which give them a sickle-shaped appearance, while swallows have broader wings and frequently maneuver their tail feathers in flight.

Swifts have tiny feet which do not allow them to perch on branches or wires, although they can cling strongly to rock walls. Interestingly, the closest relatives of swifts are the New World hummingbirds (a family absent in Africa). Swifts are typically black or dark brown in color, with white markings in some species. Tail shape is an important clue to the identification of species. The African Palm-Swift nests in the crown of tall palms, while the Little Swift builds its nest on cliff overhangs, tall buildings or beneath bridges.

Swallows and martins come to the ground to collect mud for their cup-shaped nests. Many swallows are dark blue on the back with elongated tail streamers, while martins tend to be brown or blue with square tails. The Barn Swallow visits Africa from its European breeding grounds between October and April.

AFRICAN
PALM-SWIFT
Cypsiurus parvus
6 in. (16 cm)

BARN SWALLOW
Hirundo rustica
6 in. (16 cm)

LESSER STRIPED
SWALLOW
Cercropis abyssinica
6 in. (16 cm)

LITTLE SWIFT
Apus affinis
5 in. (12 cm)

WIRE-TAILED SWALLOW
Hirundo smithii   5.5 in. (14 cm)

131

BULBULS, BABBLERS AND NICATORS

Bulbuls (including brownbuls and greenbuls) are medium-sized birds lacking bright coloration. The forest-dwelling species are known as greenbuls and are extremely difficult to tell apart. The Dark-capped Bulbul and its close relatives are birds of open country and frequently visit gardens and picnic sites where they are conspicuous and noisy. Without exception, the greenbuls are skulking birds of forest interiors or canopies where they rarely present a clear view of themselves and are best identified by their call. Most bulbuls and greenbuls tend to go about in pairs, although groups may gather at abundant food sources. Small berries and insects feature in the diet.

Babblers (and chatterers) are aptly named for their insistent calls. These medium-sized birds live in family groups in which all members raise the young and defend a fixed territory. Babblers are devoid of bright colors although some are boldly patterned in black and white. The Rufous Chatterer and Arrow-marked Babbler are among the most conspicuous members of this family.

Nicators have some physical similarities to bushshrikes, but they are thought to be more closely related to bulbuls. The Eastern Nicator is an extremely shy and skulking bird with an explosive liquid call.

DARK-CAPPED BULBUL
Pycnonotus tricolor
8 in. (20 cm)

ARROW-MARKED BABBLER
Turdoides jardineii
8.5 in. (22 cm)

RUFOUS CHATTERER
Turdoides rubiginosa
7.5 in. (19 cm)

EASTERN NICATOR
Nicator gularis
9 in. (22 cm)

THRUSHES, ROBINS AND CHATS

This is a group of small to medium-sized birds, several with bright or distinct coloration. Numerous species have fine voices, and some are accomplished mimics of other birds. All have sharp, slender bills and forage mostly on the ground where they feed on earthworms and insects. Pairs form strong bonds and defend small territories with their strident calls.

Thrushes are plump birds with somber plumage, usually seen flicking through dead leaves or hopping on lawns for their food. Rock-thrushes are birds of mountainous country where they often perch conspicuously on boulders. Robin-chats often have bright orange underparts and favor dense cover of forests, thickets and gardens. Scrub-robins are birds of dry savannah where they retreat into thickets when disturbed. Chats and wheatears are birds of open country including grasslands and deserts. Palm-thrushes (also known as morning-thrushes), stonechats, akalats and alethes also belong to this family of birds.

KURRICHANE
THRUSH
Turdus libonyanus
8.5 in. (22 cm)

WHITE-BROWED
ROBIN-CHAT
Cossypha heuglini
8 in. (20 cm)

AFRICAN STONECHAT
Saxicola torquatus
5 in. (13 cm)

MOCKING CLIFF-CHAT
Thamnolaea cinnamomeiventris
8 in. (21 cm)

SPOTTED PALM-THRUSH
Cichladusa guttata
6.5 in. (17 cm)

WARBLERS

This group of small to tiny birds includes many cryptic and furtive species, although many have loud and distinctive calls. Because most are difficult to differentiate, they are often ignored by all but the most serious of birdwatchers and often referred to as "LBJs" (Little Brown Jobs). All warblers are insectivorous and forage alone or in pairs. Some are non-breeding migrants from Eurasia.

Warblers fall into various groups. The reed-warblers are mostly brown and rarely emerge from reedbeds where they sing stridently. Tree-warblers are brown or olive-green and flit within leafy canopies. Apalisis are boldly marked with long tails and many have a dark band below the throat. Crombecs have slender, curved bills and virtually no tail. The greenish-colored camaropteras have loud bleating calls and inhabit the densest thickets. Prinias are not shy and quickly investigate any disturbance by calling loudly and flicking their long tails. Cisticolas are tan or sand-colored and the 50 or so African species show few distinguishing features. Cisticolas occupy grassland, marshland or savannah where species can be told apart by their habitat preference, call and back patterns.

TAWNY-FLANKED PRINIA
Prinia subflava
4.5 in. (11 cm)

GRAY-CAPPED WARBLER
Eminia lepida
6 in. (15 cm)

LONG-BILLED CROMBEC
Sylvietta rufescens
3.5 in. (9 cm)

ZITTING CISTICOLA
Cisticola juncidis
4 in. (10 cm)

FLYCATCHERS, BATISES AND WATTLE-EYES

Flycatchers are small to medium-sized birds which fall into two main groups: the "true flycatchers" and the "monarchs". Batises and wattle-eyes may actually be more closely related to shrikes but this relationship is under taxonomic review. Nevertheless, all these birds have broad, flat bills with bristles around their mouths which allow them to snap up insects in flight. The African Paradise-Flycatcher is one of the monarchs and the long-tailed males are among the most eye-catching of birds. All monarchs have broad tails which they regularly fan out. True flycatchers such as the Ashy, Spotted, Silverbird and White-eyed Slaty Flycatcher, hawk insects from a perch to which they return with their food. Like others of its kind, the Chin-spot Batis feeds by searching the undersides of leaves for insects and their larvae. Wattle-eyes keep to dense cover, where they forage in the manner of batises, and several species are restricted to equatorial rainforest. All flycatchers build open cup-shaped nests, which - in the case of monarchs and batises - are miniature works of art bound together with spiders' webs and decorated with lichen or moss.

SILVERBIRD
Empidornis semipartitus
7 in. (18 cm)

ASHY FLYCATCHER
Muscicapa caerulescens
6 in. (17 cm)

AFRICAN
PARADISE-FLYCATCHER
Terpsiphone viridis
14 in. incl. tail in male (36 cm)

CHIN-SPOT BATIS
Batis molitor
5 in. (12 cm)

CHESTNUT
WATTLE-EYE
Platysteira castanea
4.5 in. (10 cm)

135

Drongos, Orioles and Tits

Drongos, orioles and cuckooshrikes are medium-sized birds with sharp, slender bills used mostly for capturing insects. Drongos have hooked tips to their bills, and mouth bristles like flycatchers, which are used to hawk insects in flight. The cuckooshrikes are unobtrusive birds which search foliage and bark for their prey. The predominantly yellow orioles have a more varied diet which includes berries and nectar as well as caterpillars and insects. All of these birds build neat cup-shaped nests, bound with web and camouflaged with lichen or bark strips. The Fork-tailed Drongo is a conspicuous bird as it perches openly and frequently accompanies giraffe and other large mammals which disturb insects when they feed. Drongos are noteworthy for their bold attacks on large birds of prey, their aggressive mobbing of owls, and their ability to mimic calls of other birds. The African Golden Oriole has a beautiful liquid call typical of its family. In common with orioles, cuckooshrikes forage mostly in tree canopies and often go unseen.

Tits (same family as the American chickadees) are small, restless birds which forage among leaves and bark. They have short but strong bills which they use to pull insect larvae from seedpods and bark. Tits are mostly gray or black, have unmusical rasping calls, and nest in tree cavities.

Fork-tailed Drongo
Dicrurus adsimilis
10 in. (25 cm)

Black-headed Oriole
Oriolus larvatus
8 in. (21 cm)

Red-throated Tit
Parvus fringillinus
4.5 in. (11 cm)

White-breasted Cuckooshrike
Coracina pectoralis
10 in. (25 cm)

CROWS, PICATHARTES AND OXPECKERS

Crows and ravens (collectively known as corvids) are not closely related to starlings but have a similar anatomy and thus resemble over-sized cousins. These familiar birds are predominantly black in color and all make a living as opportunists and scavengers. Crows and ravens are among the most intelligent of all birds and most adapt readily to human developments. All have harsh, croaking calls and build large stick nests in tall trees, cliff faces or man-made structures such as electricity pylons. The starling-like Stresemann's Bush Crow is endemic to southern Ethiopia.

Picathartes (also known as rockfowl), are strange, bald-headed birds of dense tropical rainforest of western Africa, and much sought-after by dedicated birders.

Oxpeckers are specialized starlings with deep, compressed bills which they use to comb ticks from the coats of large mammals. Flocks of these bright-billed birds accompany giraffe, buffalo and most antelope species in a truly symbiotic relationship, frequently taking to flight with alarm calls when predators or people approach. Like true starlings, oxpeckers build bowl-shaped nests of straw and feathers inside tree cavities.

PIED CROW
Corvus albus
18 in. (46 cm)

GRAY-NECKED PICATHARTES
Picathartes oreas
15 in. (38 cm)

STRESEMANN'S BUSH CROW
Zavattariornis stresemanni
12 in. (30 cm)

RED-BILLED OXPECKER
Buphagus erythrorhynchus
8 in. (20 cm)

SHRIKES

Shrikes and bushshrikes are mid-sized, predatory birds with hooked bills. The true shrikes are mostly gray or black in color and perch upright on perches in open habitats where they pounce on large insects, lizards and small rodents. Some, such as the Common Fiscal, spike excess prey onto thorns or barbed-wire, to feed on later. The bushshrikes (including the boubous, gonoleks, tchagras and puffbacks) are secretive skulkers of thickets or tree canopies where pairs keep in contact with distinctive calls, often made in duet. The Gray-headed Bushshrike is the largest member of this tribe and frequently preys upon chameleons and small snakes. Most shrikes and bushshrikes eat nestling birds when the opportunity presents itself, and some prey upon waxbills and other small birds. The helmetshrikes go about in family groups of up to 12, with all members helping to raise and feed the young in a classic example of "cooperative breeding". The Magpie Shrike and Gray-backed Fiscal also breed as family groups rather than in pairs, with previous offspring assisting in nesting duties. All shrikes, bushshrikes and helmetshrikes build cup-shaped nests that are usually camouflaged with strips of bark or lichen.

BLACK-BACKED
PUFFBACK
Dryoscopus cubla
6.5 in. (17 cm)

MAGPIE SHRIKE
Urolestes melanoleuca
20 in. incl.tail (50 cm)

WHITE-CRESTED
HELMETSHRIKE
Prionops plumatus
8 in. (22 cm)

GRAY-HEADED
BUSHSHRIKE
Malaconotus blanchoti
11 in. (26 cm)

COMMON FISCAL
Lanius collaris
9 in. (23 cm)

CRIMSON-BREASTED
SHRIKE
Laniarius atrococcineus
8 in. (21 cm)

Starlings

Starlings are mid-sized birds, many with glossy aqua-blue plumage and bright yellow or red eyes. All have slender bills for a mixed diet of insects and berries. Most are gregarious and gather in large flocks when not breeding.

Many species adapt quickly to human activities, living close to people and gathering to feed at picnic sites and camp grounds. All starlings nest in cavities, either a natural tree hole, fence post or some other man-made structure. Wattled Starlings breed in large colonies, and in the Serengeti flocks follow the annual wildebeest migration to feed on insects disturbed by the herds.

Greater Blue-eared Starling
Lamprotornis chalybaens
9 in. (23 cm)

Superb Starling
Lamprotornis superbus
7.5 in. (19 cm)

Red-winged Starling
Onychognathus morio
12 in. (31 cm)

Violet-backed Starling
Cinnyicinclus leucogaster
6.5 in. (17 cm)

Burchell's Starling
Lamprotornis australis
7 in. (18 cm)

Golden-breasted Starling
Lamprotornis regius
14 in. (35 cm)

Sunbirds and White-eyes

Being specialized nectar feeders, sunbirds are the African equivalent of American hummingbirds, although they perch rather than hover while feeding. Like hummingbirds, they have long bills (and long tongues!) with which they sip nectar, and most species have a variety of specific plants which they favor (and inadvertently pollinate). The males of most sunbirds have iridescent plumage (another trait shared with hummingbirds) and aggressively chase rivals and competitors. That two unrelated bird families should be so similar in appearance and aspects of their behavior, is the result of convergent evolution, where species develop characteristics suited to a particular niche or lifestyle. The drably colored female sunbirds are confusingly similar and best identified by their bill shape, or – since they often forage in pairs or groups - by waiting for a male partner to appear. All make camouflaged purse-shaped nests suspended from plants. Sunbirds are sometimes erroneously called "sugarbirds" but this is in fact a unique family of two southern African nectivores, possibly related to Australian honeycreepers.

The white-eyes are tiny, green or yellow birds with a distinctive ring of white feathers around their eyes. They have slender, sharp bills which they use to feed on aphids and other tiny insects as well as berries and nectar.

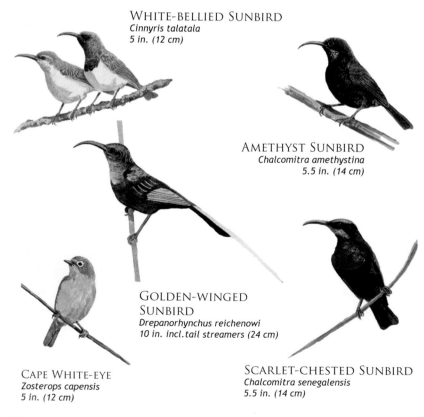

WHITE-BELLIED SUNBIRD
Cinnyris talatala
5 in. (12 cm)

AMETHYST SUNBIRD
Chalcomitra amethystina
5.5 in. (14 cm)

GOLDEN-WINGED SUNBIRD
Drepanorhynchus reichenowi
10 in. incl.tail streamers (24 cm)

CAPE WHITE-EYE
Zosterops capensis
5 in. (12 cm)

SCARLET-CHESTED SUNBIRD
Chalcomitra senegalensis
5.5 in. (14 cm)

Madagascar Endemics

Madagascar has around 250 bird species with nearly half of them being endemic to the huge island and thus found nowhere else on Earth.

Five families are unique to Madagascar (or the nearby Comores). The vangas occupy a niche similar to that of the African bushshrikes (which are absent in Madagascar), feeding on large insects and their larvae; one species, the Sickle-billed Vanga resembles and behaves like a wood-hoopoe, while the Helmet Vanga has an extraordinary and huge blue bill.

The ground-rollers are beautiful, intricately-patterned insectivores that forage on the forest floor. Cuckoo-rollers are slender, large-headed birds that hawk insects in flight. The little asities are brightly-colored berry and nectar-feeders. Mesites are terrestrial birds of the shady forest floor that hardly ever take to flight.

Sadly, many of Madagascar's birds are endangered due to shrinking forest habitats.

Madagascar Blue Vanga
Cyanolanius madagascarinus
6.5 in. (16 cm)

Pitta-like Ground-Roller
Atelornis pittoides
11 in. (26 cm)

Helmet Vanga
Euryceros prevostii
13 in. (29 cm)

Common Sunbird Asity
Neodrepanis coruscans
5 in. (11 cm)

141

WEAVERS

Weavers are among the most conspicuous of Africa's birds, not only for their brilliant yellow plumage (mostly in males) but also for their distinctive hanging nests. Each species has its own style of nest, some with lengthy entrance tubes.

Most weavers feed on seeds and have conical bills for this purpose, but they also catch insects and feed these to their nestlings.

In the Kalahari, flocks of Sociable Weavers construct a massive multi-chambered nest resembling a haystack which is insulated to keep out heat and cold. Buffalo-weavers are bulkier than true weavers and most construct untidy twig nests. Sparrow-weavers build untidy nests suspended from the outermost branches of trees. Malimbes are forest-dwelling weavers with striking black and red plumage.

VILLAGE WEAVER
Ploceus cucullatus
6 in. (15 cm)

RED-HEADED WEAVER
Anaplectes melanotis
5.5 in. (14 cm)

SOCIABLE
WEAVER
Philetarius socius
5.5 in. (14 cm)

SPECTACLED WEAVER
Ploceus ocularis
5.5 in. (14 cm)

WHITE-HEADED
BUFFALO-WEAVER
Dinemellia dinemelli
9 in. (24 cm)

Queleas, Bishops and Widowbirds

The Red-billed Quelea is regarded as the world's most numerous bird, with flocks numbering in the millions. These swarms feed on grain and can be a plague to farmers as they devastate crops within hours. Quelea breeding colonies attracts hordes of predators from snakes and storks, to mongooses and monitors, so are always well worth visiting for wildlife enthusiasts.

Bishops and widowbirds are close relatives of the weavers that favor open grassy habitats. The males have elaborate and sometimes colorful breeding plumage during the breeding season, while females are drab, sparrow-like birds that pose identification difficulties even to experienced birders. All have conical bills and feed exclusively on seeds.

Male widows perform elaborate dances designed to secure mating rights with the females which then undertake all parental duties.

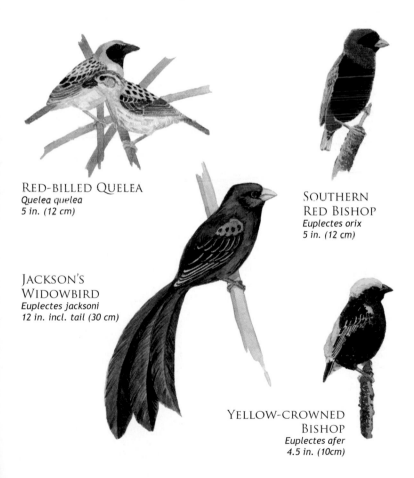

Red-billed Quelea
Quelea quelea
5 in. (12 cm)

Southern
Red Bishop
Euplectes orix
5 in. (12 cm)

Jackson's
Widowbird
Euplectes jacksoni
12 in. incl. tail (30 cm)

Yellow-crowned
Bishop
Euplectes afer
4.5 in. (10cm)

SMALL FINCHES

This group of small to tiny finches are collectively known as estrildids and most are brightly colored. All have short conical bills, ideal for feeding on grass seeds. Some go about in pairs while others are more gregarious and gather in flocks of a dozen or more. It is quite common for several species of waxbill, firefinch, pytilia or mannikin to feed together.

The mannikins (known as munias in Asia and Australia) are not to be confused with the berry-eating manakins (note different spelling) of tropical American forests. All estrildids build untidy nests made of fine grasses and lined with feathers, sometimes close to the nests of aggressive paper wasps which act as a deterrent to monkeys and other would-be nest robbers. Some commonly breed in the disused nests of weavers. Many waxbills are birds of semi-arid scrublands, while twinspots and crimsonwings are residents of forests. Whydahs and indigobirds are parasitic estrildids that lay their eggs in the nest of a particular waxbill, firefinch or twinspot.

COMMON WAXBILL
Estrilda astrild
4 in. (11 cm)

BLUE WAXBILL
Uraeginthus angolensis
4 in. (11 cm)

PIN-TAILED
WHYDAH
Vidua macroura
12 in. incl. tail (30 cm)

BRONZE MANNIKIN
Spermestes cucullatus
3.5 in. (9 cm)

RED-BILLED
FIREFINCH
Lagonosticta senegala
4 in. (10 cm)

PINK-THROATED
TWINSPOT
Hypargos margaritatus
4 in. (11 cm)

Sparrows, Buntings and Canaries

These small seed-eaters are well-known to most people as common garden or street birds (in the case of sparrows) or as singing cage birds (as with canaries). They occur in pairs or small groups, less often in flocks. All are exclusively seed-eaters, feeding mostly on the ground.

The House Sparrow is native to Europe but has spread all around the world, living in close association with people. In Africa, it occurs in towns, ports and cities and even in some remote areas around national park camps and headquarters. In general, sparrows are rather dull-colored in shades of gray, fawn and rust.

Most buntings have boldly-patterned heads, while canaries are predominantly yellow. Seed-eaters and siskins are close relatives of the canaries.

Interestingly, the African sparrows and buntings do not belong to the same families as their American namesakes; the American birds being closely allied to the cardinals and tanagers, while the African birds are finches.

CAPE SPARROW
Passer melanurus
5.5 in. (14 cm)

HOUSE SPARROW
Passer domesticus
5 5 in. (14 cm)

GOLDEN-BREASTED BUNTING
Emberiza flaviventris
6 in. (15 cm)

YELLOW-FRONTED CANARY
Crithagra mozambica
4.5 in. (12 cm)

Penguins, Albatrosses and Other Seabirds

This is a 'mixed-bag' of birds, placed together here at the end of the bird section since only a few travelers to Africa spend time birdwatching offshore. Penguins are associated with Antarctica and the cold sub-Antarctic waters of the Southern Ocean, so it comes as a surprise to many that the African Penguin breeds close to Cape Town and can also be seen on the Namibian and Garden Route coasts.

African Penguin
Spheniscus demersus
2 ft (65 cm)

The Cape Gannet is a gregarious bird that catches fish by plunging into the sea - they breed communally on offshore islands (also at Lambert's Bay on South Africa's west coast) but follow the annual "sardine run" up the east coast of South Africa.

A diversity of albatrosses, petrels, shearwaters, prions and storm-petrels visit the oceans around Africa, particularly in the cold waters of the south and these spectacular birds can be seen on specialized pelagic birding trips.

Frigatebirds and tropicbirds, as well as boobies, feed in the warmer waters off the East African coast and are frequently encountered around Seychelles and other Indian Ocean islands.

Shy Albatross
Thalassarche cauta
3 ft 2 in. (95 cm)

Cape Gannet
Morus capensis
3 ft (90 cm)

Greater Frigatebird
Fregata minor
3 ft (90 cm)

Sooty Shearwater
Puffinus griseus
1 ft 6 in. (45 cm)

AFRICAN REPTILES AND FROGS

A wide variety of reptiles and amphibians occur in sub-Saharan Africa, but the great majority are secretive and seldom seen. Reptiles evolved earlier than birds or mammals, so that some of today's species - such as the crocodile and tortoise - have ancient lineages dating back to the Jurassic era when dinosaurs (reptiles themselves) ruled the planet.

Many people have a natural fear of snakes, and dislike all other reptiles, with the possible exception of tortoises and their relatives. Naturally, all reptiles play a vital role in various ecosystems, with snakes and lizards being among the most important predators of rodents and insects, respectively. Several snakes possess venom, which they use to immobilize their prey, and mambas, cobras and adders are among those which are potentially dangerous - even lethal - to people. For this reason, it is best to leave all snakes undisturbed as they will rarely, if ever, strike if they have an escape route.

Only a few of the more conspicuous or interesting reptiles and frogs are featured on the following pages. You will be likely to see crocodiles and terrapins near water, but snakes of any kind are shy and rarely encountered. Lizards are divided into several families or groups, the most distinctive of which are featured here.

Frogs are the only amphibians native to sub-Saharan Africa, as there are no salamanders or newts. Frogs are fascinating creatures and are best looked for with a flashlight after dark, particularly in wet weather, by following their call. A chorus of calling frogs is an evocative and characteristic sound of the African night.

147

SNAKES

Africa has an extraordinary diversity of snakes, from tiny thread-like creatures which rarely come above ground, to the huge Rock-Python. All snakes are rather shy, however, and rarely encountered. This includes the venomous and potentially dangerous cobras, mambas and adders which will generally avoid humans unless cornered or aggravated in some way. All snakes are carnivorous, swallowing their prey whole and have unfused jaw bones and elastic skin.

Among the most commonly seen snakes on safari are the various tree-snakes, including the Boomslang and well-camouflaged Twig Snake, which are frequently mobbed and harassed by noisy gangs of birds and so alert people to the presence of these nest-robbers.

Adders and vipers can be rather slow-moving and might be stumbled upon on rocky hillsides, scrub and desert. The Puff Adder is notoriously sluggish and sometimes suns itself on leafy pathways. The impressive Gaboon Viper occurs in tropical forests where its coloration matches the fallen leaves in which it hides to ambush prey.

The legendary Black Mamba is diurnal and will not hesitate to strike if it has no escape route. Any bite by a cobra or mamba must be treated as a medical emergency.

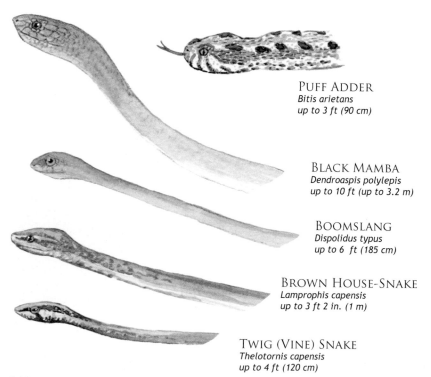

PUFF ADDER
Bitis arietans
up to 3 ft (90 cm)

BLACK MAMBA
Dendroaspis polylepis
up to 10 ft (up to 3.2 m)

BOOMSLANG
Dispolidus typus
up to 6 ft (185 cm)

BROWN HOUSE-SNAKE
Lamprophis capensis
up to 3 ft 2 in. (1 m)

TWIG (VINE) SNAKE
Thelotornis capensis
up to 4 ft (120 cm)

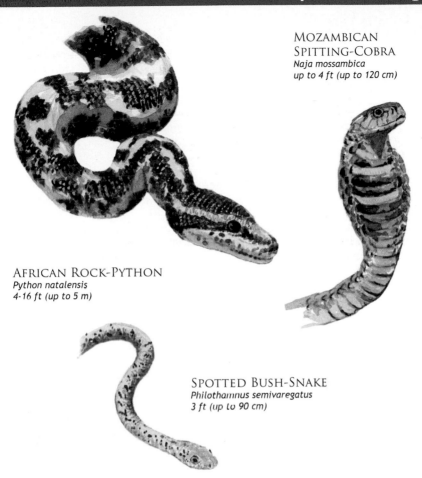

MOZAMBICAN
SPITTING-COBRA
Naja mossambica
up to 4 ft (up to 120 cm)

AFRICAN ROCK-PYTHON
Python natalensis
4-16 ft (up to 5 m)

SPOTTED BUSH-SNAKE
Philothamnus semivaregatus
3 ft (up to 90 cm)

Most cobras are primarily nocturnal, feeding on toads and rodents. These dangerous snakes are best known for their expandible "hood", but this is only visible when agitated individuals flatten their neck prior to striking. Some species are able to spit venom with incredible accuracy into the eyes of an adversary. The Snouted Cobra is widespread throughout African savannahs, while the Cape Cobra (which has a bright golden-yellow form) occurs in the Kalahari and Karoo.

The African Rock-Python is a massive snake with a broad head and geometric skin pattern. Some individuals may reach a length of 16 feet (5m) when they are capable of capturing and swallowing large prey up to the size of adult impala. Prey is killed by constriction, and literally squeezed to death. Hyraxes in rocky outcrops, and cane rats in marshes and sugarcane plantations are favored prey. These snakes are not poisonous but have long fangs capable of inflicting a severe ripping bite. Rock-Pythons lay up to 50 eggs which hatch after 65 to 80 days; females coil around the eggs to protect them, but the hatchlings must fend for themselves.

149

LIZARDS

With the exception of geckos, all lizards are diurnal and many species are frequently encountered. Almost all lizards are insectivorous, although the larger monitors will take bigger vertebrate prey.

Agamas are squat lizards with large box-shaped heads. The conspicuous males assume bright head and body colors during the breeding season, when they bob up and down on tree trunks or rocks. Females and non-breeding males are cryptically camouflaged to match their favored terrain.

Skinks are slender, snake-like lizards with short legs; some are actually legless and live beneath the ground. Many species are quite tame and sun themselves in exposed positions, but they rapidly move to cover when threatened.

Plated-lizards are denizens of large rock outcrops while girdled-lizards favor these and wooded habitats. Sand-lizards are often seen in arid and semi-arid habitats, while crag-lizards inhabit mountainous regions. Worm-lizards are rarely seen subterranean creatures.

MWANZA AGAMA
Agama mwanzae
7 in. (20 cm)

SOUTHERN
TREE-AGAMA
Acanthocercus atricollis
12 in. (32 cm)

RAINBOW AGAMA
Agama agama
7 in. (20 cm)

STRIPED SKINK
Trachylepis striata
7 in. (20 cm)

WATER (NILE) MONITOR
Varanus niloticus
3-6 ft (up to 2 m)

Monitor lizards (also known as "leguaans" in South Africa) can reach a great size. The Water Monitor is a massive semi-aquatic lizard that is most frequently seen on river banks, the branches of waterside trees and lake fringes. Adults are dark olive-brown on the back, and paler below, while juveniles are boldly patterned in yellow and black. These powerful lizards feed on virtually anything they can overpower, as well as the eggs of crocodiles, snakes and birds. They will also scavenge from the carcasses of large mammals and fish. Females have the unique habit of laying their clutch of soft-shelled eggs in an active termite mound and then leaving the social insects to close up her diggings and so create ideal conditions for incubation. The similar Rock Monitor is somewhat smaller and spends much of its time in trees.

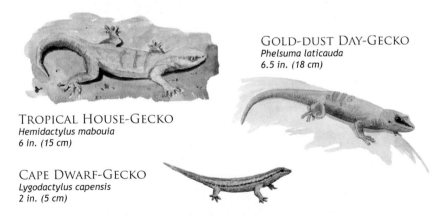

GOLD-DUST DAY-GECKO
Phelsuma laticauda
6.5 in. (18 cm)

TROPICAL HOUSE-GECKO
Hemidactylus mabouia
6 in. (15 cm)

CAPE DWARF-GECKO
Lygodactylus capensis
2 in. (5 cm)

Most geckos are strictly nocturnal and some species are familiar around lodges, hotels and homes where they capture moths and other insects attracted to lights; they have the ability to walk on smooth, vertical surfaces. Dwarf-geckos are diurnal and often seen on tree trunks and fallen logs. The Gold-dust Day-Gecko is native to Madagascar and the Comores, but has been introduced to Zanzibar and the Seychelles (as well as some Hawaiian islands). The repetitive dusk call of the Common Barking-Gecko is a distinctive sound in the Namib and Kalahari deserts.

151

CHAMELEONS

Chameleons are distinctive diurnal lizards which rely on their incredible camouflage and ability to change their skin color, in order to ambush insect prey and avoid predation. They have numerous unique anatomical adaptations including eyes that swivel independently and thus allow them to look in two places without moving their head.

Madagascar is the epicenter of chameleon evolution, with more than half of the world's 130 species endemic to this huge island that has been isolated from the African mainland for about 165 million years. The Parson's Chameleon is the largest known species, being about the length of a domestic cat, while the tiny Stump-tailed Chameleon is smaller than a match-stick.

On mainland Africa, the widespread Flap-necked Chameleon is most often encountered when it is crossing sand tracks or roads, but can also be found on night drives when roosting individuals show up whitish in spotlight beams. The Namaqua Chameleon is a resident of the arid Namib Desert, while a variety of horned-chameleons occur in eastern Africa.

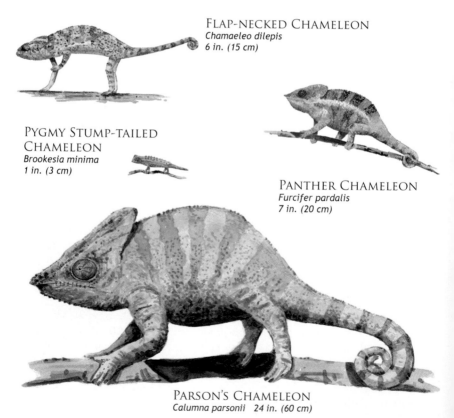

FLAP-NECKED CHAMELEON
Chamaeleo dilepis
6 in. (15 cm)

PYGMY STUMP-TAILED CHAMELEON
Brookesia minima
1 in. (3 cm)

PANTHER CHAMELEON
Furcifer pardalis
7 in. (20 cm)

PARSON'S CHAMELEON
Calumna parsonii   24 in. (60 cm)

CROCODILES

The Nile Crocodile is the largest and most dangerous of African reptiles. Although stories relating to its size and ferocity are often exaggerated, the crocodile's awesome reputation as a powerful killer cannot be contested. Individuals over 12 feet (3.5 metres) in length are opportunistic feeders and include large mammals (including humans!) in their diet. Smaller crocodiles feed on fish, frogs, aquatic birds and smaller mammals.

Crocodiles display tender parental care, rather astonishing for a primeval reptile whose bodily form has remained unchanged for the past 100 million years. Female crocodiles bury their clutch of 50 or so white eggs in a shallow burrow close to water, and then rest nearby throughout the 90-day incubation period. Once the eggs hatch and the tiny, finger-sized young emerge, they begin yelping and the caring mother carefully takes each one into her mouth. Even unhatched eggs may be picked up and gently cracked to release the young. Packed into their mother's gular pouch, the youngsters are safe until she releases them at the water's edge.

Crocodiles have been hunted for centuries as the skin on their underbellies produces the finest leather, and numerous populations have been exterminated. Crocodile farming has not only met the demand for leather, but has also allowed for the reintroduction of crocodiles into their former haunts. It remains, however, the most feared animal among rural communities.

NILE CROCODILE
Crocodylus niloticus
Up to 18 ft (up to 5.5 m);
Largest may weigh up to 1,700 lb (750 kg)

Two other species of crocodile occur in equatorial Africa: the Dwarf Crocodile of west and central Africa that reaches a maximum length of 5 feet (1.5 m), and the Slender-snouted Crocodile that feeds almost entirely on fish and attains a length of up to 12 feet (3.5 m).

TORTOISES AND TERRAPINS

Tortoises and terrapins are instantly recognized by their shield-like shell. Fossils from ancient chelonians date back over 200 million years, revealing that tortoises and their relatives have been roaming our planet even before the rise of the dinosaurs.

Tortoises live on dry land, moving about on their club-like feet and retracting their heads into their shells when threatened. The large Leopard Tortoise is the most frequently encountered species and mature specimens may weigh over 44lbs (20kg). Hinged-tortoises have a shell that hinges backwards to protect their rear. A number of small tortoises including the Geometric Tortoise and Tent Tortoise inhabit the dry parts of southern Africa, with several species being endangered.

Giant-tortoises occur on some tropical islands but only the Aldabra Giant-Tortoise survives in the wild, with several thousand on the Aldabra Atoll of the Seychelles. Many species of giant-tortoise are known to have become extinct in recent times (although the Galapagos Giant-Tortoise still flourishes on these remarkable islands in the Pacific Ocean).

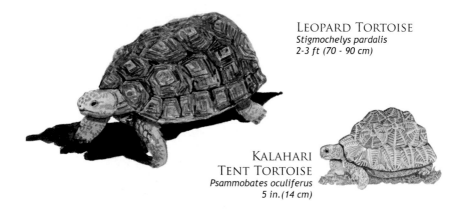

LEOPARD TORTOISE
Stigmochelys pardalis
2-3 ft (70 - 90 cm)

KALAHARI
TENT TORTOISE
Psammobates oculiferus
5 in.(14 cm)

SERRATED HINGED
TERRAPIN
Pelusios sinuatus
15 in. (35 cm)

Terrapins are semi-aquatic and live in fresh water where they feed on tadpoles, frogs and aquatic insects. Large individuals may ambush bigger prey such as doves that come to drink at waterholes. Terrapins can often be seen sunning themselves on logs or the backs of hippos, and may feed on ticks and other ectoparasites on these large mammals.

TURTLES

Turtles are marine-dwelling reptiles that spend almost all of their lives in the oceans. In contrast to tortoises and terrapins, the front limbs are greatly enlarged flippers that enable them to swim optimally.

The nesting behavior of turtles is well-known, with females crawling onto sandy beaches after dark to excavate a nest burrow, several feet about the spring high-tide limit. A clutch of round, soft-shelled eggs (up to 100) are laid then covered by scraping sand over them with the large front flippers. As with many other reptiles, the temperature of the nest determines the sex of the hatchlings. Incubation is usually between 2 and 3 months, after which the tiny hatchlings must make the often perilous journey down the exposed beach into the sea. Only a tiny percentage of hatchlings survive to maturity (at about 30 years) when females return to the beach they born to lay their own eggs. Humans have been exploiting turtle eggs as a resource for thousands of years but this - in combination with several unnatural mortality factors - has resulted in most species being classified as threatened.

The huge Leatherback Turtle is an absolute giant that can weigh up to 1,980 lbs (900 kg).

GREEN TURTLE
Chelonia mydas 3.5 ft (1.1 m)

LOGGERHEAD TURTLE
Caretta caretta 3.5 ft (1.1 m)

LEATHERBACK TURTLE
Dermochelys coricea 6 ft (1.7 m)

FROGS AND TOADS

Africa is home to a great variety of frogs and toads. Although all need water in which to breed, different species live in all kinds of environments including forest, savannah, grassland and even desert (where arid-adapted species emerge from burrows to reproduce in rain puddles). All are primarily nocturnal and more often heard than seen. Each species has a distinctive and often harsh call which is used to attract mates. At the onset of the rainy season, raucous symphonies of calling males can create a huge din in swamps and wetlands. In temperate southern Africa, many species hibernate during the dry winter months.

Frog numbers are thought to be declining all around the world. Their porous skins make them susceptible to chemical pollutants, but destruction of wetland habitats is perhaps the greatest factor. Changing climate and rainfall patterns, probably as a result of global warming, have a great impact on the breeding cycle of amphibians and may have resulted in the outbreak of chytrid fungus which is deadly to frogs and toads.

Toads are recognized by their warty skin and habit of moving freely on dry land. Tree-frogs have huge eyes and toes with sticky toe pads. Reed-frogs are tiny and often adorned in beautiful bright colors. River-frogs and grass-frogs fit the mold of the classic frog, with pointed snouts and long and muscular hind legs which allow them to leap great distances. Bullfrogs typically emerge only after rain when males aggressively defend territorial pools. The strange little rain-frogs also come out after heavy rains as their name suggests; they feast mostly on termites and inflate themselves when threatened by a predator.

The foam-nest frog often sits exposed to full sunlight and often enters buildings; its extraordinary white foam-nests are seen around waterholes.

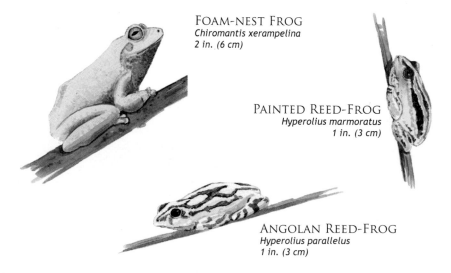

FOAM-NEST FROG
Chiromantis xerampelina
2 in. (6 cm)

PAINTED REED-FROG
Hyperolius marmoratus
1 in. (3 cm)

ANGOLAN REED-FROG
Hyperolius parallelus
1 in. (3 cm)

GUTTURAL TOAD
Amietophrynus gutturalis
3 in. (9 cm)

RED TOAD
Schismaderma carens
3 in. (9 cm)

COMMON RIVER-FROG
Amieta (Rana) angolensis
2.5 in. (7 cm)

BUSHVELD RAIN-FROG
Breviceps adspersus
1.5 in. (4 cm)

GIANT BULLFROG
Pyxicephalus adspersus
6 in. (20 cm)

AFRICAN FISH

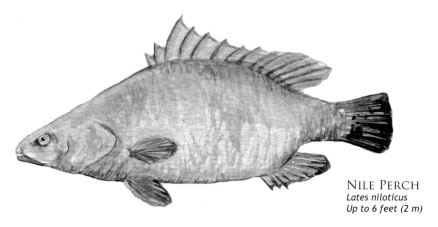

NILE PERCH
Lates niloticus
Up to 6 feet (2 m)

A remarkable diversity of fish occur in the streams, rivers, lakes and man-made dams of sub-Saharan Africa, and also – of course – in the Indian and Atlantic oceans.

Fish differ from all other vertebrates in being able to breath underwater. The majority of species are easily caught and are a much sought-after source of protein for people throughout the continent. Fish play a vital role in aquatic ecosystems as herbivores, predators and scavengers. Sadly, aquatic habitats are probably the most disturbed and fragile environments in Africa, with chemical pollution, wetland damage, damning of catchments, erosion, siltation and the impacts of alien species being among the principle problems.

Africa provides some of the world's finest sport fishing in both freshwater and marine habitats. The thrill of bringing in a large fish are these days matched by the feeling of setting it free, as "catch-and-release" is standard practice for beach resorts and waterside safari lodges.

The Rainbow Trout is native to the pacific-flowing rivers of North America and Asia, but has been introduced into many African countries where it thrives in cool, upland rivers. This relative of the salmon is the popular target of fly-fishermen such that numerous hotels and lodges have been established purely for this pursuit; unfortunately, this fish can have a negative impact on native species.

RAINBOW TROUT
Oncorhynchus mykiss
2 feet (up to 60 cm)

FRESHWATER FISH

Among the more widespread fish of African rivers and lakes are the bottom-dwelling catfish and squeakers, the largely herbivorous tilapia (bream) and their cichlid relatives, and the cyprinids (barbs, yellowfishes and labeos).

Numerous endemic cichlids occur in Lake Malawi and other rift valley lakes. The Nile Perch is native to Nile and Congo river basins but has been introduced to Lake Victoria where it has out-competed native species and caused severe environmental damage; gigantic specimens are much desired by anglers.

The predatory Tigerfish occurs in the Okavango and Zambezi rivers, while its larger cousin – the Goliath Tigerfish – is found in the Congo Basin.

Truly amazing, are the "annual" killifish that inhabit seasonal waterbodies such as floodplains and rain-filled pans; these small, brightly-colored fish complete their life cycle within a single year, laying eggs that survive desiccation to hatch during the following rainy season.

SHARP-TOOTHED CATFISH (BARBEL)
Clarias gariepinus
up to 4.5 feet (1.4 m)

BANDED TILAPIA (JEWELFISH)
Hemichromis elongatus
8 inches (20 cm)

DEMASONI CICHLID
Hemichromis elongatus
5 inches (12 cm)

TIGERFISH
Hydrocynus vittatus
2.3 feet (up to 70 cm)

SHARKS AND RAYS

These fish have skeletons composed of cartilage and skin that is smooth (rays) or rough (sharks). These features are in contrast to the "bony fish" that have bony-skeletons and scales for skin except in the case of smooth-bodied catfish and their kin.

Shark species vary in size from around 4 feet (1.2 m) to the massive Great White Shark and Tiger Shark at over 20 feet (6 m). At up to 40 feet (12 m), the simply enormous Whale Shark is the world's largest fish species, albeit a toothless filter-feeder. Most sharks are carnivorous and several are extremely dangerous to man.

Manta-rays, eagle-rays and sting-rays have flattened bodies that act as "wings" underwater and some species have whip-like tails with a barb or sting tip.

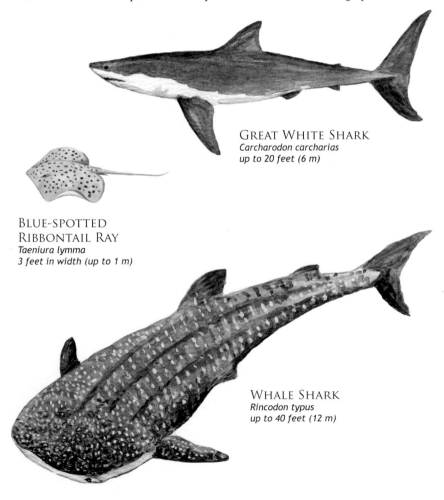

GREAT WHITE SHARK
Carcharodon carcharias
up to 20 feet (6 m)

BLUE-SPOTTED
RIBBONTAIL RAY
Taeniura lymma
3 feet in width (up to 1 m)

WHALE SHARK
Rincodon typus
up to 40 feet (12 m)

PELAGIC FISH

Pelagic fish are those that live in deep, open water - offshore, away from reefs. These fish are typically silver-gray in color (in contrast to the multicolored reef fish) are the target of commercial fishing operations, as well as sport fishermen.

Included among the pelagics are the billfish such as the Black Marlin, Blue Marlin and Sailfish; also, such well-known groups as tuna, mackerel, trevally and sardine. All around the world, these fish have been subjected to over-utilization by man which has led to great changes in the balance of life for many marine species. Stricter controls are required and consumers can contribute by purchasing only those species with a particular rating.

In southern Africa, the annual (mid-winter) "sardine run" is a dramatic event as millions of these small fish move from Namibia to KwaZulu-Natal, with thousands of dolphins, gannets and other predators in their wake. In equatorial waters, the fascinating flying-fish are often seen when boating between tropical islands.

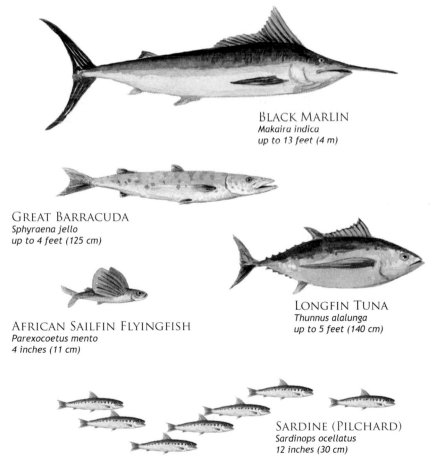

BLACK MARLIN
Makaira indica
up to 13 feet (4 m)

GREAT BARRACUDA
Sphyraena jello
up to 4 feet (125 cm)

AFRICAN SAILFIN FLYINGFISH
Parexocoetus mento
4 inches (11 cm)

LONGFIN TUNA
Thunnus alalunga
up to 5 feet (140 cm)

SARDINE (PILCHARD)
Sardinops ocellatus
12 inches (30 cm)

CORAL REEF FISH

Coral reefs occur along the east coast of Africa from the Red Sea south to Sodwana Bay in South Africa; also, around the Indian Ocean islands of Seychelles and Mauritius, as well as Madagascar.

Coral reefs can be compared to tropical rainforests in terms of their incredible biodiversity but - like the rainforests - they are threatened due to human impacts. Coral reefs are living structures composed of hard and soft corals belonging to the phylum *cnidaria* (which includes jellyfish and sea anemones); all are filter feeders of microscopic organisms. A bewildering array of spectacular and colorful fish occur around coral reefs and are viewed by snorkeling or scuba diving. Many corals are very fragile and easily damaged by careless operators.

On these pages, just a few of the eye-catching reef fish of the Indian Ocean are illustrated.

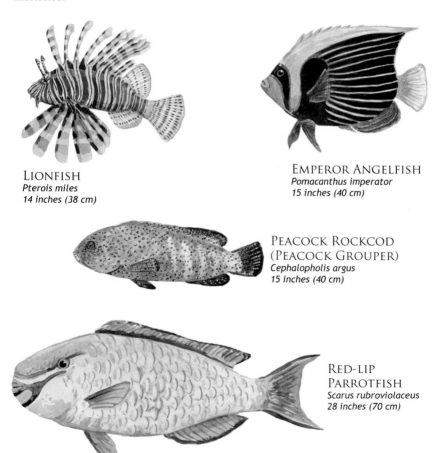

LIONFISH
Pterois miles
14 inches (38 cm)

EMPEROR ANGELFISH
Pomacanthus imperator
15 inches (40 cm)

PEACOCK ROCKCOD
(PEACOCK GROUPER)
Cephalopholis argus
15 inches (40 cm)

RED-LIP
PARROTFISH
Scarus rubroviolaceus
28 inches (70 cm)

THREAD-FIN BUTTERFLYFISH
Chaetodon auriga
up to 9 inches (24 cm)

POWDER-BLUE SURGEONFISH
Acanthurus leucosternon
9 inches (24 cm)

CLOWN TRIGGERFISH
Balistoides conspiucillum
20 inches (50 cm)

SIX-BAR WRASSE
Thalassoma hardwicke
8 inches (20 cm)

BLUE-LINED SNAPPER
Lutjanus kasmiri
14 inches (35 cm)

INDIAN OCEAN BIRD-WRASSE
Gomphosus caeruleus
11 inches (28 cm)

SHORT-SPINED PORCUPINEFISH
Diodon luturosus
15 inches (40 cm)

CORAL REEF FISH

BLUE-GREEN CHROMIS
Chromis viridis
3.5 inches (9 cm)

TWO-TONE CHROMIS (CHOCOLATE DIP)
Chromis dimidiata
3.5 inches (9 cm)

HUMBUG DASCYLLUS
Dascyllus aruanus
3 inches (8 cm)

TWO-BAR ANEMONEFISH
Amphiprion allardi
5.5 inches (14 cm)

YELLOW BOXFISH
Ostracion cubicus
5 inches (12 cm)

MOORISH IDOL
Zanclus cornutus
6.2 inches (16 cm)

BLUE-STREAK CLEANER-WRASSE
Labroides dimidiatus
4 inches (10 cm)

FIRE DARTFISH
Nemateleotris magnifica
3 inches (8 cm)

AFRICAN INVERTEBRATES

HOUSE MOSQUITO
Culex pipiens

With such a spectacular diversity of large mammals and birds, not to mention reptiles, frogs and fish, it is easy to overlook most smaller life forms when on an African safari.

Invertebrates are animals that lack a backbone and they account for about 97% of all known animal species. Most are small, and many are microscopic. They play a vital role as parasites, decomposers, pollinators and predators without which ecosystems could not function.

The largest group of invertebrates are the arthropods which are characterised by an exoskeleton that covers a segmented body, and jointed legs. Insects, centipedes, millipedes, crustaceans and arachnids are the most familiar arthropods.

Insects can be distinguished from other arthropods by their three-part bodies (head, thorax and abdomen) and three pairs of jointed legs; most insects have two pairs of wings. Caterpillars and grubs are the young (larval stage) of butterflies, moths, beetles and certain others, and do not resemble adults at all. There may be as many as 30 million different insect species worldwide, although fewer than one million have been scientifically described.

Most people see insects as little more than pests to be destroyed at any opportunity. While it is true that many species bring harm to mankind by attacking crops, gardens and wooden structures, and that flies, fleas and mosquitoes transmit diseases, the majority of insects are useful and harmless. There are also a great many insects that perform vital ecological functions, including pollination, pest-control and waste-disposal, upon which human societies are dependent.

While on safari you will encounter a host of colorful, unusual and fascinating insects, as well as a few annoying ones! Learning a little about them can enrich your experience and understanding of the ecosystems in which lions and elephants are just a part. Many insects are attracted to lights after dark, and you are sure to see many strange and fascinating creatures around your lodge and hotel accommodations. Needless to say, biting insects such as mosquitoes can be inhibited by means of repellant spray, or the burning of mosquito coils.

Butterflies and Moths

Colorful and active on bright sunny days, butterflies are often the first insects which attract the interest of people. Some African butterflies are extremely beautiful and make fine photographic subjects. Your guide may be able to help you identify some species, but comprehensive illustrated guide books are available.

AFRICAN MONARCH
Danaus chrysippus

Moths differ from butterflies in that most species are nocturnal (these too make ideal photographic subjects as they are drawn to lights around safari lodges and camps). Moths tend to lay their wings flat when at rest, and usually have feathery rather than clubbed antennae (feelers). Most butterflies fold their wings vertically above their body and have clubbed antennae. All butterflies and moths lay eggs on particular "food plants" upon which their offspring will hatch and feed as developing caterpillars. Adult butterflies and moths feed on plant sap or nectar which they suck up with a long, tubular proboscis.

VINE HAWK-MOTH
Hippotion celerio

GOLD-BANDED FORESTER
Euphaedra neophron

AFRICAN LUNAR MOTH
Argema mimosae

GUINEAFOWL BUTTERFLY
Hamanumida daedalus

Termites

Harvester Termite
Hodotermes mossambicus

The conspicuous mounds made by termites are a distinctive feature of African savannahs and, though tiny and practically blind, these sociable insects play a major role in the functioning of ecosystems. Impressive towers of clay built by some termite species provide a home for a variety of other creatures and are often colonized by plants to create new habitats such as thickets.

Termites typically feed on dead plant material such as wood, bark and straw, being able to digest woody fibers with the help of bacteria that live in their stomachs. Acting as highly efficient decomposers, the termites return the plant nutrients to the soil through their feces and saliva. Lacking pigment and a protective exoskeleton, termites operate mostly underground, but some species forage above ground after dark. In some parts of Africa, there may be as many as 10,000 termites to a square yard of soil surface, so it is not surprising that these insects also feature in the diet of numerous other species. Termites are often incorrectly referred to as "white ants" or "flying ants" although they are not closely related to ants at all. But, like ants, they live in well-ordered colonies with soldiers, workers and reproductives. A new colony begins when two winged alates, of opposite sexes, manage to avoid predation on their risky nuptial flight (birds, toads and bats consume most) and burrow into a suitable substrate. The offspring of this "royal pair" will then become the workers and soldiers required to build the mound.

Ants

Ants are considered to be the most advanced of social insects, with colonies containing a single queen and numbers of wingless workers and soldiers. Black or red are the typical colors of African ants. Most species create colonies underground, which may contain tens of thousands of members, but other species occur in smaller numbers in hollow twigs or acacia thorns. The round mud-ball nests of cocktail ants are conspicuous in some regions. Most ants are carnivorous, boldly attacking other

Carpenter Ant
Camponotus ligniperda

insects or consuming dead animals of all kinds, but some feed on seeds, plant sap or "honeydew" secreted by aphids and sap-sucking bugs. Army ants form hunting parties which overpower and eat other insects; these formidable creatures are known as "siafu" in eastern Africa. Ants are not dangerous to humans although some can deliver a painful bite.

WASPS

Although some species are aggressive and capable of injecting venom, wasps are a fascinatingly diverse group of insects. It is advisable to leave the large paper-wasps and hornets well alone, as these fearless creatures attack and sting in defense of their nests. Similar in shape, but not aggressive or venomous, are the mason- and potter-wasps which construct beautiful clay pot egg chambers, or large many-celled dormitories.

GIANT PAPER-WASP
Belonogaster dubia

The largest of wasps are the spider-hunting wasps which have the interesting but macabre habit of capturing spiders, injecting them with paralyzing venom, and then laying their eggs into the body of their victim. Once the wasp egg hatches, it will feed on the flesh of the paralyzed spider. Iridescent cuckoo-wasps are kleptoparasites which lay their eggs into the nests of other wasp species.

A great variety of tiny wasps lay their own eggs inside the eggs or larvae of other insects. In this way, these parasites control the numbers of their host insects, some of which would otherwise assume plague proportions. The small and delicate fig-wasps perform a critical pollination function for fig trees, which – through their bounty of fruit – are a vital source of food for an entire web of wildlife.

PRAYING MANTIS

Well known for their unique body form and characteristic pose of upheld front limbs (which recalls somebody at prayer), the mantises are carnivorous insects with fascinating lifestyles. There are thought to be two or three hundred species in sub-Saharan Africa. Mantises have distinctive triangular heads and long wings which fold flat over their abdomen. The head can be rotated with more flexibility than that of any other insect, while the front legs are equipped with hook-like spines on their inner surface, which hold prey securely. All mantises are extremely well camouflaged in colors which blend into their natural habitats. Most species are plain green or brown, but some are ornately colored in shades of pink and yellow. The typical means of capturing prey is for the mantis to sit patiently in wait until a suitable insect or spider comes within range. Like many insects, they can often be seen around the artificial lights of buildings after dark.

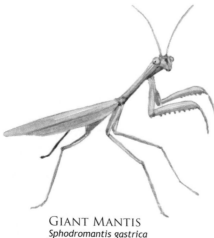

GIANT MANTIS
Sphodromantis gastrica

DRAGONFLIES

Due to their bright coloration and conspicuous behavior, dragonflies quickly attract attention. It is not unusual to see six or more species at any suitable wetland. Dragonflies and their damselfly relatives, belong to the insect order Odonata. They are most active in warm weather and the majority of adults die at the onset of winter. Their eggs and larvae, however, can withstand the cold and a new generation of adults emerge each year.

RED-VEINED DROPWING
Trithemis arteriosa

There are several distinctive groups of dragonflies. Massive emperors course low above the surface in pursuit of flies, bees and even smaller dragonflies. Skimmers and dropwings perch conspicuously on fringing grass or reeds, bursting out to chase rivals or capture prey. Impossibly brilliant jewels glitter alongside rapids, and delicate sprites dance above shallows. Hawkers rest among branches and often emerge at dusk to hunt. Many dragonfly species return to favored perches and make rewarding photographic subjects.

BEETLES

There are more varieties of beetles than any other insect group, but it is the fascinating dung-beetles which are most likely to attract your attention on safari. Ranging in size from three-inch (7.5 cm) "monsters" to tiny, metallic green miniatures, dung-beetles are attracted to the fresh droppings of large mammals. The beetles are uniquely adapted to extract dung and roll it into a ball which is then pushed backwards to a burrow where it is either eaten or used as a fertile egg chamber. A pause at a rhino-midden or clump of elephant droppings will provide you with a captivating experience as large and small dung-beetles jostle with one another for a share of the spoils.

Other conspicuous beetles include the horned rhinoceros-beetles, ground-hunting tiger-beetles, desert-dwelling darkling-beetles, and the large and nocturnal longicorn (or longhorn) beetles with their extended antennae.

FLIGHTLESS DUNG-BEETLE
Circellium bacchus

ARACHNIDS

Arachnids differ from insects in having two body segments (cephalothorax and abdomen) and four pairs of legs (all insects have three pairs of legs).

Scorpions, recognized by their clawed pincers and sting-bearing tails, are the most ancient group of arachnids. Scorpions are nocturnal predators of ants, beetles and other insects. The sting is used in defense, with members of Buthidae family having powerful venom dangerous to humans; these scorpions have small pincers but fat tails. The more fearsome-looking scorpions with large pincers are less venomous. All scorpions give birth to live young which are carried on the female's back.

Solifuges (also known as Sun-spiders or Roman-spiders) might be taken for a hybrid between a spider and a scorpion but they are unique arachnids active by day and night. They lack poison glands so capture and kill prey with their large pincers.

THICK-TAILED SCORPION
Parabuthus capensis

ROCK SCORPION
Hadogenes troglodytes

KALAHARI SOLIFUGE (SUN-SPIDER)
Solpugema spectralis

Spiders are among the least-popular of invertebrates among people. This fear is rather irrational, however, for although most species are venomous, only a handful pose any danger to man. Nevertheless, the fast, dashing movement of spiders (not to mention their eight eyes) sends a chill down many a human spine!

There are over 40,000 described species of spider and Africa has its fair share.

All spiders are predatory, capturing prey in webs made of silk, or through ambush or pursuit.

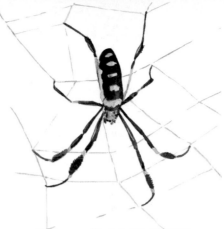

GOLDEN ORB-WEB SPIDER
Nephila senegalensis

Perhaps the most impressive and noticeable of African spiders is the Golden Orb web Spider of savannah woodland; these impressive hunters string their huge webs of golden silk across tree gaps of several feet.

Crab-spiders are ambush predators that hide in flowers that match their own body color, to trap bees and other pollinating insects. Jumping-spiders feed largely on ants and are capable of prodigious leaps to escape geckos and birds. Baboon-spiders are members of the tarantula family and rely on their large size to overpower prey that wanders past their silken burrows. Fishing-spiders hunt small frogs, fishes and dragonflies. Kite-spiders are forest-dwellers with brilliantly colored abdomens often adorned with spikes or "horns". Bark-spiders create magnificent webs – often across quiet roads – in savannah.

The black widow and violin-spider have powerful venom and are potentially dangerous to humans, but they are generally very shy and keep to dark corners, so seldom encountered.

Collectively, spiders are among the most efficient predators of flies, mosquitoes, midges and other insects and thus play a vital role in regulating populations.

KITE SPIDER
Gasteracantha milvoides

BLACK WIDOW
Latrodectus indistinctus

AFRICAN TREES

There are so many different tree species in Africa, that it takes years of study and field work to be able to identify the majority. In addition to leaf structure (*simple* or *compound* is the most basic division), it is often necessary to examine the growth form, bark texture, flower parts, and fruit, in order to accurately identify a tree.

While on safari, it is nevertheless worthwhile to be able to recognize some of the more conspicuous and interesting trees. Thorn trees *(Acacia)* are often the most abundant trees in flat countryside, with many similar species occurring side-by-side. In hilly terrain, various species of bushwillow *(Combretum)* tend to dominate. Naturally, trees reach greater proportions when their roots are able to reach underground water supplies, and evergreen species often prevail along rivers and seasonal watercourses. In savannah and woodland, many African trees shed their leaves in the dry winter months. Some species have beautiful yellow and amber foliage prior to shedding, although this is never as striking as the fall (autumn) shows in North America and Europe. In African forests, trees shed and replace their leaves throughout the year, so they are never devoid of green foliage.

Many African trees have spectacular colorful flowers, which attract pollinators and provide a rich nectar source for birds and insects. Trees of any one species flower simultaneously, putting on remarkable floral displays in savannah and other habitats. The seeds and pods of many species often take on distinctive shapes and forms, none more so than the extraordinary Sausage Tree.

Trees play a major role in African culture and livelihood, for they provide food in the way of berries, nuts and fruit, bark for medicine, as well as shelter and sometimes the main source of fuel. Certain large fig trees are regarded as sacred by the Maasai and others.

Compound leaf shape

Simple leaf shape

ACACIAS (THORN TREES)

With their flat crowns and spreading
branches, thorn trees – such as the Umbrella
Thorn – are the embodiment of Africa.
Spaced out on the park-like savannah,
with giraffe browsing on their foliage and
wildebeest resting in their shade, they form
the backdrop for many an African scene.

WHISTLING THORN
Acacia drepanolobium

Acacia trees are typified by feathery,
compound leaves, divided in numerous
pairs of tiny leaflets. All African species
have thorns, whether straight or hooked. Their foliage and pods are relished by all
browsers. Although the often fierce thorns do act as a deterrent for some browsers,
it is the colonies of cocktail ants which more aggressively defend these trees. By and
large, ants are abundant in thorn trees where they are provided with sweet nectar
in return for their vigorous defense; even large antelope such as kudu can tolerate
biting ants only for a period of time before moving on elsewhere. Most thorn trees are
tolerant of fire and have thick or corky bark to withstand heat. The hard seeds of these
leguminous trees actually benefit from fire as the heat splits the outer covering and
speeds up germination.

Acacia flowers are either bright yellow or cream in color, and may be ball- or spike
-shaped depending upon the species. Bees and other insects are attracted in their
thousands during the flowering period. Most thorn trees exude a sweet sticky gum
from their bark and this is relished by bushbabies and people alike. Smaller birds
frequently build their nests in thorn trees and shrubs, as the armory deters would-be
predators of the eggs and nestlings. Large flat-topped thorn trees are favored sites for
eagles, vultures and storks.

UMBRELLA THORN *Acacia tortilis*

173

PALMS

Africa does not have a great variety of palm trees, but these stately and instantly recognizable plants occur in many habitats, often near water.

Palms are distinctive in that almost all species have a single unbranched stem or trunk (the Doum Palm of eastern Africa is a notable exception). The large leathery leaves are either fan- or feather-shaped,

IVORY PALM *Hyphaene coriacea*

and droop down in a spiral from the crown. The Wild Date Palm is widely distributed, occurring on stream and river banks and the fringes of Okavango Delta islands. Baboons and civets relish the dates, while elephants strip the tough leaves. Tall Fan (or Lala) Palms are a feature of the Okavango Delta, where elephants feed on the bell-shaped or spherical fruits; the seed is encased in an ivory-like kernel which may be carved into jewelry or ornaments. Borassus Palms are the tallest of African palms and noted for their swollen trunks. The Raphia Palm of lagoon fringes has leaves that are up to 60 feet (18 m) in length – the longest of any plant! Coconut Palms fringe beaches in Tanzania and Kenya, as well as on Indian Ocean islands.

EUPHORBIAS

Euphorbias are succulent plants armed with sharp spines. In shape and form many varieties strongly resemble cacti. The larger tree-like species are sometimes referred to as candelabras in view of their distinctive shape. All euphorbias contain a sticky, milky latex which can cause temporary blindness. Euphorbia flowers are small and inconspicuous but produce copious nectar and attract large numbers of bees and other insects, as well as birds. The only animal known to eat euphorbia stems is the Black Rhinoceros.

CANDELABRA TREE *Euphorbia ingens*

BAOBAB

These huge, broad-trunked trees are unmistakable, particularly when they lose their leaves in the dry season. It is then that they suit their nickname of "upside-down tree" as their bare branches resemble roots. Baobabs are among the oldest of life forms with some specimens aged at well over 1,000 years. The smooth bark and soft pulpy fiber is relished by elephants which may destroy even the largest specimens. The huge showy white flowers open at night to be pollinated by fruit-bats. Baobab seeds are surrounded by a white pulp within a large velvety pod. Mature baobabs typically have many holes and crevices which provide homes for bushbabies, owls and many other creatures. Large hollow specimens may even be used as rooms, or grain houses by rural people.

BAOBAB *Adansonia digitata*

SAUSAGE TREE

This is a large deciduous tree that favors riverside habitats. The extraordinary fruits may grow up to 2 feet (60 cm) in length, and hang in clusters from the outer branches. Baboons eat the pulp inside the sausage-shaped fruits, and so disperse the seeds. Interestingly, the sap from these fruits is used as a skin care product.

The Sausage Tree has spectacular burgundy flowers shaped like trumpets. Sunbirds visit these flowers for nectar during the day, while fruit-bats and hawk-moths feast at night. The short-lived flowers fall to the ground after pollination, leaving an extravagant wine-red carpet beneath the tree. These trees often take on a wide-spreading shape which makes their broad branches ideal resting places for Leopard.

SAUSAGE TREE *Kigelia africana*

FIGS

There are many species of *Ficus* in Africa, with the sulphur-barked Sycamore Fig being one of the most impressive. Fig flowers are hidden within the figs, which only ripen when these tiny flowers have been pollinated by a particular species of fig-wasp. This unique mutual relationship between tree and insect sets in motion a great food web, as the abundance of juicy figs are fed upon by all manner of creatures from fish and duiker, to hornbills and green-pigeons. Unlike most other tree species that flower and fruit in a particular season, figs produce their crop at random so that there is usually at least one productive tree in an area.

SYCAMORE FIG *Ficus sycomorus*

The majority of African fig trees fall into one of two categories: the rock-splitters and the stranglers. The tenacious aerial roots of these trees enable them to take hold in impossibly small cracks, or wrap themselves around, and ultimately squeeze to death, even the largest of host trees.

ALOES

Only a few aloe species assume the proportions of a tree, but several species stand as tall as a man, and decorate hillsides and valleys with their distinctive form and bright flower heads. These are succulent plants able to withstand dry conditions. Many African species are grown in sub-tropical gardens around the world. *Aloe vera* is a north African species which is now widely cultivated for its medicinal value; the clear sap is a cure for skin rashes and blemishes.

ROCK ALOE
Aloe spicata

Aloes carry hundreds of tubular flowers on candelabra-shaped stalks, attracting sunbirds and bees to their nectar.

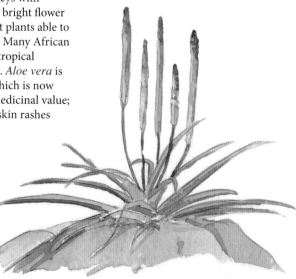

176

SOME OTHER DISTINCTIVE TREES

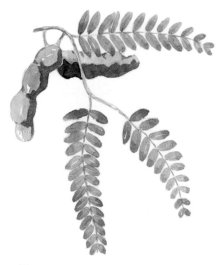

TAMARIND *Tamarindus indica*

POD MAHOGANY *Afzelia quanzensis*

MIOMBO *Brachystegia species*

MOPANE *Colophospermum mopane*

SOME OTHER DISTINCTIVE TREES

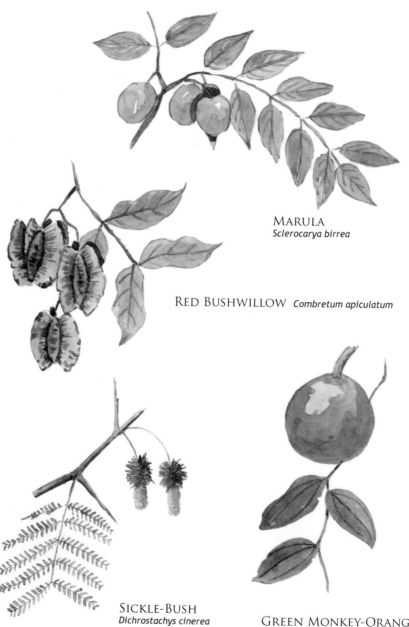

MARULA
Sclerocarya birrea

RED BUSHWILLOW *Combretum apiculatum*

SICKLE-BUSH
Dichrostachys cinerea

GREEN MONKEY-ORANGE
Strychnos spinosa

SOME OTHER DISTINCTIVE TREES

SACRED CORAL-TREE
Erythrina lysistemon

JACKALBERRY
Diospyros mespiliformis

WEEPING BOERBEAN
Schotia brachypetala

SILVER CLUSTER-LEAF
Terminalia sericea

SOME OTHER DISTINCTIVE TREES

IMPALA-LILY
Adenium multiflorum

CABBAGE TREE
Cussonia spicata

WOODEN-BANANA TREE
Entandrophragma caudatum

AFRICAN ROSEWOOD
Hagenia abyssinica

AFRICAN FLAME TREE
Spathodea campanulata

MAP DIRECTORY

On the following pages are a selection of maps featuring Africa's top wildlife countries, as well as the most popular wildlife reserves. You can use these to orientate yourself while traveling and to help plan your next safari!

Map Legend
- Lodge
- Luxury Tented Camp
- International Airport
- Regional Airport
- Airstrip
- Hot Air Balloon Launch Site

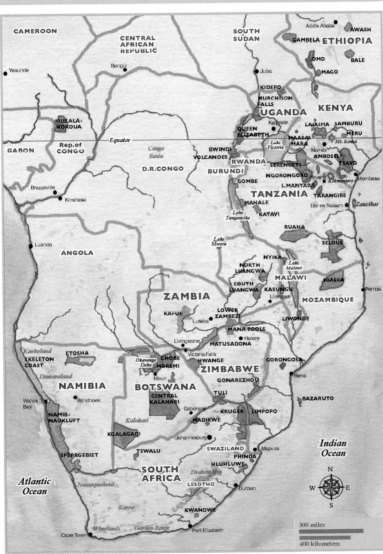

Northern Tanzania and Southern Kenya

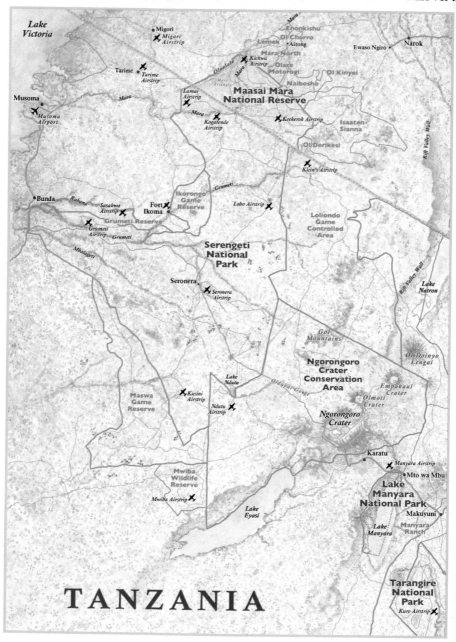

TANZANIA

Northern Tanzania and Southern Kenya

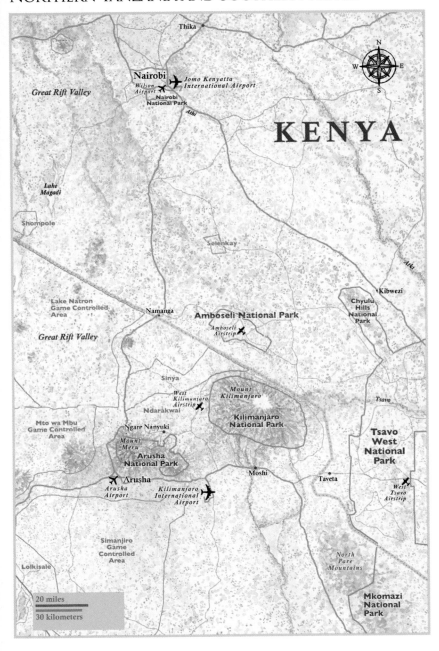

KENYA

From the warm tropical waters of the Indian Ocean to the icy heights of Mount Kenya at 17,058 feet (5,199 m), this is truly "a world in one country". Desert and arid savannah prevails in the northern frontier and southeast, while remnant forests extend over the high country and wetter west. Covering 225,000 square miles (582,750 km²), Kenya is about the same size as Texas or France. The population numbers some 47 million, with over 3 million in the capital city of Nairobi. KiSwahili and English are the official languages. Currency is the Kenyan Shilling.

Maasai Mara National Reserve and Conservancies

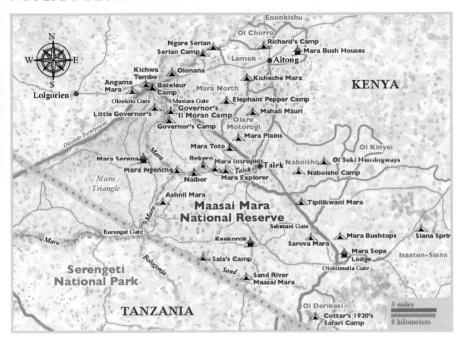

Amboseli National Park

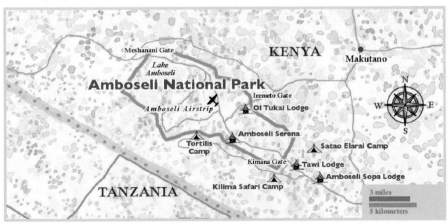

SAMBURU AND BUFFALO SPRINGS

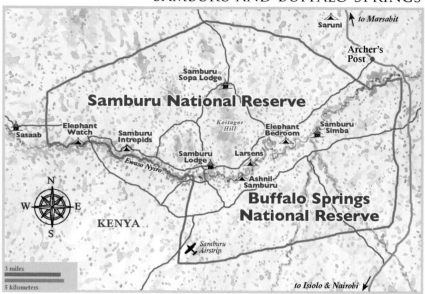

LAIKIPIA WILDLIFE CONSERVANCY

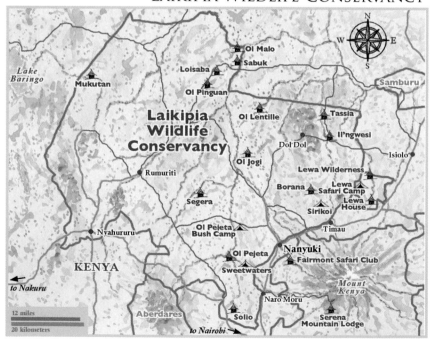

TSAVO WEST AND CHYULU HILLS

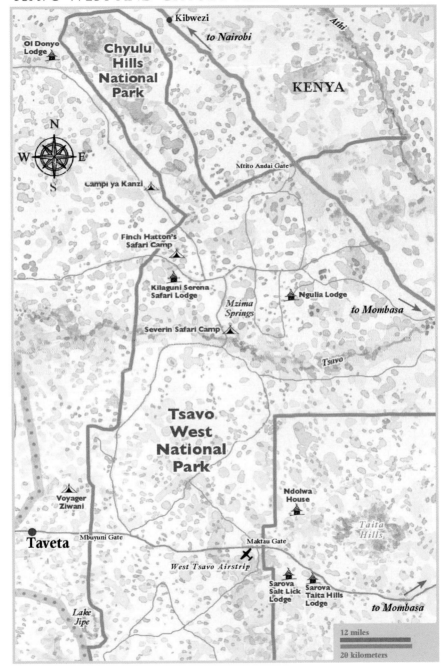

187

TANZANIA

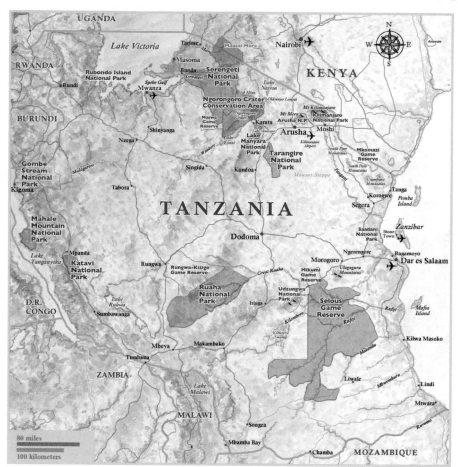

Set between the tropical Indian Ocean and the two arms of the Rift Valley, Tanzania is one of Africa's most scenically beautiful countries. It also has some of the most extensive protected areas including the fabled Serengeti. The landscape rises from sea level to nearly 19,000 feet (5,894 m) at the summit of Kilimanjaro.

Covering 365,000 square miles (945,000 km²), Tanzania is about the same size as Texas and Oklahoma combined. The population numbers some 51 million, with Dodoma as the administrative capital. The famous port city of Dar es Salaam is the largest with a population of over 4 million, and has been a key trading center for centuries. KiSwahili is the most widely spoken language, but English is also commonly used. The currency is the Tanzanian Shilling.

SERENGETI NATIONAL PARK AND THE GREAT MIGRATION

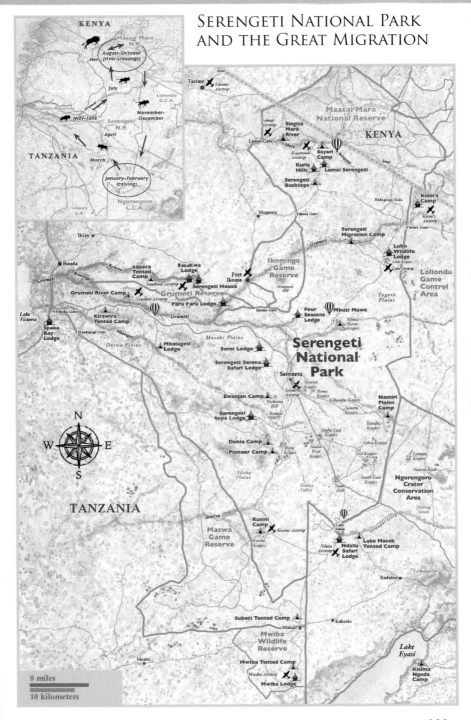

KENYA

Maasai Mara N.P.

August–October (river crossings)

July

Loliondo G.C.A.

Grumeti Reserve

November–December

May–June

April

Serengeti N.P.

TANZANIA

March

January–February (calving)

Ngorongoro L.C.A.

Maswa G.R.

Sirari

Tarime • ✕ Tarime Airstrip

Lamai Airstrip

Singita Mara River

Maasai Mara National Reserve

KENYA

Lamai Gate

Mara

Kogatende Airstrip

Sayari Camp

Kurla Hills

Lamai Serengeti

Serengeti Bushtops

Sand

Balagonja Gds.

Klein's Camp

Klein's Airstrip

Klein's Gate

Mugumu •

Tabora Gate

Grumeti

Serengeti Migration Camp

Loliondo Game Control Area

Ikizu •

Ikorongo Game Reserve

Loliondo Wildlife Lodge

Lobo Airstrip

Bunda •

Rubana

Sabora Tented Camp

Sasakwa Lodge

Fort Ikoma

Manyuni Hill

Togoro Plains

Grumeti

Kawiruri

Sasakwa Airstrip

Serengeti House

Four Seasons Lodge

Mbuzi Mawe

Grumeti River Camp

Grumeti Airstrip

Faru Faru Lodge

Grumeti Reserve

Ikoma Gate

Mbuzi Mawe Kopjes

Lake Victoria

Ndabaka Gate

Kirawira Tented Camp

Grumeti

Mbalageti

Handajega Gate

Speke Bay Lodge

Mbalageti Lodge

Musabi Plains

Sorol Lodge

Serengeti National Park

Dutwa Plains

Serengeti Serena Safari Lodge

Seronera

Maasai Kopjes

Boma Kopjes

Serengeti Airstrip

Namiri Plains Camp

Ewanjan Camp

Mukoma Hill

Ramoni Hill

Kihumbu Kopjes

Semetu Kopjes

Serengeti Sopa Lodge

Simba East Kopjes

Barafu Kopjes

Zebra Kopjes

Dunia Camp

Pioneer Camp

Moru Kopjes

Simba West Kopjes

Simba Kopjes

Gol Kopjes

Lemuta Kopjes

Nasera Rock

Ndoha Plains

Hidden Valley

Naabi Hill

South East Kopjes

Ngorongoro Crater Conservation Area

Shifting Sands

Simiyu

Kusini Camp

✕ Kusini Airstrip

Lake Ndutu

Didagani Gorge

Maswa Game Reserve

Kusini Kopjes

Ndutu Airstrip

Ndutu Safari Lodge

Lake Masek Tented Camp

Endulen •

Lemagarut

TANZANIA

Subeti Tented Camp

Makao

• Kakesio

Mwiba Wildlife Reserve

Lake Eyasi

Meatu •

Mwiba Tented Camp

Mwiba Airstrip

Mwiba Lodge

Kisima Ngeda Camp

8 miles

10 kilometers

189

NGORONGORO CRATER

LAKE MANYARA AND TARANGIRE

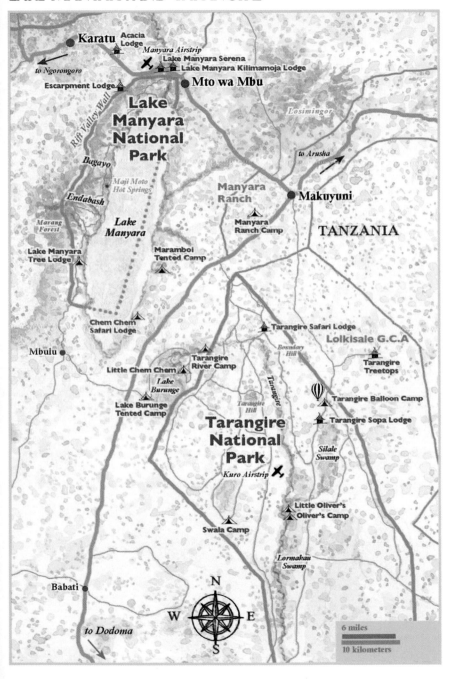

Karatu
Acacia Lodge
to Ngorongoro
Manyara Airstrip
Lake Manyara Serena
Lake Manyara Kilimamoja Lodge
Escarpment Lodge
Mto wa Mbu
Rift Valley Wall
Lake Manyara National Park
Eosimingor
Dugayo
Maji Moto Hot Springs
to Arusha
Endabash
Manyara Ranch
Makuyuni
Marang Forest
Lake Manyara
Manyara Ranch Camp
TANZANIA
Lake Manyara Tree Lodge
Maramboi Tented Camp
Chem Chem Safari Lodge
Tarangire Safari Lodge
Lolkisale G.C.A
Mbulu
Boundary Hill
Tarangire River Camp
Little Chem Chem
Tarangire Treetops
Lake Burunge
Tarangire
Lake Burunge Tented Camp
Tarangire Hill
Tarangire Balloon Camp
Tarangire Sopa Lodge
Tarangire National Park
Silale Swamp
Kuro Airstrip
Little Oliver's
Oliver's Camp
Swala Camp
Lormakau Swamp
Babati
N
W E
S
to Dodoma
6 miles
10 kilometers

ARUSHA NATIONAL PARK

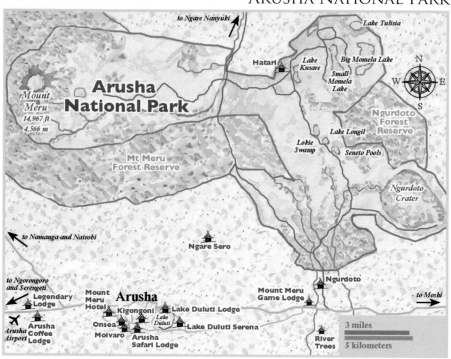

ARUSHA, MOSHI AND KILIMANJARO

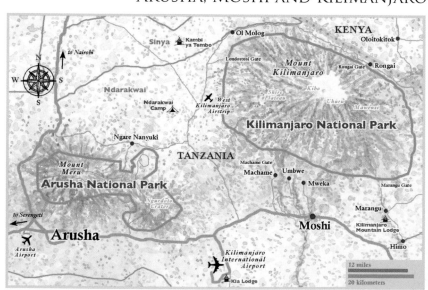

KILIMANJARO CLIMBING ROUTES

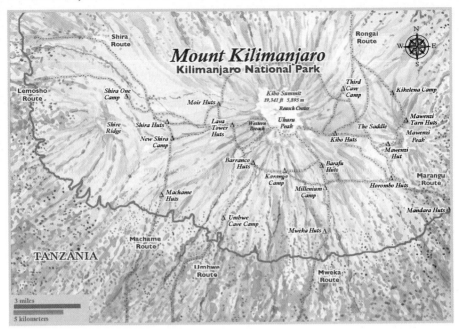

KIBO SUMMIT OF KILIMANJARO

SELOUS GAME RESERVE (NORTHERN SECTOR)

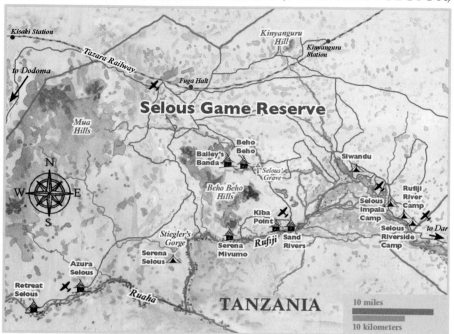

RUAHA NATIONAL PARK (SOUTHERN SECTOR)

ZANZIBAR (TANZANIA)

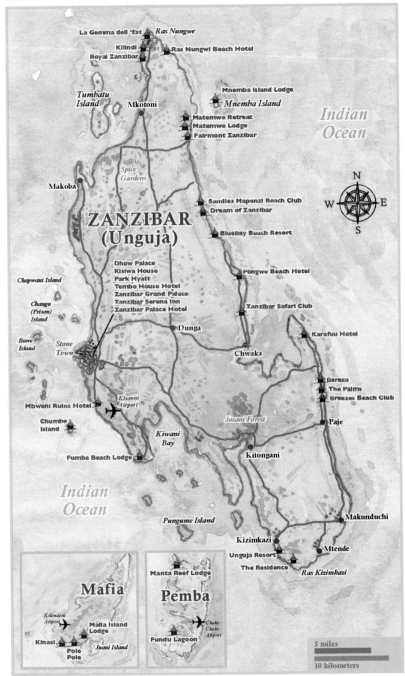

La Gemma dell 'Est   *Ras Nungwe*
Kilindi   Ras Nungwi Beach Hotel
Royal Zanzibar

Tumbatu Island   Mkotoni

Mnemba Island Lodge
Mnemba Island
Matemwe Retreat
Matemwe Lodge
Fairmont Zanzibar

Indian Ocean

Spice Gardens

Makoba

ZANZIBAR (Unguja)

Sandies Maponzi Beach Club
Dream of Zanzibar

Bluebay Beach Resort

N
W   E
S

Dhow Palace
Kisiwa House
Park Hyatt
Tembo House Hotel
Zanzibar Grand Palace
Zanzibar Serena Inn
Zanzibar Palace Hotel

Pongwe Beach Hotel

Chapwani Island

Changu (Prison) Island

Zanzibar Safari Club

Dunga

Karafuu Hotel

Bawe Island

Stone Town

Chwaka

Baraza
The Palms
Breezes Beach Club

Mbweni Ruins Hotel
Kisauni Airport

Chumbe Island

Josani Forest

Paje

Kiwani Bay

Fumba Beach Lodge

Kitongani

Indian Ocean

Pungume Island

Makunduchi

Kizimkazi

Mtende

Unguja Resort
The Residence

Ras Kizimkazi

Manta Reef Lodge

Mafia

Pemba

Kilondoni Airport

Mafia Island Lodge

Kinasi

Juani Island

Pole Pole

Fundu Lagoon

Chake Chake Airport

5 miles

10 kilometers

195

UGANDA & RWANDA

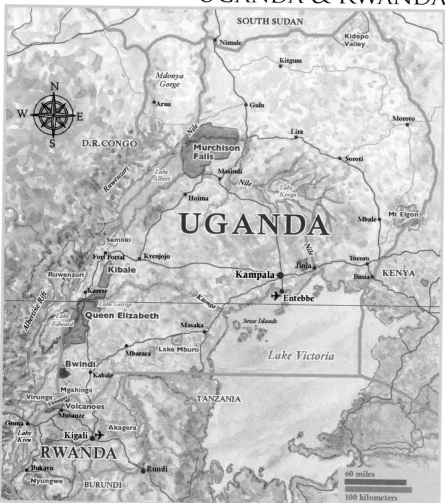

Straddling the equator, most of Uganda is an upland plateau averaging 3,000 feet (1,000 m) above sea level. The enormous Lake Victoria , other Rift Valley lakes and the mighty Nile River are key features. Approximately the size of Oregon (or Great Britain) Uganda covers 93,000 square miles (240, 000 km²). Almost all of the 42 million population are either subsistence farmers or employed in agriculture. Kampala is the capital city with about 1.6 million inhabitants. Lugenda and English are the main languages. The currency is the Ugandan Shilling.

Rwanda is characterized by rolling hills and volcanic peaks, with altitude varying from 3,960 feet (1,207 m) to 14,786 feet (4,500 m) above sea level. Mount Karisimbi in northern Rwanda's Virunga range is the highest peak. At around 10,000 square miles (26,700 km²) Rwanda has a population of about 12 million, with about 1 million in the capital city of Kigali. Kinyarawanda is the predominant language but French and English are widely understood. The currency is the Rwandan Franc.

MOUNTAIN GORILLA RESERVES - BWINDI AND VIRUNGA

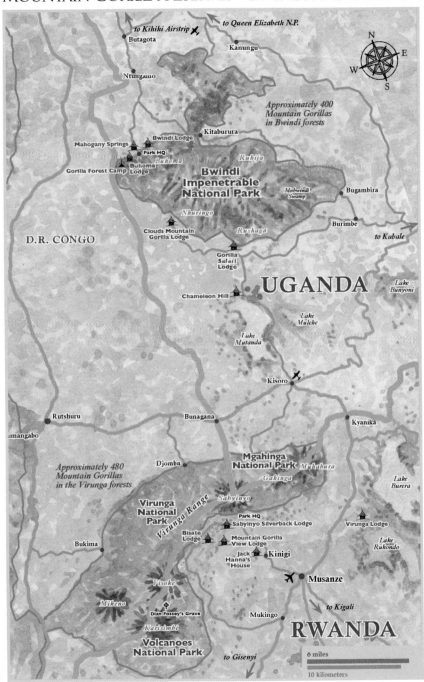

QUEEN ELIZABETH NATIONAL PARK

to Kibale Forest
National Park

Kasese

D.R. CONGO

Rwenzori Mountains

Lake George

Bwera

Kasenyi

Katwe

Kyambura Wildlife Reserve

Kazinga Channel

Kyambura Gorge
Kyambura Gorge Lodge

Mweya Safari Lodge

Kyambura Game Lodge

Lake Edward

Kazinga

Katara Lodge

Queen Elizabeth National Park

Jacana Safari Lodge

Kisenyi

N
W   E
S

Maramagambo Forest

Ishasha Wilderness Camp

UGANDA

Kigezi Game Reserve

Ishaka

to Kabale

10 miles

10 kilometers

KIBALE NATIONAL PARK

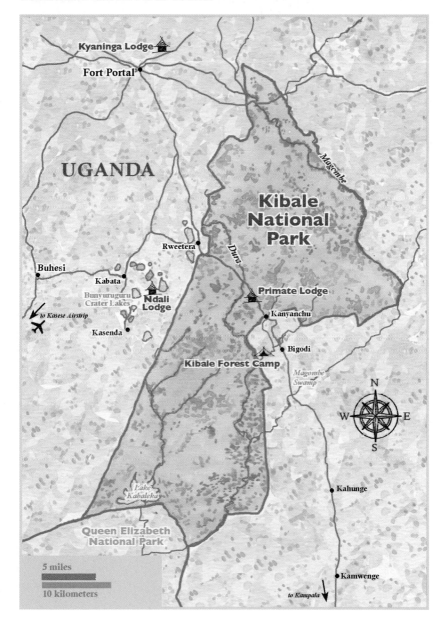

MURCHISON FALLS NATIONAL PARK

ETHIOPIA

Ethiopia is a mountainous country situated in the Horn of Africa, covering some 435,070 square miles (1,127,127 km²) about twice the size of Texas. It has three distinct climate zones relative to topography.

The highest peaks in the Simien Mountains rise above 14,400 feet (4,400 m), while those in the Bale Mountains are just slightly lower. These cool temperate uplands are in stark contrast to the low lying Danakil and Ogaden deserts which are among the hottest places on Earth. A number of endemic mammals, birds and other species are confined to Ethiopia.

There are 84 indigenous languages, but English is widely used. The population is estimated at 104 million, with some 3.3 million in the capital city of Addis Adaba. The currency is the Ethiopian Birr.

REPUBLIC OF CONGO

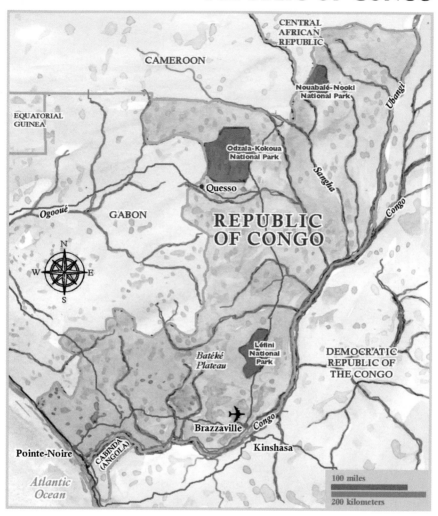

The Republic of Congo (also known simply as Congo, or Congo-Brazzaville) is a different country to the Democratic Republic of Congo (D.R.C. – formerly Zaire) that it borders to the east and south. Congo was formerly part of French Equatorial Africa and French remains the official language.

The country covers some 132,000 square miles (342,000 km²) in the Congo Basin. Rainforest remains mostly in the northern part of the country. The climate is fairly consistent, with a dry season from June to August. The population is estimated at around 4.8 million, with 1.3 million in the capital city of Brazzaville. The currency is the Central African Franc (CFA).

MALAWI

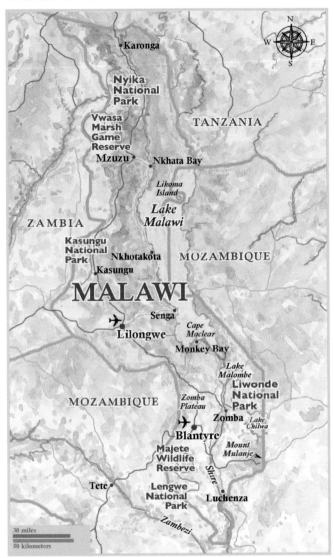

Known to many as the "Warm Heart of Africa", Malawi is a country dominated by the great lake of the same name. The altitude varies from 120 feet (37 m) in the Shire Valley to 9,847 feet (3,002 m) on the summit of Mount Mulanje. *Brachystegia* (miombo) woodland prevails over most of the country, with open grassland and moorland on higher ground.

The population of Malawi is around 18 million, with about 1 million in the capital of Lilongwe. The majority of the population are subsistence farmers. Chichewa and English are the official languages. The currency is the Malawian Kwacha.

ZAMBIA

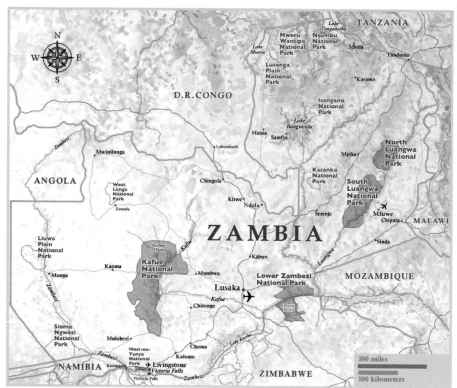

Zambia is one of Africa's least developed countries, with vast areas of wilderness and a comprehensive network of national parks protecting its wildlife. The landscape is an upland plateau ranging in altitude from 3,000 to 5,000 feet above sea level (915 to 1,525 m) with dry savannah and miombo woodland predominating. North and South Luangwa as well as Lower Zambezi National Park are in low-lying valleys between 1,000 (300m) and 1,500 feet (450m) above sea level, with mopane, dry savannah and riparian woodland dominating.

Zambia's economy is based on copper mining, agriculture and tourism. At 290,586 square miles (752,614 km²), Zambia is larger than Texas (or France) but has a population of some 16 million. Lusaka is the capital city with around 2 million inhabitants. English is the official language, with Bemba, Tonga, Ngoni and Lozi widely spoken. The currency is the Zambian Kwacha.

SOUTH LUANGWA NATIONAL PARK

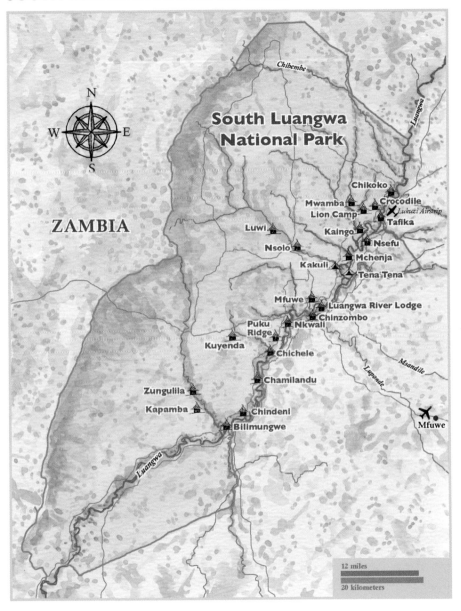

NORTH LUANGWA NATIONAL PARK

Livingstone - Victoria Falls
Mosi-oa-Tunya & Zambezi National Park (Zimbabwe)

Lower Zambezi National Park and Mana Pools National Park (Zimbabwe)

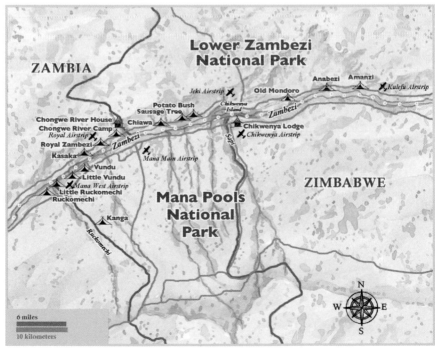

KAFUE NATIONAL PARK

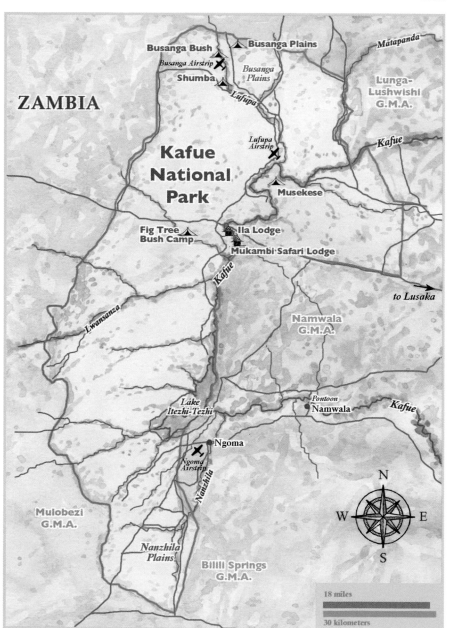

ZIMBABWE

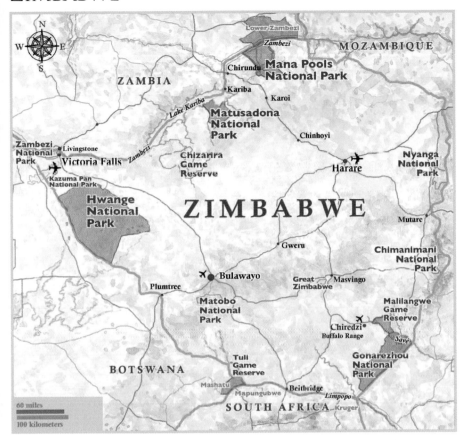

Zimbabwe is a scenic land consisting of a central plateau which drops down to the Zambezi and Limpopo River valleys in the north and south respectively. The average altitude is about 3,300 feet (1,000 m) on the plateau, rising to 8,000 feet (2,400 m) in the Eastern Highlands. The plateau is dominated by Miombo (*Brachystegia*) woodland, with thorn tree and mopane savannah in the larger valleys. A mosaic of grassland and forest occurs in the eastern Highlands.

With an area of 150,872 square miles (390,759 km^2), Zimbabwe is about the size of California (or Great Britain). The population is estimated at around 16 million, with the capital of Harare having some 2 million inhabitants. Shona, Ndebele and English are the main languages. The currency is the U.S. Dollar.

HWANGE NATIONAL PARK

to Victoria Falls

ZIMBABWE

Hwange

Hwange Airport

Khulu Ivory Lodge

Ivory Lodge

Robins Camp

Sinamatella Camp

Dete

Dete Vlei

Hwange Safari Lodge

to Harare and Bulawayo

Camp Hwange

Hwange Main Camp

Nehimba

The Hide

Giraffe Pan

Somalisa Camp

Somalisa Airstrip

Somalisa Acacia

Davison's Camp

Hwange National Park

Makalolo Plains

Little Makalolo

Linkwasha

Ngamo Pan

Makalolo Airstrip

Ziga School

N

W   E

S

Libuti Pan

BOTSWANA

12 miles

20 kilometers

210

Matusadona National Park

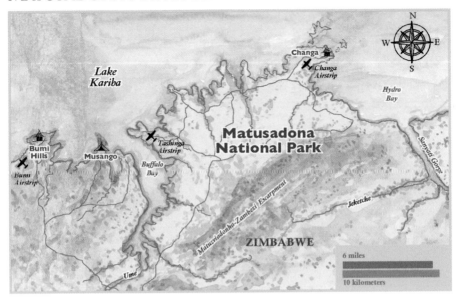

Malilangwe and Gonarezhou National Park

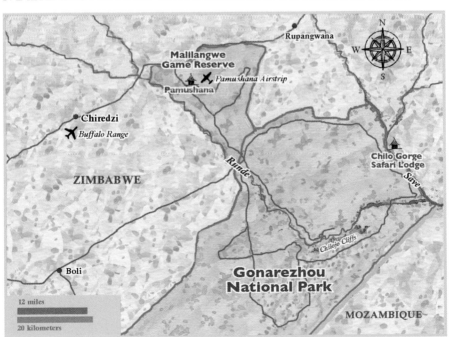

BOTSWANA

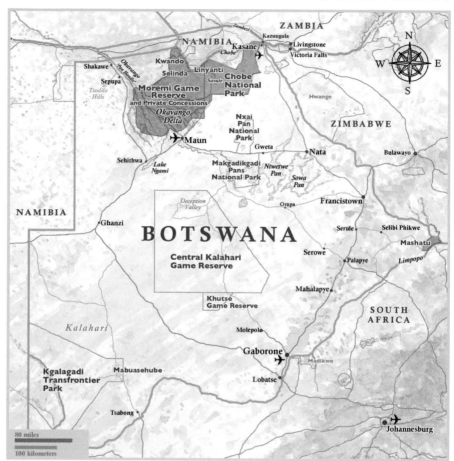

Botswana is dominated by the great Kalahari desert which is actually a varied landscape of grasslands, bush scrub and savannah. In the far northwest, the Okavango River spills out onto the deep Kalahari sands to create the magical Okavango Delta - one of the continent's great wilderness regions.

At some 224,606 square miles (581,730 km²) Botswana is about the size of Texas (or France). The average elevation is around 3,300 feet (1,000 m) above sea level. Botswana's population numbers about 2.1 million, with the great majority living in the southeast, including the capital city of Gaborone. Setswana and English are the official languages. The currency is the Pula.

Okavango Delta

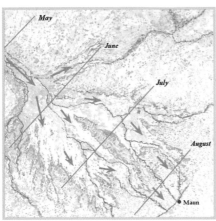

The Okavango Delta is a giant watery oasis within the Kalahari Basin - an otherwise flat, parched landscape of deep, wind-blown sands. Having traveled some 600 miles (1,000 km) from its source in the Angolan highlands, the Okavango River is channeled through a 'pan handle' before fanning out into the basin. Here, it transforms the Kalahari into a tapestry of marshes, woodlands, grasslands, forested islands and seasonal pans that support an immense variety and abundance of wildlife.

The northern part of the Delta and the areas along the main channels are wet throughout the year and regarded as permanent swamp, while the rest is a seasonal swamp that only becomes inundated between May and October - the actual 'dry season' when no rain falls in the Delta. In general, the seasonal Okavango floodwaters take about four months to travel the 150 miles (250 km) from Mohembo to Maun - a gradient of just 230 feet (70 m).

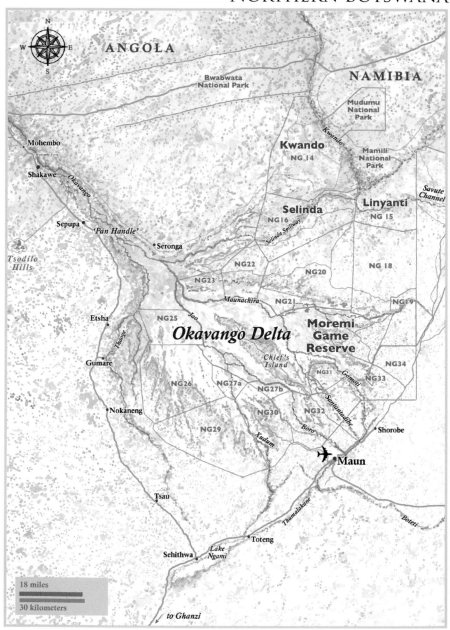

Northern Botswana

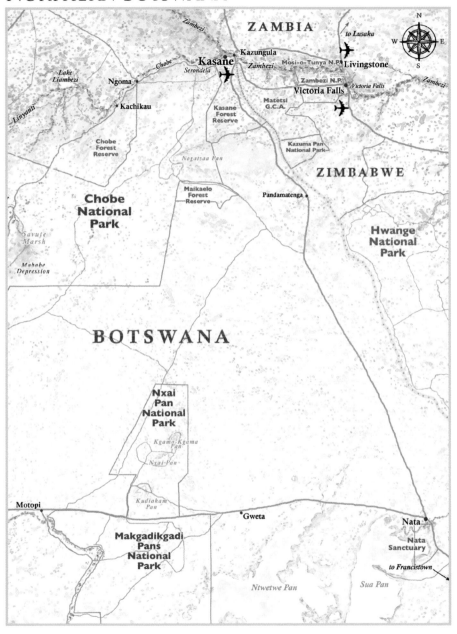

CHOBE NATIONAL PARK (NORTHERN SECTOR)

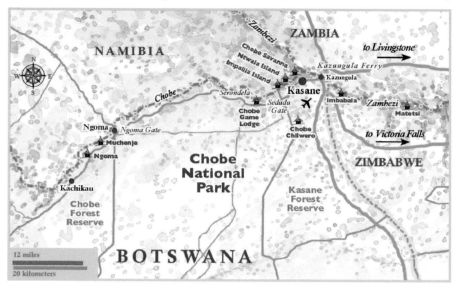

KWANDO, SELINDA, LINYANTI AND SAVUTE

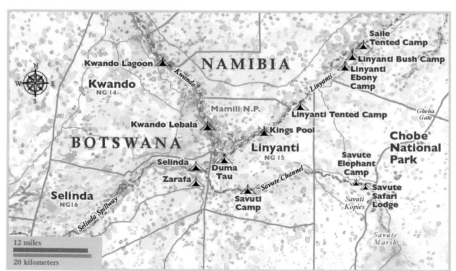

Nxai Pan and Makgadikgadi Pans

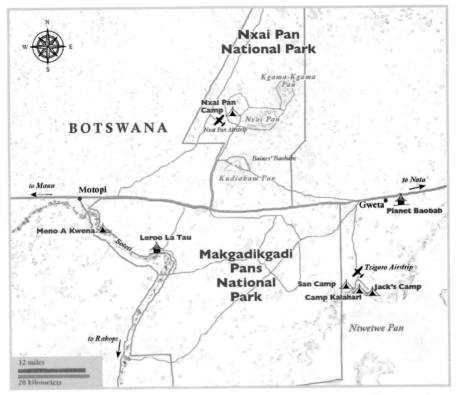

Central Kalahari Game Reserve (Northern Sector)

NAMIBIA

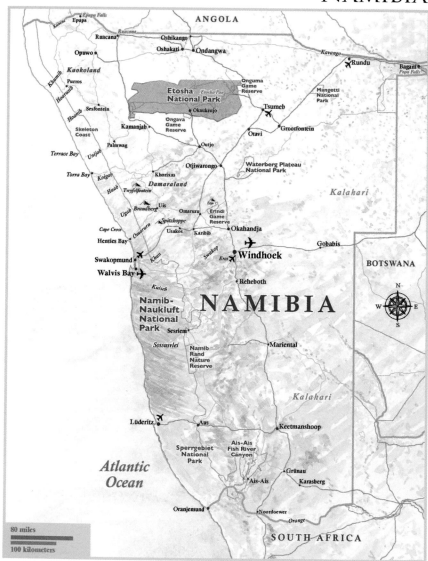

Namibia is one of Africa's driest countries, with the Namib and Kalahari deserts dominating the landscape. Elevation ranges from sea level on the Atlantic seaboard to some 5,410 feet (1,650 m) at Windhoek on the central plateau. In the far north, the permanent water of the Kunene and Okavango Rivers allows for productive agriculture and it is here that most of the population lives. Approximately 2.3 million people inhabit the 318,250 square miles (824,268 km²) of Namibia which is about twice the size of California. Windhoek is the capital city. English is the official language. The currency is the Namibian Dollar.

NAMIBIA (NORTH-EAST CAPRIVI REGION)

KAOKOLAND

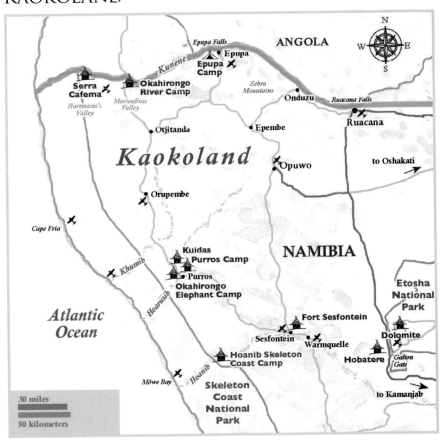

DAMARALAND

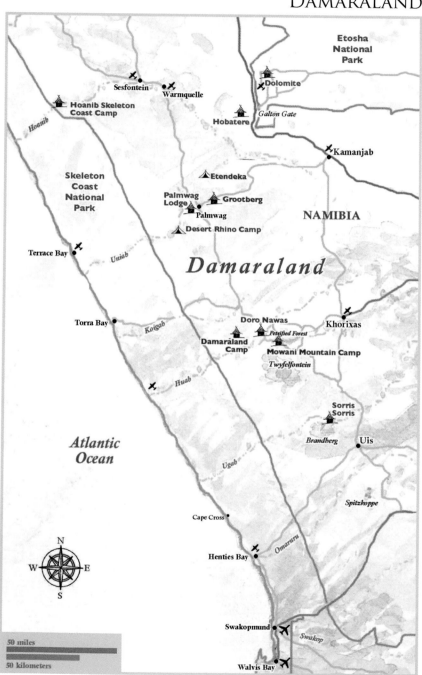

Etosha National Park

Sesfontein

Warmquelle

Dolomite

Hoanib Skeleton Coast Camp

Hoanib

Hobatere

Galton Gate

Skeleton Coast National Park

Kamanjab

Etendeka

Palmwag Lodge

Grootberg

Palmwag

NAMIBIA

Desert Rhino Camp

Terrace Bay

Uniab

Damaraland

Torra Bay

Koigab

Doro Nawas

Khorixas

Petrified Forest

Damaraland Camp

Mowani Mountain Camp

Twyfelfontein

Huab

Sorris Sorris

Brandberg   Uis

Atlantic Ocean

Ugab

Spitzkoppe

Cape Cross

Omaruru

Henties Bay

N
W   E
S

Swakopmund

Swakop

50 miles

50 kilometers

Walvis Bay

220

Etosha National Park

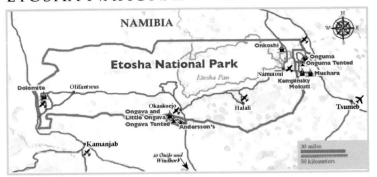

Namib-Naukluft National Park

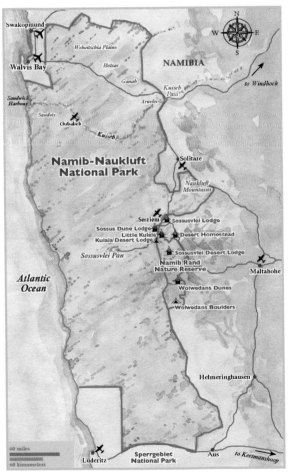

SOUTH AFRICA (WESTERN)

At the southern end of the continent, South Africa is an extremely diverse country with temperate highlands, sub-tropical savannah, alpine-like mountains, semi-desert and unique Mediterranean-like heathlands known as "fynbos". Much of the country is a high plateau averaging some 4,800 feet (1,500 m) above sea level, with the Drakensberg rising to 11,400 feet (3,450 m). The country is flanked by the cool Atlantic and warm Indian Oceans, each of which has a strong bearing on the climate. South Africa is the most industrialized nation on the continent but still has large protected areas including the famous Kruger National Park and surrounding areas which occupy most of the "lowveld". Covering some

471,445 square miles (1.2 million km²), South Africa is twice the size of Texas. English is the official language, with Zulu, Tswana, Xhosa, Sotho and Afrikaans all widely spoken. The population is estimated at around 55 million. Pretoria and Cape Town are the capital cities but Johannesburg is the business hub. The currency is the Rand (ZAR).

BOTSWANA

Nossob

Kgalagadi Transfrontier Park

McCarthy's Rest

Twee Rivieren

Ashkam

Hotazel

Kalahari

Tswalu

Kuruman

NAMIBIA

Richtersveld National Park

Oranjemund

Upington

Viool sdrif

Orange

Augrabies National Park

Mokala National Park

Springbok

Orange

Prieska

SOUTH AFRICA

Namaqua National Park

Namaqualand

Britstown

Atlantic Ocean

Victoria West

Vanrhynsdorp

Calvinia

Karoo

Lambert's Bay

Cedarberg

Clanwilliam

St Helena Bay

Tankwa Karoo National Park

Sutherland

Karoo National Park

Beaufort West

Camdeboo National Park

Graaf-Reinet

Langebaan

West Coast National Park

Berg

Swartberg

Paarl

Worcester

Franschhoek

Langeberg

Oudtshoorn

George

Tsitsikamma National Park

Cape Town

Stellenbosch

False Bay

Bontebok

Swellendam

Gourits

Knysna

Plettenberg Bay

Table Mountain National Park

Hermanus

De Hoop

Mossel Bay

Walker Bay

Gansbaai

Arniston

Cape Agulhas

SOUTH AFRICA (EASTERN)

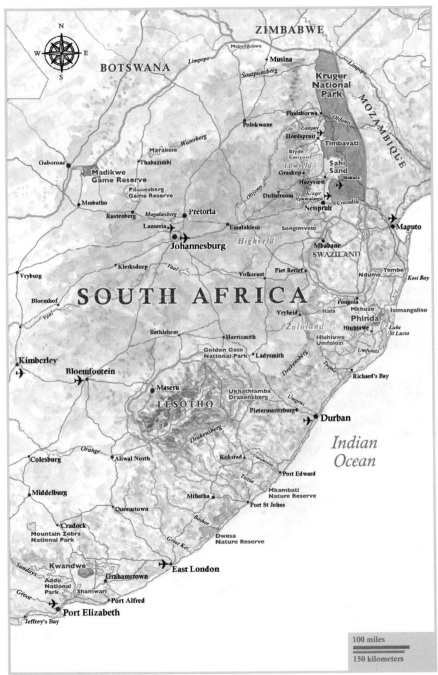

KRUGER NATIONAL PARK

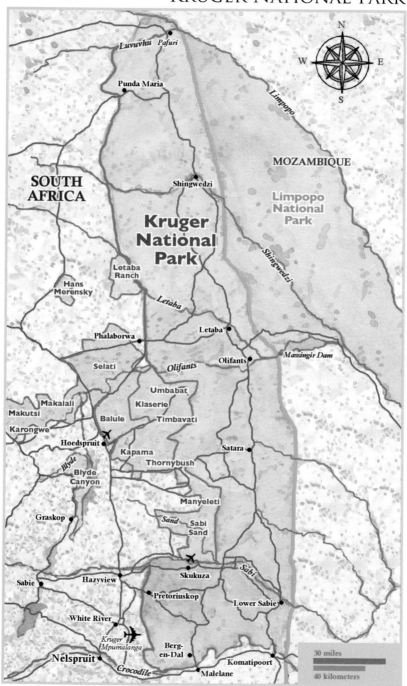

Luvuvhu   Pafuri

Punda Maria

Limpopo

N
W   E
S

MOZAMBIQUE

SOUTH
AFRICA

Shingwedzi

Limpopo
National
Park

**Kruger
National
Park**

Letaba
Ranch

Shingwedzi

Hans
Merensky

Letaba

Phalaborwa

Letaba

Olifants

Olifants

Massingir Dam

Selati

Umbabat

Klaserie

Makalali
Makutsi
Karongwe

Balule

Timbavati

Hoedspruit

Kapama

Satara

Blyde

Blyde
Canyon

Thornybush

Manyeleti

Graskop

Sand   Sabi
Sand

Sabie

Hazyview

Skukuza

Sabi

Pretoriuskop

White River

Lower Sabie

Kruger
Mpumalanga

Berg-
en-Dal

Nelspruit

Crocodile

Malelane

Komatipoort

30 miles

40 kilometers

224

Sabi Sand, Timbavati and other Private Reserves bordering Kruger National Park

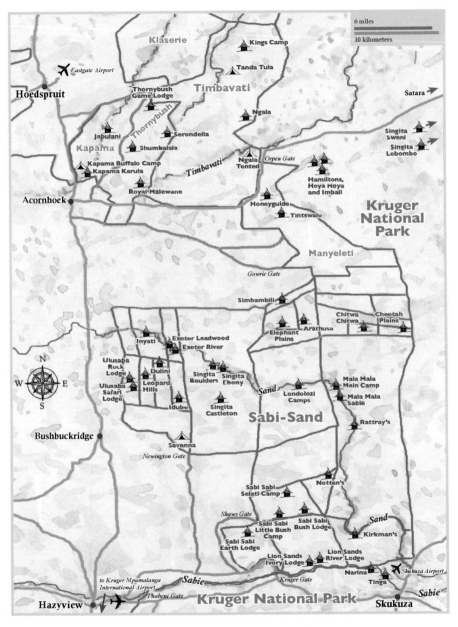

225

CAPE PENINSULA

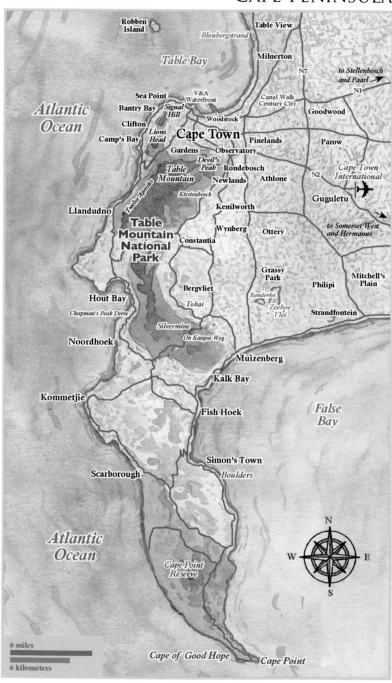

CAPE WINELANDS

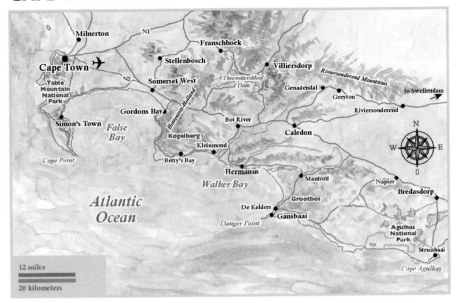

GARDEN ROUTE AND KAROO

MADAGASCAR

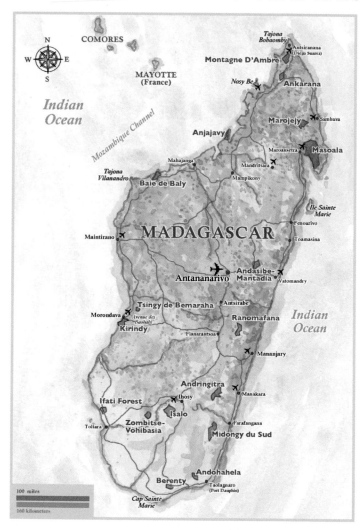

Madagascar is an island country in the Indian Ocean off Africa's southeastern coast. Madagascar split from India around 88 million years ago, after the larger Gondwanan landmass (of which they were a part along with Africa and South America) had broken up some 40 million years earlier; this explains the unique fauna of which 90% occurs nowhere else.

At 228,900 square miles (587,000 km²), Madagascar is the 5th largest island on the planet. The center of the island is a plateau from 2,400 to 4,900 feet (750 to 1,500 m) above sea level, with an escarpment along the length of the east coast. Most of the remaining tropical forest exists along and to the east of this escarpment. The southwest is semi-arid. The population is around 25 million, with 90% living below the poverty line. Malagasy and French are the official languages. The currency is the Madagascar Ariary (MGA).

SEYCHELLES

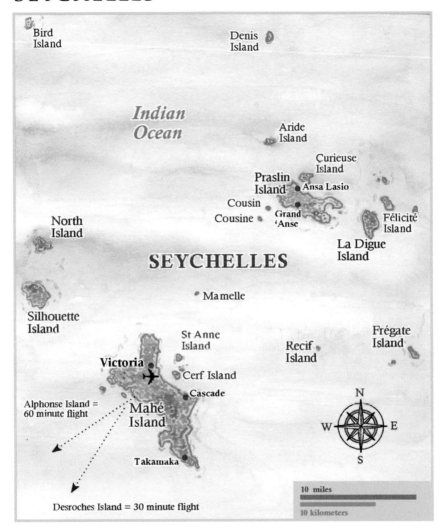

Bird Island

Denis Island

Indian Ocean

Aride Island

Curieuse Island

Praslin Island Ansa Lasio

Cousin

Cousine Grand 'Anse

North Island

Félicité Island

La Digue Island

SEYCHELLES

Mamelle

Silhouette Island

St Anne Island

Recif Island

Frégate Island

Victoria

Cerf Island

Cascade

Alphonse Island = 60 minute flight

Mahé Island

Takamaka

N

W   E

S

Desroches Island = 30 minute flight

10 miles

10 kilometers

The Seychelles comprise 115 islands which cover a collective area of just 171 square miles (433 km²) in the western Indian Ocean. Mahé, the largest of the islands, is located 4 degrees south of the equator. The islands are made of either granite or coral, with the former having peaks rising up to 2,970 feet (905 m). Most of the coraline or "outer" islands are just a few feet above sea level.

Due to its geographic isolation, most of the flora and fauna is unique, but plants and animals introduced by man have greatly altered the landscape and endangered many species. The resident population is less than 100,000 with Creole, French and English widely spoken. The currency is the Seychelles Rupee.

MAURITIUS

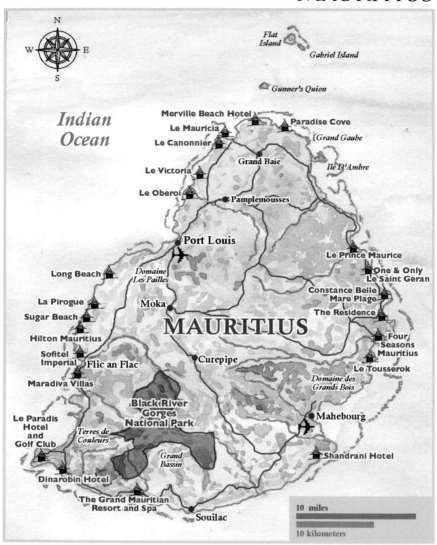

Mauritius is a volcanic island in the south-western Indian Ocean, 520 miles (840 km) east of Madagascar. The island extends over 720 square miles (1,865 km²), which is about the size of Rhode Island (or Luxembourg). The terrain of Mauritius is hilly with some small but spectacular mountains, the highest of which rise to some 2,700 feet (824 m). The 124 mile (200 km) coastline is fringed by coral reef although much of this is not in a pristine state. The island was previously forested but – along with much of the native fauna – much of this has been lost to development. The extinct Dodo was a tragic victim of colonization by humans. The resident population is estimated at 1.3 million. Creole, French and English are the predominant languages. The currency is the Mauritian Rupee.

STAR GAZING ON SAFARI

Breathtaking views of the night sky are a typical feature of clear nights in African wilderness areas. A cloudless night provides a glorious opportunity to become familiar with several interesting constellations and noteworthy stars, as well as up to five planets in our own solar system. The position of the stars and the constellations is constant, but their place in the night sky is determined by the position of our own planet which, of course, revolves around the sun, as well as the time of night at which observations are made. So it is, that the position of the stars appears different to us at different times of the night and throughout the year. Gazing up at the night sky certainly provides a clear indication of the Earth's mobile state, and an understanding of this was the foundation for the human-invented calendar.

Highly sophisticated applications for tablets and smart phones now make it possible to obtain a precise picture of the night sky, based on any particular position, at any particular time.

The old-fashioned revolving "planisphere" (two adjustable polyvinyl wheels) is another reliable way to read the night sky.

Duncan Butchart

Even just viewing the moon through a good pair of binoculars can be mesmerizing!

231

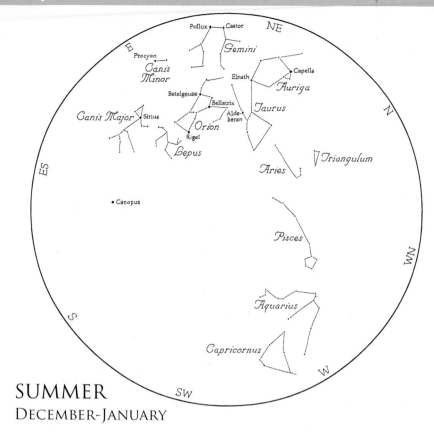

SUMMER
DECEMBER-JANUARY

With so many hundreds of thousands of stars, it is quite impossible for the novice to gain anything but a general picture of the night sky, and most people will be happy to be able to locate and identify the Southern Cross (or Crux) and other major constellations such as Orion's Belt and Scorpio. One or more of the planets, Venus, Jupiter or Mars, will be visible at any given time of year.

Planets (including our own) do not emit light, but reflect light from the Sun, around which all planets in our solar system revolve. Because of this, planets appear as constant, unblinking bright spots. Stars, on the other hand, are sources of light (like our Sun) and appear as flickering bright spots when we view them (although in many cases we are viewing light from stars that may have burned out decades ago!).

The diagrams on these pages provide a simplistic picture of the Southern Sky in summer (December-January) and winter (June-July). They are not intended as precise tools, but merely an indication of what you might look for.

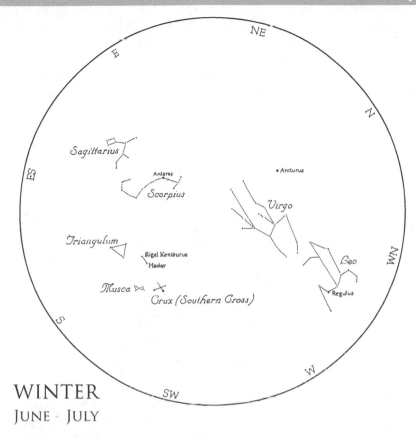

WINTER
JUNE - JULY

Many safari guides possess a good knowledge of the night sky and will be able to point out some of the constellations and planets, and perhaps even relate interesting fables and stories regarding the origin of their names.

A good pair of binoculars will greatly enhance sky watching, as you'll see up to ten times as many stars! Even seemingly "blank" or "sparse" parts of the sky will be seen to be filled with hundreds of distant stars when you use binoculars. Scanning the Milky Way can be truly astounding. To avoid tired arms and binocular shake when looking upwards for more than a few minutes, it is advisable to lie flat on the ground and brace your binoculars with your elbows.

The Moon itself is magnificent to view through binoculars, as various craters and the "Sea of Tranquility" are easily seen. Because it is so bright, detail on the surface of the moon is best viewed early in the evening before it becomes totally dark.

Mammal Spoor

Leopard

Lion

Cheetah

Spotted Hyena

African Wild Dog

African Elephant

Giraffe

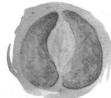

Cape Buffalo

Plains Zebra

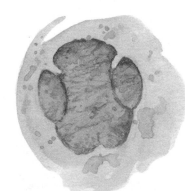

White Rhinoceros

Warthog

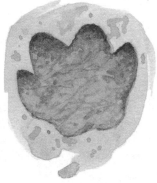

Hippopotamus

MAMMAL CHECKLIST

This is a comprehensive checklist of all the larger mammal species that occur in southern, central and eastern Africa. Species restricted to the Congo Basin and the unique mammals of Madagascar are listed separately. It can be used from South Africa to Ethiopia, and from Congo Republic to Madagascar and Seychelles. Marine mammals are also included for those who venture offshore. Names listed here follow the most recent taxonomic changes including the major revision of the ungulates (Groves & Grubb, 2011).

Aardvark	Colobus, Iringa Red	Duiker, Eastern White-bellied
Aardwolf	Colobus, Tana Red	Duiker, Itombwe
Baboon, Chacma	Colobus, Zanzibar Red	Duiker, Lestrade's
Baboon, Gelada	Dikdik, Cavendish's	Duiker, Natal Red
Baboon, Hamadryas (Sacred)	Dikdik, Damara	Duiker, Peters' Red
Baboon, Olive	Dikdik, Gunther's	Eland, Common
Baboon, Yellow	Dikdik, Hinde's	Elephant, African Savannah
Bat, Angola Fruit-	Dikdik, Kirk's	Elephant-Shrew, Bushveld
Bat, Epauletted Fruit-	Dikdik, Lawrence's	Elephant-Shrew, Cape
Bat, Hammer	Dikdik, Smith's	Elephant-Shrew, Checkered
Bat, Mauritian Tomb-	Dikdik, Swayne's	Elephant-Shrew, Dusky
Bat, Mountain Fruit-	Dikdik, Thomas'	Elephant-Shrew, Dusky-footed
Bat, Slit-faced	Dolphin, Common	Elephant-Shrew, Eastern Rock
Bat, Straw-colored Fruit-	Dolphin, Dusky	Elephant-Shrew, Four-toed
Bat, Egyptian Fruit-	Dolphin, Fraser's	Elephant-Shrew, Golden-rumped
Bat, Yellow-winged	Dolphin, Heaviside's	Elephant-Shrew, Karoo Rock
Blesbok	Dolphin, Hourglass	Elephant-Shrew, Rufous
Bongo	Dolphin, Indo-Pacific Bottlenose	Elephant-Shrew, Short-eared
Bontebok	Dolphin, Melon-headed	Elephant-Shrew, Zanj
Buffalo, Cape	Dolphin, Pantropical Spotted	Fox, Bat-eared
Bushbuck, Common	Dolphin, Risso's	Fox, Cape (Silver)
Bushbuck, Harnessed	Dolphin, Rough-toothed	Galago, Greater
Bushpig	Dolphin, Southern Right Whale	Galago, Matundu
Cane Rat, Marsh	Dolphin, Striped	Galago, Mozambique
Cane Rat, Savannah	Dolphin, Spinner	Galago, Mweru
Caracal	Dormouse, Rock	Galago, Rondo
Cat, African Wild	Dormouse, Spectacled	Galago, Senegal Lesser
Cat, Golden	Dormouse, Woodland	Galago, Silver
Cat, Small-spotted	Dugong (Manatee)	Galago, Small-eared
Cheetah	Duiker, Abbott's	Galago, Somali Lesser
Chimpanzee	Duiker, Aders'	Galago, Southern
Civet, African	Duiker, Black-fronted	Galago, Spectacled Lesser
Civet, African Palm-	Duiker, Blue	Galago, Thomas's
Colobus, Black-and-white	Duiker, Gray (Common)	Galago, Usambara

235

Galago, Zanzibar	Impala, Black-faced	Monkey, Grivet
Gazelle, Grant's	Impala, Common	Monkey, L'Hoest's
Gazelle, Soemmerring's	Jackal, Black-backed	Monkey, Patas
Gazelle, Thomson's	Jackal, Golden	Monkey, Red-(Copper-)tailed
Genet, Blotched (Large-spotted)	Jackal, Side-striped	Monkey, Samango
Genet, Common (Small-spotted)	Klipspringer	Monkey, Sykes'
Genet, Ethiopian	Kob, Ugandan	Monkey, Vervet
Genet, Miombo	Kob, White-eared (Nile)	Oribi
Genet, Servaline	Kongoni	Oryx, Beisa
Gerenuk	Kudu, Greater	Oryx, Fringe-eared
Gemsbok (Southern Oryx)	Kudu, Lesser	Oryx, Southern (Gemsbok)
Giraffe, Maasai	Nyala, Common	Otter, African (Cape) Clawless
Giraffe, Reticulated	Nyala, Mountain	Otter, Spot-necked
Giraffe, Rothchild's (Nubian)	Lechwe, Black (Bangweulu)	Pangolin, Ground
Giraffe, Southern	Lechwe, Kafue	Porcupine, African
Giraffe, Thornicroft's (Luangwa)	Lechwe, Red	Potto
Gorilla, Mountain	Lechwe, Nile	Puku
Grysbok, Cape	Leopard	Rabbit, Jameson's Red Rock-
Grysbok, Sharpe's	Lion	Rabbit, Natal Rock-
Hare, African Savannah	Mangabey, Sanje	Rabbit, Riverine
Hare, Cape	Mangabey, Tana	Rabbit, Smith's Red Rock-
Hare, Scrub	Meerkat (Suricate)	Rat, Acacia
Hare, Starck's (Ethiopian)	Mongoose, Banded	Rat, African Giant
Hare, Ugandan Grass	Mongoose, Bushy-tailed	Rat, Angoni Vlei
Hartebeest, Coke's (Kongoni)	Mongoose, Dwarf	Rat, Brants' Whistling
Hartebeest, Lichtenstein's	Mongoose, Egyptian	Rat, Common Vlei
Hartebeest, Red	Mongoose, Jackson's	Rat, Gambian Pouched
Hedgehog, African	Mongoose, Marsh	Rat, Malagasy Giant
Hippopotamus	Mongoose, Meller's	Rat, Sloggett's Vlei
Hirola	Mongoose, Savannah	Reedbuck, Bohor
Hog, Giant Forest-	Mongoose, Selous'	Reedbuck, Common
Honey-Badger (Ratel)	Mongoose, Slender	Reedbuck, Eastern Mountain
Hyena, Brown	Mongoose, Small Gray	Reedbuck, Southern Mountain
Hyena, Spotted	Mongoose, Sokoke Dog	Rhebok, Gray (Vaal)
Hyena, Striped	Mongoose, White-tailed	Rhinoceros, Black
Hyrax, Rock	Mongoose, Yellow	Rhinoceros, Northern White
Hyrax, Southern Tree	Monkey, Bale	Rhinoceros, Southern White
Hyrax, Western Tree	Monkey, Blue	Roan Antelope
Hyrax, Yellow-spotted Bush	Monkey, Crowned	Sable Antelope
Ibex, Nubian	Monkey, De Brazza's	Seal, Antarctic Fur

Seal, Cape Fur	Whale, False Killer-	Duiker, Black
Seal, Crab-eater	Whale, Fin	Duiker, Congo Bay
Seal, Leopard	Whale, Giant Beaked	Duiker, Itombwe
Seal, Southern Elephant	Whale, Gray's Beaked-	Duiker, Red-flanked
Seal, Subantarctic Fur	Whale, Hector's Beaked-	Duiker, White-legged
Seal, Weddell	Whale, Humpback	Duiker, Yellow-backed
Serval	Whale, Killer (Orca)	Elephant, Forest
Sitatunga	Whale, Layard's Beaked-	Galago, Demidoff's
Springbok	Whale, Longman's Beaked	Genet, Aquatic
Springhare	Whale, Minke	Genet, Giant Servaline
Squirrel, Damara Ground	Whale, Pilot	Gorilla, Western Lowland
Squirrel, Mutable Sun	Whale, Pygmy Blue	Hog, Red River
Squirrel, Ochre Dush	Whale, Pygmy Right	Linsang, Central African
Squirrel, Red-bellied Coast	Whale, Pygmy Killer-	Mandrill
Squirrel, Red-legged Sun	Whale, Pygmy Sperm	Mangabey, Agile
Squirrel, Rope	Whale, Sei	Mangabey, Black
Squirrel, Rwenzori Sun	Whale, Shepherd's Beaked	Mangabey, Gray-cheeked
Squirrel, Smith's Bush	Whale, Southern Right	Mangabey, Red-capped
Squirrel, S. African Ground	Whale, True's Beaked-	Monkey, Allen's Swamp
Squirrel, Striped Bush	Wildebeest, Black (White-tailed)	Monkey, Crowned
Squirrel, Striped Ground	Wildebeest, Blue (Brindled)	Monkey, De Brazza's
Squirrel, Tanganyika Mountain	Wildebeest, White-bearded (Serengeti)	Monkey, Mustached
Squirrel, Unstriped Ground	Wild Dog, African	Monkey, Northern Talapoin
Squirrel, Zanj Sun	Wolf, Ethiopian	Monkey, Owl-faced
Steenbok	Zebra, Cape Mountain	Monkey, Putty-nosed
Suni	Zebra, Grevy's	Monkey, Tantalus
Tiang	Zebra, Hartmann's Mountain-	Monkey, Wolf's
Topi	Zebra, Plains (Burchell's)	Okapi
Tsessebe	Zorilla (Striped Polecat)	Otter, Swamp
Warthog, Common		Pangolin, Giant
Warthog, Desert	**Mammals restricted to**	Pangolin, Tree
Waterbuck, Common	**the Congo Basin**	Porcupine, Brush-tailed
Waterbuck, Defassa	Anomalure, Beecroft's	Porcupine, Crested
Weasel, Striped	Anomalure, Lord Derby's	Rat, Gambian Pouched
Whale, Blainville's Beaked-	Antelope, Dwarf	Squirrel, African Giant
Whale, Blue	Buffalo, Forest	Squirrel, African Pygmy
Whale, Bottlenose	Cat, Golden	Squirrel, Alexander's Dwarf
Whale, Bryde's	Chevrotain, Water	
Whale, Cuvier's Beaked	Colobus, Black (Satanic)	
Whale, Dwarf Sperm	Cusimanse, Alexander's	

Mammals restricted to the Congo Basin

237

Mammals Restricted to Madagascar

Angwantibo, Golden
Aye-aye
Bat, Madagascan Fruit-
Civet, Malagasy
Falanouc
Fossa
Indri
Lemur, Amber Mountain
Lemur, Black
Lemur, Black-and-white-ruffed
Lemur, Blue-eyed Black
Lemur, Brown Mouse-
Lemur, Collared Brown
Lemur, Common Brown
Lemur, Coquerel's Dwarf-
Lemur, Crowned
Lemur, Eastern Fork-marked
Lemur, Eastern Gray Bamboo-
Lemur, Fat-tailed Dwarf-
Lemur, Golden Bamboo-
Lemur, Golden-brown Mouse-
Lemur, Gray-backed Sportive-
Lemur, Gray Mouse-
Lemur, Greater Bamboo-
Lemur, Greater Dwarf-
Lemur, Hairy-eared Dwarf-
Lemur, Lake Alaotra Gentle
Lemur, Milne-Edward's Sportive-
Lemur, Northern Sportive-
Lemur, Pale Fork-marked
Lemur, Pariente's Fork-marked
Lemur, Pygmy Mouse-

Lemur, Red-bellied
Lemur, Red-fronted Brown
Lemur, Red-ruffed
Lemur, Red-tailed Sportive-
Lemur, Ring-tailed
Lemur, Sanford's Brown
Lemur, Small-toothed Sportive-
Lemur, Weasel Sportive-
Lemur, Western Gray Bamboo-
Lemur, White-collared Brown
Lemur, White-footed Sportive-
Lemur, White-fronted Brown
Mongoose, Broad-striped Malagasy
Mongoose, Brown-tailed
Mongoose, Grandidier's
Mongoose, Long-snouted
Mongoose, Narrow-striped
Mongoose, Ring-tailed

Sifaka, Coquerel's
Sifaka, Crowned
Sifaka, Diademed
Sifaka, Eastern
Sifaka, Golden-crowned
Sifaka, Milne-Edward's
Sifaka, Silky
Sifaka, Verreaux's
Sifaka, Von der Decken's
Sifaka, Western
Tenrec, Common
Tenrec, Greater Hedgehog
Tenrec, Highland Streaked
Tenrec, Large-eared
Tenrec, Lesser Hedgehog
Tenrec, Lowland Streaked
Tenrec, Tailless
Tenrec, Web-footed

Red-fronted Brown Lemur

BIRD CHECKLIST

This is a comprehensive checklist of all the bird species that occur in southern, central and eastern Africa, as well as those of the Congo Basin and the Indian Ocean islands. As such, it can be used in all of Africa's "top wildlife countries" from South Africa to Ethiopia, and from Congo Republic to Madagascar and Seychelles. Seabirds are also included for those who venture into deeper waters off the continental shelf south of the Cape.

Akalat, Bocage's	Apalis, Karamoja	Babbler, White-rumped
Akalat, East Coast (Gunning's)	Apalis, Kungwe	Barbet, Acacia Pied
Akalat, Equatorial	Apalis, Lowland Masked	Barbet, Anchieta's
Akalat, Gray-winged	Apalis, Mountain Masked	Barbet, Banded
Akalat, Iringa	Apalis, Namuli	Barbet, Black-backed
Akalat, Lowland	Apalis, Rudd's	Barbet, Black-billed
Akalat, Rubeho	Apalis, Rwenzori	Barbet, Black-breasted
Akalat, Sharpe's	Apalis, Taita	Barbet, Black-collared
Akalat, Usambara	Apalis, White-winged	Barbet, Black-throated
Albatross, Atlantic Yellow-nosed	Apalis, Yellow-breasted	Barbet, Bristle-nosed
Albatross, Black-browed	Apalis, Yellow-throated	Barbet, Brown-breasted
Albatross, Gray-headed	Asity, Common Sunbird-	Barbet, Chaplin's (Zambian)
Albatross, Indian Yellow-nosed	Asity, Schlegel's	Barbet, Crested
Albatross, Shy	Asity, Velvet	Barbet, D'Arnaud's (Usambara)
Albatross, Wandering	Asity, Yellow-bellied Sunbird-	Barbet, Double-toothed
Alethe, Brown-chested	Avadavat, Red *	Barbet, Green
Alethe, Fire-crested	Avocet, Pied	Barbet, Gray-throated
Alethe, Red-throated	Babbler, African Hill-	Barbet, Miombo Pied
Alethe, Thyolo	Babbler, Arrow-marked	Barbet, Naked-faced
Alethe, White-chested	Babbler, Bare-cheeked	Barbet, Red-and-yellow
Antpecker, Jameson's	Babbler, Blackcap	Barbet, Red-faced
Antpecker, Woodhouse's	Babbler, Black-faced	Barbet, Red-fronted
Apalis, Bar-throated	Babbler, Black-lored	Barbet, Sladen's
Apalis, Black-capped	Babbler, Brown	Barbet, Spot-flanked
Apalis, Black-collared	Babbler, Capuchin	Barbet, Streaky-throated
Apalis, Black-headed	Babbler, Crossley's	Barbet, Viellot's
Apalis, Black-throated	Babbler, Dusky	Barbet, White-eared
Apalis, Brown-headed	Babbler, Hartlaub's	Barbet, White-headed
Apalis, Buff-throated	Babbler, Hinde's	Barbet, Whyte's
Apalis, Chapin's	Babbler, Northern Pied	Barbet, Yellow-billed
Apalis, Chestnut-throated	Babbler, Red-collared	Barbet, Yellow-breasted
Apalis, Chirinda	Babbler, Scaly	Barbet, Yellow-spotted
Apalis, Gosling's	Babbler, Southern Pied	Bateleur
Apalis, Gray	Babbler, White-headed	Batis, Angola

Batis, Cape	Bishop, Southern Red	Bulbul, Cope
Batis, Chinspot	Bishop, Yellow (Cape)	Bulbul, Common
Batis, Dark	Bishop, Yellow-crowned (Golden)	Bulbul, Comoro
Batis, Eastern Black-headed	Bishop, Zanzibar Red	Bulbul, Dark-capped
Batis, Gabon	Bittern, Dwarf	Bulbul, Dodson's
Batis, Gray-headed	Bittern, Eurasian	Bulbul, Madagascar
Batis, Ituri	Bittern, Little	Bulbul, Mauritius
Batis, Malawi	Blackcap	Bulbul, Reunion
Batis, Margaret's	Blackstart	Bulbul, Seychelles
Batis, Pale	Bluebill, Grant's	Bulbul, Swamp Palm
Batis, Pririt	Bluebill, Red-headed	Bunting, Brown-rumped
Batis, Pygmy	Bluebill, Western	Bunting, Cabanis'
Batis, Rwenzori	Bluethroat	Bunting, Cape
Batis, Short-tailed	Bokmakierie	Bunting, Cinerous
Batis, Western Black-headed	Booby, Brown	Bunting, Cinnamon-breasted
Batis, Woodward's	Booby, Masked	Bunting, Golden-breasted
Bee-eater, Black	Booby, Red-footed	Bunting, Lark-like
Bee-eater, Black-headed	Boubou, East Coast	Bunting, Ortolan
Bee-eater, Blue-breasted	Boubou, Ethiopian	Bunting, Somali
Bee-eater, Blue-cheeked	Boubou, Fulleborn's (Black)	Bunting, Striated
Bee-eater, Blue-headed	Boubou, Lowland Sooty	Bunting, Vincent's
Bee-eater, Böhm's	Boubou, Mountain Sooty	Bush-Blackcap
Bee-eater, Cinnamon-chested	Boubou, Slate-coloured	Bustard, Arabian
Bee-eater, European	Boubou, Southern	Bustard, Black-bellied
Bee-eater, Little	Boubou, Swamp	Bustard, Buff-crested
Bee-eater, Little Green	Boubou, Tropical	Bustard, Denham's (Stanley's)
Bee-eater, Madagascar (Olive)	Boubou, Willard's	Bustard, Hartlaub's
Bee-eater, Northern Carmine	Bristlebill, Red-tailed	Bustard, Heuglin's
Bee-eater, Red-throated	Bristlebill, Yellow-eyed	Bustard, Kori
Bee-eater, Rosy	Bristlebill, Yellow-lored	Bustard, Little Brown
Bee-eater, Somali	Broadbill, African	Bustard, Ludwig's
Bee-eater, Southern Carmine	Broadbill, African Green	Bustard, White-bellied (Northern)
Bee-eater, Swallow-tailed	Broadbill, Gray-headed	Buttonquail, Black-rumped
Bee-eater, White-fronted	Broadbill, Rufous-sided	Buttonquail, Hottentot
Bee-eater, White-throated	Brownbul, Northern	Buttonquail, Kurrichane (Small)
Bishop, Black	Brownbul, Terrestrial	Buttonquail, Madagascar
Bishop, Black-winged	Brubru	Buzzard, Augur
Bishop, Fire-fronted	Bulbul, African Red-eyed	Buzzard, Common
Bishop, Northern Red (Orange)	Bulbul, Black-collared	Buzzard, European Honey-

Buzzard, Forest	Chat, Mocking Cliff-	Cisticola, Luapula
Buzzard, Grasshopper	Chat, Moorland (Alpine)	Cisticola, Lynes'
Buzzard, Jackal	Chat, Northern Ant-eater	Cisticola, Madagascar
Buzzard, Lizard	Chat, Ruaha	Cisticola, Pale-crowned
Buzzard, Long-legged	Chat, Rüppell's Black	Cisticola, Pectoral-patch
Buzzard, Madagascar	Chat, Sickle-winged	Cisticola, Rattling
Buzzard, Mountain	Chat, Sombre Rock-	Cisticola, Red-faced
Buzzard, Red-necked	Chat, Sooty	Cisticola, Red-pate
Buzzard, Steppe	Chat, Southern Ant-eating	Cisticola, Rock-loving
Camaroptera, Green-backed	Chat, Tractrac	Cisticola, Rufous-winged
Camaroptera, Gray-backed	Chat, White-fronted Black	Cisticola, Short-winged (Siffling)
Camaroptera, Olive-green	Chat, White-winged Cliff-	Cisticola, Singing
Camaroptera, Yellow-browed	Chatterer, Rufous	Cisticola, Stout
Canary, Black-faced	Chatterer, Scaly	Cisticola, Tana River
Canary, Black-headed	Chiffchaff	Cisticola, Tinkling (Gray)
Canary, Black-throated	Chough, Red-billed	Cisticola, Tiny
Canary, Brimstone (Bully)	Cisticola, Aberdare	Cisticola, Trilling
Canary, Cape	Cisticola, Ashy	Cisticola, Wailing
Canary, Forest	Cisticola, Black-backed	Cisticola, Whistling
Canary, Lemon-breasted	Cisticola, Black-lored	Cisticola, White-tailed
Canary, Northern Grosbeak-	Cisticola, Boran	Cisticola, Winding
Canary, Papyrus	Cisticola, Carruthers's	Cisticola, Wing-snapping (Ayres')
Canary, Southern Grosbeak-	Cisticola, Chattering	Cisticola, Zitting (Fan-tailed)
Canary, White-bellied	Cisticola, Chirping	Citril, African
Canary, White-throated	Cisticola, Chubb's	Citril, Southern
Canary, Yellow	Cisticola, Churring	Citril, Western
Canary, Yellow-crowned	Cisticola, Cloud	Coot, Eurasian
Canary, Yellow-fronted	Cisticola, Coastal	Coot, Red-knobbed
Catbird, Abyssinian	Cisticola, Croaking	Cordonbleu, Blue-capped
Chaffinch, Common *	Cisticola, Dambo	Cordonbleu, Red-cheeked
Chat, Angola Cave-	Cisticola, Desert	Cormorant, Bank
Chat, Arnot's	Cisticola, Ethiopian	Cormorant, Cape
Chat, Boulder	Cisticola, Foxy	Cormorant, Crowned
Chat, Brown-tailed Rock-	Cisticola, Gray-backed	Cormorant, Reed
Chat, Buff-streaked	Cisticola, Hunter's	Cormorant, White-breasted
Chat, Congo Moor	Cisticola, Kilombero (Melodious)	Coua, Blue
Chat, Familiar	Cisticola, Lazy	Coua, Coquerel's
Chat, Herero	Cisticola, Levaillant's	Coua, Crested
Chat, Karoo	Cisticola, Long-tailed (Tabora)	Coua, Giant

241

Coua, Green-capped	Crimsonwing, Shelley's	Cuckooshrike, Petit's
Coua, Red-breasted	Crombec, Green	Cuckooshrike, Purple-throated
Coua, Red-capped	Crombec, Lemon-bellied	Cuckooshrike, Red-shouldered
Coua, Red-fronted	Crombec, Long-billed	Cuckooshrike, Reunion
Coua, Running	Crombec, Northern	Cuckooshrike, White-breasted
Coua, Verreaux's	Crombec, Red-capped	Curlew, Eurasian
Coucal, Black	Crombec, Red-faced	Darter, African
Coucal, Black-throated	Crombec, Somali	Dove, Adamawa Turtle-
Coucal, Blue-headed	Crombec, White-browed	Dove, African Collared (Rose-gray)
Coucal, Burchell's	Crow, Cape (Black)	Dove, African Mourning
Coucal, Coppery-tailed	Crow, House *	Dove, African White-winged
Coucal, Gabon	Crow, Pied	Dove, Black-billed Wood-
Coucal, Madagascar	Crow, Stresemann's Bush-	Dove, Blue-headed Wood-
Coucal, Senegal	Cuckoo, African	Dove, Blue-spotted Wood-
Coucal, White-browed	Cuckoo, African Emerald	Dove, Cape Turtle-
Courser, Bronze-winged	Cuckoo, Barred Long-tailed	Dove, Dusky Turtle-
Courser, Burchell's	Cuckoo, Black	Dove, Emerald-spotted Wood-
Courser, Cream-coloured	Cuckoo, Common (Eurasian)	Dove, European Turtle-
Courser, Double-banded	Cuckoo, Diderick	Dove, Laughing (Palm)
Courser, Somali	Cuckoo, Dusky Long-tailed	Dove, Lemon (Cinnamon)
Courser, Temminck's	Cuckoo, Great Spotted	Dove, Madagascar Turtle-
Courser, Three-banded (Heuglin's)	Cuckoo, Jacobin	Dove, Namaqua
Crab-Plover	Cuckoo, Klaas's	Dove, Red-eyed
Crake, African	Cuckoo, Lesser	Dove, Rock (Feral Pigeon) *
Crake, Baillon's	Cuckoo, Levaillant's (Striped)	Dove, Seychelles Turtle-
Crake, Black	Cuckoo, Madagascar	Dove, Spotted *
Crake, Corn-	Cuckoo, Olive Long-tailed	Dove, Tambourine
Crake, Little	Cuckoo, Red-chested	Dove, Vinaceous
Crake, Spotted	Cuckoo, Thick-billed	Dove, Zebra (Barred) *
Crake, Striped	Cuckoo, Yellow-throated	Drongo, Aldabra
Crane, Black Crowned-	Cuckoo-Roller, Comoro	Drongo, Crested
Crane, Blue	Cuckoo-Roller, Madagascar	Drongo, Fork-tailed
Crane, Demoiselle	Cuckooshrike, Black	Drongo, Grande Comore
Crane, Gray Crowned-	Cuckooshrike, Blue	Drongo, Mayotte
Crane, Wattled	Cuckooshrike, Comoro	Drongo, Shining
Creeper, Spotted	Cuckoooshrike, Eastern Wattled	Drongo, Square-tailed
Crimsonwing, Abyssinian	Cuckooshrike, Gray	Drongo, Velvet-mantled
Crimsonwing, Dusky	Cuckooshrike, Madagascar	Duck, African Black
Crimsonwing, Red-faced	Cuckooshrike, Mauritius	Duck, Comb (Knob-billed)

Duck, Ferruginous	Egret, Little	Firefinch, Brown
Duck, Fulvous Whistling-	Egret, Slaty	Firefinch, Jameson's
Duck, Hartlaub's	Egret, Yellow-billed	Firefinch, Red-billed
Duck, Maccoa	Emutail, Brown	Fiscal, Common
Duck, Mallard	Emutail, Gray	Fiscal, Gray-backed
Duck, Meller's	Eremomela, Black-necked	Fiscal, Long-tailed
Duck, Tufted	Eremomela, Burnt-necked	Fiscal, Mackinnon's
Duck, White-backed	Eremomela, Green-backed	Fiscal, Somali
Duck, White-faced Whistling-	Eremomela, Green-capped	Fiscal, Taita
Duck, Yellow-billed	Eremomela, Karoo	Fiscal, Uhehe
Dunlin	Eremomela, Rufous-crowned	Flamingo, Greater
Eagle, African Crowned	Eremomela, Salvadori's	Flamingo, Lesser
Eagle, African Fish	Eremomela, Turner's	Flufftail, Buff-spotted
Eagle, African Hawk-	Eremomela, Yellow-bellied	Flufftail, Chestnut-headed
Eagle, Ayres' Hawk-	Eremomela, Yellow-vented	Flufftail, Madagascar
Eagle, Beaudouin's Snake-	Falcon, African Pygmy	Flufftail, Red-chested
Eagle, Black-chested Snake-	Falcon, Amur (Kestrel)	Flufftail, Slender-billed
Eagle, Booted	Falcon, Barbary	Flufftail, Streaky-breasted
Eagle, Brown Snake-	Falcon, Eleanora's	Flufftail, Striped
Eagle, Cassin's Hawk-	Falcon, Lanner	Flufftail, White-spotted
Eagle, Congo Serpent-	Falcon, Peregrine	Flufftail, White-winged
Eagle, Eastern Imperial	Falcon, Red-footed (Kestrel)	Flycatcher, Abyssinian Slaty
Eagle, Golden	Falcon, Red-necked	Flycatcher, African Blue-
Eagle, Greater Spotted	Falcon, Saker	Flycatcher, African Dusky
Eagle, Lesser Spotted	Falcon, Sooty	Flycatcher, African Gray
Eagle, Long-crested	Falcon, Taita	Flycatcher, African Paradise-
Eagle, Madagascar Fish-	Finch, Cuckoo	Flycatcher, African Shrike
Eagle, Madagascar Serpent-	Finch, Cut-throat	Flycatcher, Ashy (Blue-gray)
Eagle, Martial	Finch, Oriole	Flycatcher, Bates' Paradise-
Eagle, Short-toed Snake-	Finch, Pale Rock	Flycatcher, Black-and-white (Vanga)
Eagle, Southern Banded Snake-	Finch, Red-headed	Flycatcher, Blue-headed Crested-
Eagle, Steppe	Finch, Scaly-feathered	Flycatcher, Blue-mantled Crested-
Eagle, Tawny	Finch, Spice *	Flycatcher, Böhm's
Eagle, Verreaux's (Black)	Finch, Trumpeter	Flycatcher, Cassin's
Eagle, Wahlberg's	Finfoot, African	Flycatcher, Chapin's
Eagle, Western Banded Snake-	Firefinch, African (Blue-billed)	Flycatcher, Chat
Egret, Cattle	Firefinch, Bar-breasted	Flycatcher, Chestnut-naped
Egret, Dimorphic	Firefinch, Black-bellied	Flycatcher, Collared
Egret, Great White	Firefinch, Black-faced	Flycatcher, Dusky-blue

Flycatcher, Dusky Crested	Fody, Mauritius	Goshawk, Gabar
Flycatcher, Fairy	Fody, Rodrigues	Goshawk, Henst's
Flycatcher, Fiscal	Fody, Seychelles	Goshawk, Long-tailed
Flycatcher, Fraser's Forest	Francolin, Archer's	Goshawk, Pale Chanting
Flycatcher, Gambaga	Francolin, Coqui	Goshawk, Red-chested
Flycatcher, Gray Tit-	Francolin, Crested	Grassbird, Cape
Flycatcher, Gray-throated Tit-	Francolin, Finsch's	Grebe, Alaotra
Flycatcher, Humblot's	Francolin, Forest (Latham's)	Grebe, Black-necked
Flycatcher, Little Gray	Francolin, Gray *	Grebe, Great Crested
Flycatcher, Little Yellow	Francolin, Gray-winged	Grebe, Little (Dabchick)
Flycatcher, Livingstone's	Francolin, Moorland	Grebe, Madagascar Little
Flycatcher, Madagascar Paradise-	Francolin, Orange River	Greenbul, Ansorge's
Flycatcher, Marico	Francolin, Red-winged	Greenbul, Appert's
Flycatcher, Mascarene Paradise-	Francolin, Ring-necked	Greenbul, Black-headed Mountain
Flycatcher, Northern Black	Francolin, Shelley's	Greenbul, Dusky
Flycatcher, Olivaceous	Frigatebird, Greater	Greenbul, Eastern Bearded
Flycatcher, Pale	Frigatebird, Lesser	Greenbul, Falkenstein's
Flycatcher, Pied	Fulmar, Antarctic	Greenbul, Fischer's
Flycatcher, Red-bellied Paradise-	Gadwall	Greenbul, Golden
Flycatcher, Rufous-vented Paradise-	Gallinule, Allen's (Lesser)	Greenbul, Gray-crowned
Flycatcher, Semi-collared	Gallinule, American Purple	Greenbul, Gray-olive
Flycatcher, Seychelles Black Paradise-	Gannet, Australian	Greenbul, Honeyguide
Flycatcher, Sooty	Gannet, Cape	Greenbul, Icterine
Flycatcher, Southern Black	Gargany	Greenbul, Joyful
Flycatcher, Spotted	Go-away-bird, Bare-faced	Greenbul, Kakamega
Flycatcher, Swamp	Go-away-bird, Gray	Greenbul, Little
Flycatcher, Tessmann's	Go-away-bird, White-bellied	Greenbul, Little Gray
Flycatcher, Ward's	Godwit, Bar-tailed	Greenbul, Long-billed
Flycatcher, White-bellied Crested-	Godwit, Black-tailed	Greenbul, Olive-breasted Mountain
Flycatcher, White-browed Forest	Godwit, Hudsonian	Greenbul, Olive-headed
Flycatcher, White-eyed Slaty	Gonolek, Black-headed	Greenbul, Placid
Flycatcher, White-tailed Blue-	Gonolek, Papyrus	Greenbul, Plain
Flycatcher, White-tailed Crested-	Goose, African Pygmy-	Greenbul, Red-tailed
Flycatcher, Yellow-eyed Black	Goose, Blue-winged	Greenbul, Sharpe's
Flycatcher, Yellow-footed	Goose, Egyptian	Greenbul, Shelley's
Fody, Aldabra	Goose, Spur-winged	Greenbul, Simple (Leaf-love)
Fody, Comoro	Goshawk, African	Greenbul, Slender-billed
Fody, Forest	Goshawk, Dark Chanting	Greenbul, Sombre
Fody, Madagascar	Goshawk, Eastern Chanting	Greenbul, Southern Mountain

Greenbul, Spectacled	Gull, White-eyed	Honeyguide, Wilcock's
Greenbul, Spotted	Hamerkop	Honeyguide, Zencker's
Greenbul, Stripe-cheeked	Harrier, African Marsh-	Hoopoe, African
Greenbul, Stripe-faced	Harrier, Black	Hoopoe, Eurasian
Greenbul, Tiny (Slender)	Harrier, Montagu's	Hoopoe, Madagascar
Greenbul, Toro Olive	Harrier, Pallid	Hornbill, African Gray
Greenbul, Uluguru Mountain	Harrier, Reunion	Hornbill, African Pied
Greenbul, Usambara	Harrier, Western Marsh-	Hornbill, Black Dwarf
Greenbul, White-bearded	Harrier-Hawk, African (Gymnogene)	Hornbill, Black-and-white Casqued
Greenbul, White-throated	Harrier-Hawk, Madagascar	Hornbill, Black-casqued Wattled-
Greenbul, Xavier's	Hawk, African Cuckoo-	Hornbill, Bradfield's
Greenbul, Yellow-bellied	Hawk, Bat	Hornbill, Crowned
Greenbul, Yellow-streaked	Heron, Black	Hornbill, Damara Red-billed
Greenbul, Yellow-throated Mountain	Heron, Black-crowned Night-	Hornbill, Eastern Yellow-billed
Greenbul, Yellow-whiskered	Heron, Black-headed	Hornbill, Hemprich's
Greenshank, Common	Heron, Goliath	Hornbill, Jackson's
Grenadier, Purple	Heron, Green-backed (Striated)	Hornbill, Monteiro's
Ground-Roller, Long-tailed	Heron, Gray	Hornbill, Northern Ground-
Ground-Roller, Pitta-like	Heron, Humblot's	Hornbill, Northern Red-billed
Ground-Roller, Rufous-headed	Heron, Madagascar Pond-	Hornbill, Pale-billed
Ground-Roller, Scaly	Heron, Purple	Hornbill, Piping
Ground-Roller, Short-legged	Heron, Rufous-bellied	Hornbill, Red-billed Dwarf
Guineafowl, Black	Heron, Squacco	Hornbill, Silvery-cheeked
Guineafowl, Crested	Heron, White-backed Night-	Hornbill, Southern Ground-
Guineafowl, Helmeted	Heron, White-crested Tiger-	Hornbill, Southern Red-billed
Guineafowl, Plumed	Hobby, African	Hornbill, Southern Yellow-billed
Guineafowl, Vulturine	Hobby, Eurasian	Hornbill, Tanzanian Red-billed
Gull, Caspian	Honeybird, Brown-backed	Hornbill, Trumpeter
Gull, Common Black-headed	Honeybird, Cassin's	Hornbill, Von der Decken's
Gull, Franklin's	Honeybird, Green-backed	Hornbill, White-crested
Gull, Gray-headed	Honeyguide, Dwarf	Hornbill, White-thighed
Gull, Hartlaub's	Honeyguide, Greater	Hylia, Green
Gull, Heuglin's	Honeyguide, Least	Hyliota, Southern (Mashona)
Gull, Kelp	Honeyguide, Lesser	Hyliota, Usambara
Gull, Lesser Black-backed	Honeyguide, Lyre-tailed	Hyliota, Violet-backed
Gull, Pallas's	Honeyguide, Pallid	Hyliota, Yellow-bellied
Gull, Sabine's	Honeyguide, Scaly-throated	Ibis, African Sacred
Gull, Slender-billed	Honeyguide, Spotted	Ibis, Glossy
Gull, Sooty (Hemprich's)	Honeyguide, Thick-billed	Ibis, Hadeda

Ibis, Madagascar Crested	Kestrel, Mauritius	Lapwing, Long-toed
Ibis, Madagascar Sacred	Kestrel, Rock	Lapwing, Senegal
Ibis, Olive	Kestrel, Seychelles	Lapwing, Sociable
Ibis, Southern Bald	Kingfisher, African Dwarf-	Lapwing, Spot-breasted
Ibis, Spot-breasted	Kingfisher, African Pygmy-	Lapwing, Spur-winged
Ibis, Wattled	Kingfisher, Blue-breasted	Lapwing, White-crowned
Illadopsis, Blackcap	Kingfisher, Brown-hooded	Lapwing, White-tailed
Illadopsis, Brown	Kingfisher, Chocolate-backed	Lark, Agulhas Long-billed
Illadopsis, Gray-chested	Kingfisher, Giant	Lark, Athi Short-toed
Illadopsis, Mountain	Kingfisher, Gray-headed	Lark, Barlow's
Illadopsis, Pale-breasted	Kingfisher, Half-collared	Lark, Beesley's
Illadopsis, Puvel's	Kingfisher, Madagascar	Lark, Benguela Long-billed
Illadopsis, Scaly-breasted	Kingfisher, Madagascar Pygmy-	Lark, Bimaculated
Indigobird, Baka	Kingfisher, Malachite	Lark, Botha's
Indigobird, Dusky	Kingfisher, Mangrove	Lark, Cape Clapper
Indigobird, Jambandu	Kingfisher, Pied	Lark, Cape Long-billed
Indigobird, Purple	Kingfisher, Shining-blue	Lark, Collared
Indigobird, Village	Kingfisher, Striped	Lark, Crested
Indigobird, Wilson's	Kingfisher, White-bellied	Lark, Dune
Indigobird, Zambezi	Kingfisher, Woodland	Lark, Dusky
Irania	Kite, Black	Lark, Eastern Clapper
Jacana, African	Kite, Black-shouldered	Lark, Eastern Long-billed
Jacana, Lesser	Kite, Scissor-tailed	Lark, Erlanger's
Jacana, Madagascar	Kite, Yellow-billed	Lark, Fawn-coloured
Jaeger, Long-tailed	Knot, Great	Lark, Flappet
Jaeger, Parasitic	Knot, Red	Lark, Friedmann's
Jaeger, Pomarine	Korhaan, Blue	Lark, Gillett's
Jery, Common	Korhaan, Karoo	Lark, Gray's
Jery, Green	Korhaan, Northern Black	Lark, Karoo
Jery, Stripe-throated	Korhaan, Red-crested	Lark, Karoo Long-billed
Jery, Wedge-tailed	Korhaan, Rüppell's	Lark, Liben (Sidamo)
Kestrel, Banded	Korhaan, Southern Black	Lark, Madagascar
Kestrel, Common	Korhaan, White-bellied (Barrow's)	Lark, Malbrant's
Kestrel, Dickinson's	Lapwing, African Wattled	Lark, Masked
Kestrel, Fox	Lapwing, Black-headed	Lark, Melodious
Kestrel, Greater	Lapwing, Blacksmith	Lark, Monotonous
Kestrel, Gray	Lapwing, Black-winged	Lark, Pink-billed
Kestrel, Lesser	Lapwing, Brown-chested	Lark, Pink-breasted
Kestrel, Madagascar	Lapwing, Crowned	Lark, Red

Lark, Red-capped	Magpie-Robin, Seychelles	Newtonia, Archibold's
Lark, Red-winged	Malimbe, Cassin's	Newtonia, Common
Lark, Rudd's	Malimbe, Crested	Newtonia, Dark
Lark, Rufous-naped	Malimbe, Gray-billed	Newtonia, Red-tailed
Lark, Sabota	Malimbe, Rachel's	Nicator, Eastern
Lark, Sclater's	Malimbe, Red-bellied	Nicator, Western
Lark, Short-clawed	Malimbe, Red-crowned	Nicator, Yellow-throated
Lark, Short-tailed	Malimbe, Red-headed	Nightingale, Common
Lark, Singing Bush	Malkoha, Blue	Nightingale, Thrush
Lark, Somali Short-toed	Malkoha, Green	Nightjar, Bates'
Lark, Spike-heeled	Mannikin, Black-and-white	Nightjar, Black-shouldered
Lark, Stark's	Mannikin, Bronze	Nightjar, Brown
Lark, Theleka	Mannikin, Madagascar	Nightjar, Collared
Lark, White-tailed	Mannikin, Magpie (Pied)	Nightjar, Donaldson-Smith's
Lark, Williams's	Mannikin, Red-backed	Nightjar, Egyptian
Leaf-love, Red-tailed	Martin, African River-	Nightjar, European
Leaf-love, Yellow-throated	Martin, Banded	Nightjar, Fiery-necked
Locustfinch	Martin, Brazza's	Nightjar, Freckled
Longbill, Gray	Martin, Brown-throated	Nightjar, Long-tailed
Longbill, Kretschmer's	Martin, Common House	Nightjar, Madagascar
Longbill, Yellow	Martin, Congo	Nightjar, Montane
Longclaw, Abyssinian	Martin, Eurasian Crag	Nightjar, Nechisar
Longclaw, Cape (Orange-throated)	Martin, Mascarene	Nightjar, Nubian
Longclaw, Fulleborn's	Martin, Rock	Nightjar, Pennant-winged
Longclaw, Pangani	Martin, Sand (Eurasian)	Nightjar, Plain
Longclaw, Rosy-breasted (Pink throat.)	Mesite, Brown	Nightjar, Prigogine's
Longclaw, Sharpe's	Mesite, Subdesert	Nightjar, Rufous-cheeked
Longclaw, Yellow-throated	Mesite, White-breasted	Nightjar, Ruwenzori
Lovebird, Black-cheeked	Modulatrix, Spot-throat	Nightjar, Slender-tailed
Lovebird, Black-cheeked	Moorhen, Common	Nightjar, Sombre (Dusky)
Lovebird, Black-collared	Moorhen, Lesser	Nightjar, Square-tailed
Lovebird, Black-winged	Mountain-Robin, Dappled	Nightjar, Standard-winged
Lovebird, Fischer's	Mousebird, Blue-naped	Nightjar, Star-spotted
Lovebird, Gray-headed	Mousebird, Red-faced	Nightjar, Swamp
Lovebird, Lilian's (Nyasa)	Mousebird, Speckled	Nigrita, Chestnut-breasted
Lovebird, Red-headed	Mousebird, White-backed	Nigrita, Gray-headed
Lovebird, Rosy-faced	Mousebird, White-headed	Nigrita, Pale-fronted
Lovebird, Yellow-collared	Myna, Common (Indian) *	Nigrita, White-breasted
Magpie-Robin, Madagascar	Neddicky (Piping Cisticola)	Noddy, Brown (Common)

Noddy, Lesser	Owl, Short-eared	Partridge, Chukar *
Oliveback, Gray-headed	Owl, Sokoke Scops-	Partridge, Madagascar
Oliveback, White-collared	Owl, Southern White-faced Scops-	Partridge, Stone
Oriole, African Golden	Owl, Spotted Eagle-	Partridge, Udzungwa Forest
Oriole, Black-headed	Owl, Usambara Eagle-	Peacock, Congo
Oriole, Black-winged	Owl, Vermiculated Fishing-	Pelican, Great White
Oriole, Ethiopian	Owl, Verreaux's Eagle-	Pelican, Pink-backed
Oriole, Eurasian Golden	Owl, White-browed	Penguin, African
Oriole, Green-headed	Owlet, African Barred	Penguin, Northern Rockhopper
Oriole, Mountain	Owlet, Albertine	Petrel, Barau's
Oriole, Western Black-headed	Owlet, Pearl-spotted	Petrel, Black-bellied Storm-
Osprey	Owlet, Red-chested	Petrel, Bulwer's
Ostrich, Common	Owlet, Sjostedt's	Petrel, European Storm-
Ostrich, Somali	Oxpecker, Red-billed	Petrel, Gray
Owl, Abyssinian Long-eared	Oxpecker, Yellow-billed	Petrel, Great-winged
Owl, African Grass-	Oxylabes, White-throated	Petrel, Jouanin's
Owl, African Scops-	Oxylabes, Yellow-browed	Petrel, Leach's Storm-
Owl, African Wood-	Oystercatcher, African Black	Petrel, Northern Giant-
Owl, Akun Eagle-	Oystercatcher, Eurasian	Petrel, Pintado
Owl, Anjouan Scops-	Palm-Thrush, Collared	Petrel, Reunion
Owl, Barn	Palm-Thrush, Rufous-tailed	Petrel, Soft-plumaged
Owl, Cape Eagle-	Palm-Thrush, Spotted	Petrel, Southern Giant-
Owl, Congo Bay-	Parakeet, Mauritius (Echo)	Petrel, Spectacled
Owl, European Scops-	Parakeet, Rose-ringed (Ring-necked)*	Petrel, Trinidade
Owl, Fraser's Eagle-	Parisoma, Banded	Petrel, White-bellied Storm-
Owl, Grayish Eagle-	Parisoma, Brown	Petrel, White-chinned
Owl, Karthala Scops-	Parrot, African Orange-bellied	Petrel, White-faced Storm-
Owl, Little	Parrot, Brown-headed	Petrel, Wilson's Storm-
Owl, Madagascar Long-eared	Parrot, Cape	Petronia, Bush
Owl, Madagascar Red	Parrot, Gray (African Gray)	Petronia, Yellow-spotted
Owl, Madagascar Scops-	Parrot, Greater Vasa	Petronia, Yellow-throated
Owl, Maned	Parrot, Gray-headed	Phalarope, Red
Owl, Marsh	Parrot, Lesser Vasa	Phalarope, Red-necked
Owl, Northern White-faced Scops-	Parrot, Meyer's (Brown)	Phalarope, Wilson's
Owl, Pel's Fishing-	Parrot, Red-fronted	Piapiac
Owl, Pemba Scops-	Parrot, Rüppell's	Picathartes, Gray-necked
Owl, Sandy Scops-	Parrot, Senegal	Piculet, African
Owl, Seychelles Scops-	Parrot, Seychelles Black	Pigeon, Afep
Owl, Shelley's Eagle-	Parrot, Yellow-fronted	Pigeon, African Green-

Pigeon, African Olive-	Plantain-eater, Western Gray	Puffback, Northern
Pigeon, Bruce's Green-	Plover, American Golden	Puffback, Pink-footed
Pigeon, Comoro Blue-	Plover, Caspian	Puffback, Pringle's
Pigeon, Comoro Green-	Plover, Chestnut-banded	Puffback, Red-eyed
Pigeon, Comoro Olive-	Plover, Common Ringed	Puffback, Sabine's
Pigeon, Eastern Bronze-naped	Plover, Egyptian	Pytilia, Green-winged (Melba)
Pigeon, Madagascar Blue-	Plover, Forbe's	Pytilia, Orange-winged
Pigeon, Madagascar Green-	Plover, Gray	Pytilia, Red-billed
Pigeon, Pink	Plover, Greater Sand	Quail-plover
Pigeon, Seychelles Blue-	Plover, Kentish	Quail, Blue
Pigeon, Speckled	Plover, Kittlitz's	Quail, Common
Pigeon, Western Bronze-naped	Plover, Lesser Sand	Quail, Harlequin
Pigeon, White-collared	Plover, Little Ringed	Quailfinch, African
Pigeon, White-naped	Plover, Pacific Golden	Quailfinch, Black-chinned
Pintail, Northern	Plover, Three-banded	Quelea, Cardinal
Pipit, African (Grassveld)	Plover, White-fronted	Quelea, Red-billed
Pipit, African Rock	Pochard, Common	Quelea, Red-headed
Pipit, Buffy	Pochard, Madagascar	Rail, African
Pipit, Bushveld	Pochard, Red-crested	Rail, Aldabra
Pipit, Golden	Pochard, Southern	Rail, Gray-throated
Pipit, Jackson's	Pratincole, Black-winged	Rail, Madagascar
Pipit, Kimberley	Pratincole, Collared	Rail, Madagascar Wood-
Pipit, Long-billed	Pratincole, Gray	Rail, Nkulengu
Pipit, Long-legged	Pratincole, Madagascar	Rail, Rouget's
Pipit, Long-tailed	Pratincole, Rock	Rail, Sakalava
Pipit, Malindi	Prinia, Banded	Rail, White-throated
Pipit, Mountain	Prinia, Black-chested	Raven, Dwarf (Somali Crow)
Pipit, Plain-backed	Prinia, Drakensberg	Raven, Fan-tailed
Pipit, Red-throated	Prinia, Karoo (Spotted)	Raven, Thick-billed
Pipit, Short-tailed	Prinia, Namaqua	Raven, White-necked
Pipit, Sokoke	Prinia, Pale	Redshank, Common
Pipit, Striped	Prinia, Tawny-flanked	Redshank, Spotted
Pipit, Tawny	Prinia, White-chinned	Redstart, Black
Pipit, Tree	Prion, Antarctic	Redstart, Common
Pipit, Woodland	Prion, Broad-billed	Robin, Forest
Pipit, Yellow-breasted	Prion, Fairy	Robin, Swynnerton's
Pitta, African	Prion, Salvin's	Robin, White-starred
Pitta, Green-breasted	Prion, Slender-billed	Robin-Chat, Archer's
Plantain-eater, Eastern Gray	Puffback, Black-backed	Robin-Chat, Blue-shouldered

Robin-Chat, Cape	Sandpiper, Pectoral	Shearwater, Audubon's
Robin-Chat, Chorister	Sandpiper, Terek	Shearwater, Cory's
Robin-Chat, Olive-flanked	Sandpiper, White-rumped	Shearwater, Flesh-footed
Robin-Chat, Red-capped (Natal)	Sandpiper, Wood	Shearwater, Great
Robin-Chat, Rüppell's	Saw-wing, Black	Shearwater, Little
Robin-Chat, Snowy-crowned	Saw-wing, Eastern	Shearwater, Manx
Robin-Chat, White-bellied	Saw-wing, Square-tailed	Shearwater, Mascarene
Robin-Chat, White-browed (Heuglin's)	Saw-wing, White-headed	Shearwater, Sooty
Robin-Chat, White-crowned	Scimitarbill, Abyssinian	Shearwater, Tropical
Robin-Chat, White-throated	Scimitarbill, Black	Shearwater, Wedge-tailed
Rock-jumper, Cape	Scimitarbill, Common	Sheathbill, Greater
Rock-jumper, Drakensberg	Scrub-Robin, Bearded	Shelduck, Ruddy
Rockrunner	Scrub-Robin, Black	Shelduck, South African
Roller, Abyssinian	Scrub-Robin, Brown	Shikra (Little Banded Goshawk)
Roller, Blue-throated	Scrub-Robin, Brown-backed	Shoebill
Roller, Broad-billed	Scrub-Robin, Kalahari	Shoveller, Cape
Roller, European	Scrub-Robin, Miombo	Shoveller, Northern
Roller, Lilac-breasted	Scrub-Robin, Rufous-tailed	Shrike, Black-fronted Bush-
Roller, Purple (Rufous-crowned)	Scrub-Robin, White-browed	Shrike, Chestnut-fronted Helmet-
Roller, Racket-tailed	Secretarybird	Shrike, Crimson-breasted
Ruff	Seedcracker, Black-bellied	Shrike, Doherty's Bush-
Sanderling	Seedcracker, Lesser	Shrike, Emin's
Sandgrouse, Black-faced	Seedeater, Black-eared	Shrike, Fiery-breasted Bush-
Sandgrouse, Burchell's	Seedeater, Brown-rumped	Shrike, Gorgeous Bush-
Sandgrouse, Chestnut-bellied	Seedeater, Kipengere	Shrike, Gray-crested Helmet-
Sandgrouse, Double-banded	Seedeater, Protea	Shrike, Gray-green Bush-
Sandgrouse, Four-banded	Seedeater, Reichard's	Shrike, Gray-headed Bush-
Sandgrouse, Lichtenstein's	Seedeater, Reichenow's	Shrike, Lagden's Bush-
Sandgrouse, Madagascar	Seedeater, Salvadori's	Shrike, Lesser Gray
Sandgrouse, Namaqua	Seedeater, Streaky	Shrike, Lühder's Bush-
Sandgrouse, Spotted	Seedeater, Streaky-headed	Shrike, Magpie (Long-tailed)
Sandgrouse, Yellow-throated	Seedeater, Thick-billed	Shrike, Many-coloured Bush-
Sandpiper, Baird's	Seedeater, West African	Shrike, Masked
Sandpiper, Broad-billed	Seedeater, White-rumped	Shrike, Northern White-crowned
Sandpiper, Buff-breasted	Seedeater, White-throated	Shrike, Olive Bush-
Sandpiper, Common	Seedeater, Yellowbrowed	Shrike, Orange-breasted Bush-
Sandpiper, Curlew	Seedeater, Yellow-rumped	Shrike, Perrin's Bush-
Sandpiper, Green	Seedeater, Yellow-throated	Shrike, Red-backed
Sandpiper, Marsh	Shearwater, Arabian	Shrike, Red-naped Bush-

Shrike, Red-tailed (Isabelline)	Sparrow, Southern Gray-headed	Spurfowl, Natal
Shrike, Retz's Helmet-	Sparrow, Sudan Golden	Spurfowl, Red-billed
Shrike, Rosy-patched Bush-	Sparrow, Swahili	Spurfowl, Red-necked
Shrike, Rufous-bellied Helmet-	Sparrow, Swainson's	Spurfowl, Scaly
Shrike, Southern Gray	Sparrowhawk, Black (Great)	Spurfowl, Swainson's
Shrike, Southern White-crowned	Sparrowhawk, Chestnut-flanked	Spurfowl, Yellow-necked
Shrike, Souza's	Sparrowhawk, Eurasian	Starling, Abbott's
Shrike, Uluguru Bush-	Sparrowhawk, France's	Starling, African Pied
Shrike, White-crested Helmet-	Sparrowhawk, Levant	Starling, Ashy
Shrike, White-tailed	Sparrowhawk, Little	Starling, Black-bellied
Shrike, Woodchat	Sparrowhawk, Madagascar	Starling, Bristle-crowned
Shrike, Yellow-billed	Sparrowhawk, Ovambo	Starling, Bronze-tailed
Shrike, Yellow-crested Helmet-	Sparrowhawk, Red-thighed	Starling, Burchell's
Silverbill, African	Sparrowhawk, Rufous-chested	Starling, Cape Glossy
Silverbill, Gray-headed	Sparrowlark, Black-crowned	Starling, Chestnut-bellied
Silverbird	Sparrowlark, Black-eared	Starling, Chestnut-winged
Siskin, Cape	Sparrowlark, Chestnut-backed	Starling, Common (European) *
Siskin, Drakensberg	Sparrowlark, Chestnut-headed	Starling, Fischer's
Siskin, Ethiopian	Sparrowlark, Fischer's	Starling, Golden-breasted
Skimmer, African	Sparrowlark, Gray-backed	Starling, Greater Blue-eared
Skua, Great	Spinetail, Black (Chapin's)	Starling, Hildebrandt's
Skua, South Polar	Spinetail, Böhm's	Starling, Kenrick's
Skua, Subantarctic	Spinetail, Cassin's	Starling, Lesser Blue-eared
Snipe, African	Spinetail, Madagascar	Starling, Madagascar
Snipe, Common	Spinetail, Mottled	Starling, Magpie
Snipe, Great	Spinetail, Sabine's	Starling, Meves's
Snipe, Greater Painted-	Spoonbill, African	Starling, Miombo Blue-eared
Snipe, Jack	Spurfowl, Cape	Starling, Narrow-tailed
Snipe, Madagascar	Spurfowl, Chestnut-naped	Starling, Pale-winged
Sparrow, Cape	Spurfowl, Clapperton's	Starling, Purple Glossy
Sparrow, Chestnut	Spurfowl, Erckel's	Starling, Purple-headed
Sparrow, Great	Spurfowl, Gray-breasted	Starling, Red-winged
Sparrow, House *	Spurfowl, Handsome	Starling, Rüppell's
Sparrow, Java *	Spurfowl, Hartlaub's	Starling, Sharpe's
Sparrow, Kenya Rufous	Spurfowl, Harwood's	Starling, Sharp-tailed
Sparrow, Northern Gray-headed	Spurfowl, Heuglin's	Starling, Shelley's
Sparrow, Parrot-billed	Spurfowl, Hildebrandt's	Starling, Slender-billed
Sparrow, Shelley's Rufous	Spurfowl, Jackson's	Starling, Somali
Sparrow, Somali	Spurfowl, Nahan's	Starling, Splendid Glossy

Starling, Stuhlmann's	Sunbird, Bronzy	Sunbird, Pemba
Starling, Superb	Sunbird, Carmelite	Sunbird, Plain-backed
Starling, Violet-backed (Plum-col.)	Sunbird, Collared	Sunbird, Purple-banded
Starling, Waller's	Sunbird, Comoro Green	Sunbird, Purple-breasted
Starling, Wattled	Sunbird, Congo	Sunbird, Pygmy
Starling, White-billed	Sunbird, Copper	Sunbird, Red-chested
Starling, White-collared	Sunbird, Dusky	Sunbird, Regal
Starling, White-crowned	Sunbird, Eastern Double-collared	Sunbird, Reichenbach's
Starling, White-winged Babbling	Sunbird, Eastern Violet-backed	Sunbird, Rockerfeller's
Stilt, Black-winged	Sunbird, Forest Double-collared	Sunbird, Rufous-winged
Stint, Little	Sunbird, Fraser's	Sunbird, Rwenzori Double-collared
Stint, Long-toed	Sunbird, Golden-winged	Sunbird, Scarlet-chested
Stint, Red-necked	Sunbird, Greater Double-collared	Sunbird, Scarlet-tufted
Stint, Temminck's	Sunbird, Green-headed	Sunbird, Seychelles
Stonechat, African	Sunbird, Green-throated	Sunbird, Shelley's
Stonechat, Common	Sunbird, Gray	Sunbird, Shining
Stonechat, Reunion	Sunbird, Gray-chinned	Sunbird, Souimanga
Stonechat, Siberian	Sunbird, Gray-headed	Sunbird, Southern Double-collared
Stork, Abdim's	Sunbird, Humblot's	Sunbird, Splendid
Stork, African Openbill	Sunbird, Hunter's	Sunbird, Superb
Stork, Black	Sunbird, Johanna's	Sunbird, Tacazze
Stork, Marabou	Sunbird, Little Green	Sunbird, Tiny
Stork, Saddle-billed	Sunbird, Loveridge's	Sunbird, Tsavo
Stork, White	Sunbird, Ludwig's Double-collared	Sunbird, Uluguru Violet-backed
Stork, Woolly-necked	Sunbird, Madagascar Green	Sunbird, Usambara Double-collared
Stork, Yellow-billed	Sunbird, Malachite	Sunbird, Variable
Sugarbird, Cape	Sunbird, Mangrove (Brown)	Sunbird, Violet-breasted
Sugarbird, Gurney's	Sunbird, Marico	Sunbird, Violet-tailed
Sunbird, Abbott's	Sunbird, Mayotte	Sunbird, Western Violet-backed
Sunbird, Amani	Sunbird, Miombo Double-collared	Sunbird, White-bellied
Sunbird, Amethyst (Black)	Sunbird, Moreau's	Swallow, Angola
Sunbird, Anchieta's	Sunbird, Neergaard's	Swallow, Barn (European)
Sunbird, Anjouan	Sunbird, Nile Valley	Swallow, Black-and-rufous
Sunbird, Banded (Green)	Sunbird, Northern Double-collared	Swallow, Blue
Sunbird, Bates'	Sunbird, Olive	Swallow, Ethiopian
Sunbird, Beautiful	Sunbird, Olive-bellied	Swallow, Forest
Sunbird, Black-bellied	Sunbird, Orange-breasted	Swallow, Greater Striped
Sunbird, Blue-headed	Sunbird, Orange-tufted	Swallow, Gray-rumped
Sunbird, Blue-throated Brown	Sunbird, Oustalet's	Swallow, Lesser Striped

Swallow, Mosque	Tern, Antarctic	Thrush, Littoral Rock-
Swallow, Pearl-breasted	Tern, Arctic	Thrush, Miombo Rock-
Swallow, Red-breasted	Tern, Black	Thrush, Mountain
Swallow, Red-chested	Tern, Black-naped	Thrush, Oberlaender's Ground-
Swallow, Red-rumped	Tern, Bridled	Thrush, Olive
Swallow, South African Cliff	Tern, Caspian	Thrush, Orange Ground-
Swallow, White-tailed	Tern, Common	Thrush, Red-tailed Ant-
Swallow, White-throated	Tern, Damara	Thrush, Rufous-tailed Rock-
Swallow, White-throated Blue	Tern, Gull-billed	Thrush, Sentinel Rock-
Swallow, Wire-tailed	Tern, Lesser Crested	Thrush, Short-toed Rock-
Swamphen, African Purple	Tern, Little	Thrush, Song
Swift, African Black	Tern, Roseate	Thrush, Spotted Ground-
Swift, African Palm-	Tern, Royal	Thrush, Usambara
Swift, Alpine	Tern, Sandwich	Thrush, White-tailed Rufous
Swift, Bates'	Tern, Saunders'	Thrush, Taita
Swift, Bradfield's	Tern, Sooty	Tinkerbird, Green
Swift, Common (European)	Tern, Swift	Tinkerbird, Moustached
Swift, Horus	Tern, Whiskered	Tinkerbird, Red-fronted
Swift, Little	Tern, White (Fairy)	Tinkerbird, Red-rumped
Swift, Madagascar Black	Tern, White-cheeked	Tinkerbird, Speckled
Swift, Mottled	Tern, White-winged	Tinkerbird, Western
Swift, Nyanza	Thick-knee, Eurasian	Tinkerbird, Yellow-fronted
Swift, Pallid	Thick-knee, Senegal	Tinkerbird, Yellow-rumped
Swift, Scarce	Thick-knee, Spotted	Tinkerbird, Yellow-throated
Swift, Schouteden's	Thick-knee, Water	Tit, Acacia (Somali)
Swift, White-rumped	Thrush, Abyssinian Ground-	Tit, Ashy
Swiftlet, Mascarene	Thrush, African	Tit, Cape Penduline-
Swiftlet, Seychelles	Thrush, Amber Mountain Rock-	Tit, Cinnamon-breasted
Tchagra, Anchieta's	Thrush, Bare-eyed	Tit, Dusky
Tchagra, Black-crowned	Thrush, Black-eared Ground-	Tit, Forest Penduline-
Tchagra, Brown-crowned	Thrush, Blue Rock-	Tit, Gray
Tchagra, Marsh	Thrush, Cape Rock-	Tit, Gray (African) Penduline-
Tchagra, Southern	Thrush, Comoro	Tit, Miombo
Tchagra, Three-streaked (James')	Thrush, Forest Rock-	Tit, Mouse-coloured Penduline-
Teal, Bernier's	Thrush, Fraser's Rufous	Tit, Red-throated
Teal, Cape	Thrush, Groundscraper	Tit, Rufous-bellied
Teal, Common	Thrush, Karoo	Tit, Southern Black
Teal, Hottentot	Thrush, Kurrichane	Tit, Stripe-breasted
Teal, Red-billed	Thrush, Little Rock-	Tit, White-backed

Tit, White-bellied	Vanga, Lafresnaye's	Warbler, Broad-tailed
Tit, White-shouldered Black	Vanga, Madagascar Blue	Warbler, Brown Woodland
Tit, White-winged Black	Vanga, Nuthatch	Warbler, Buff-bellied
Tit-Babbler, Chestnut-vented	Vanga, Pollen's	Warbler, Cinnamon Bracken
Tit-Babbler, Layard's	Vanga, Red-shouldered	Warbler, Cinnamon-breasted
Tit-Hylia	Vanga, Red-tailed	Warbler, Common Grasshopper
Trogon, Bare-cheeked	Vanga, Rufous	Warbler, Comoro Brush
Trogon, Bar-tailed	Vanga, Sickle-billed	Warbler, Cryptic
Trogon, Narina	Vanga, Tylas	Warbler, Dark-capped Yellow
Tropicbird, Red-billed	Vanga, Van Dam's	Warbler, Eastern Olivaceous
Tropicbird, Red-tailed	Vanga, White-headed	Warbler, Eastern Orphean
Tropicbird, White-tailed	Vulture, Bearded	Warbler, Eurasian Reed
Turaco, Black-billed	Vulture, Cape (Griffon)	Warbler, Evergreen Forest
Turaco, Fischer's	Vulture, Egyptian	Warbler, Garden
Turaco, Great Blue	Vukture, Eurasian (Griffon)	Warbler, Grauer's Swamp
Turaco, Guinea	Vulture, Hooded	Warbler, Great Reed
Turaco, Hartlaub's	Vulture, Lappet-faced	Warbler, Greater Swamp
Turaco, Knysna	Vulture, Palm-nut	Warbler, Gray Wren-
Turaco, Livingstone's	Vulture, Rüppell's (Griffon)	Warbler, Gray-capped
Turaco, Purple-crested	Vulture, White-backed	Warbler, Icterine
Turaco, Ross'	Vulture, White-headed	Warbler, Knysna
Turaco, Ruspoli's	Wagtail, African Pied	Warbler, Laura's Woodland
Turaco, Rwenzori	Wagtail, Cape	Warbler, Lesser Swamp (Cape Reed)
Turaco, Schalow's	Wagtail, Citrine	Warbler, Little Rush
Turaco, Violet	Wagtail, Gray	Warbler, Long-billed Forest-
Turaco, White-cheeked	Wagtail, Madagascar	Warbler, Madagascar Brush
Turaco, White-crested	Wagtail, Mountain (Long-tailed)	Warbler, Madagascar Swamp
Turaco, Yellow-billed	Wagtail, White	Warbler, Marsh
Turnstone, Ruddy	Wagtail, Yellow	Warbler, Mountain Yellow
Twinspot, Brown	Warbler, African Reed	Warbler, Moustached Grass-
Twinspot, Dusky	Warbler, Aldabra Brush	Warbler, Neumann's (Short-tailed)
Twinspot, Green	Warbler, Bamboo	Warbler, Olive-Tree
Twinspot, Pink-throated	Warbler, Barratt's	Warbler, Oriole
Twinspot, Red-throated	Warbler, Barred	Warbler, Pale Wren-
Vanga, Bernier's	Warbler, Barred Wren-	Warbler, Papyrus Yellow
Vanga, Chabert's	Warbler, Basra Reed	Warbler, Rand's
Vanga, Comoro Blue	Warbler, Benson's Brush	Warbler, Red-capped Forest-
Vanga, Helmet	Warbler, Black-faced Rufous-	Warbler, Red-faced Woodland
Vanga, Hook-billed	Warbler, Black-headed Rufous-	Warbler, Red-fronted

Warbler, Red-winged	Waxbill, Kandt's	Weaver, Northern Masked
Warbler, Red-winged Gray	Waxbill, Orange-breasted	Weaver, Olive-headed
Warbler, River	Waxbill, Orange-cheeked	Weaver, Orange
Warbler, Roberts'	Waxbill, Swee	Weaver, Preuss's
Warbler, Rodrigues	Waxbill, Violet-eared	Weaver, Red-billed Buffalo-
Warbler, Rufous-eared	Waxbill, Yellow-bellied	Weaver, Red-headed
Warbler, Savi's	Weaver, Baglafecht	Weaver, Rufous-tailed
Warbler, Sedge	Weaver, Bar-winged	Weaver, Rüppell's
Warbler, Seychelles	Weaver, Bertram's	Weaver, Saklava
Warbler, Stierling's Wren-	Weaver, Black-billed	Weaver, Slender-billed
Warbler, Subdesert Brush	Weaver, Black-capped Social-	Weaver, Sociable
Warbler, Thamnornis	Weaver, Black-chinned	Weaver, Southern Brown-throated
Warbler, Uganda Woodland	Weaver, Black-headed	Weaver, Southern Masked
Warbler, Upcher's	Weaver, Bob-tailed	Weaver, Speckle-fronted
Warbler, Victorin's Scrub	Weaver, Bocage's	Weaver, Spectacled
Warbler, White-winged Swamp	Weaver, Brown-capped	Weaver, Speke's
Warbler, Willow	Weaver, Cape	Weaver, Strange
Warbler, Winifred's	Weaver, Chestnut	Weaver, Tanzania Masked
Warbler, Wood	Weaver, Chestnut-backed Sparrow-	Weaver, Taveta
Warbler, Yellow-throated Woodland	Weaver, Chestnut-crowned Sparrow-	Weaver, Thick-billed (Grosbeak)
Wattle-eye, Black-necked	Weaver, Clarke's	Weaver, Usambara
Wattle-eye, Black-throated	Weaver, Compact	Weaver, Viellot's Black
Wattle-eye, Brown-throated	Weaver, Dark-backed (Forest)	Weaver, Village
Wattle-eye, Chestnut	Weaver, Donaldson-Smith's Sparrow-	Weaver, Vitteline Masked
Wattle-eye, Jameson's	Weaver, Fox's	Weaver, Weyns'
Wattle-eye, White-spotted	Weaver, Golden (Holub's)	Weaver, White-browed Sparrow-
Wattle-eye, Yellow-bellied	Weaver, Golden Palm	Weaver, White-headed Buffalo-
Waxbill, Abyssinian	Weaver, Golden-backed	Weaver, Yellow
Waxbill, Black-cheeked	Weaver, Golden-naped	Weaver, Yellow-capped
Waxbill, Black-crowned	Weaver, Gray-capped Social-	Weaver, Yellow-legged
Waxbill, Black-faced	Weaver, Heuglin's Masked	Weaver, Yellow-mantled
Waxbill, Black-headed	Weaver, Juba (Salvadori's)	Wheatear, Abyssinian Black
Waxbill, Black-rumped	Weaver, Katanga Masked	Wheatear, Black-eared
Waxbill, Blue	Weaver, Kilombero	Wheatear, Capped
Waxbill, Cinderella	Weaver, Little	Wheatear, Cyprus
Waxbill, Common	Weaver, Loango	Wheatear, Desert
Waxbill, Crimson-rumped	Weaver, Maxwell's Black	Wheatear, Heuglin's
Waxbill, Fawn-breasted	Weaver, Nelicourvi	Wheatear, Isabelline
Waxbill, Gray	Weaver, Northern Brown-throated	Wheatear, Northern

Wheatear, Pied	Whydah, Broad-tailed Paradise-	Woodpecker, Brown-backed
Wheatear, Red-breasted	Whydah, Long-tailed Paradise-	Woodpecker, Brown-eared
Wheatear, Schalow's	Whydah, Pin-tailed	Woodpecker, Buff-spotted
Wheatear, Somali	Whydah, Sahel Paradise-	Woodpecker, Cardinal
Whimbrel, Common	Whydah, Shaft-tailed	Woodpecker, Elliot's
White-eye, Abyssinian	Whydah, Steel-blue	Woodpecker, Gabon
White-eye, African Yellow	Whydah, Straw-tailed	Woodpecker, Golden-tailed
White-eye, Cape	Widowbird, Fan-tailed (Red-should.)	Woodpecker, Gray
White-eye, Forest (Green)	Widowbird, Jackson's	Woodpecker, Green-backed
White-eye, Karthala	Widowbird, Long-tailed	Woodpecker, Ground
White-eye, Kirk's	Widowbird, Marsh (Hartlaub's)	Woodpecker, Knysna
White-eye, Kulal	Widowbird, Montane	Woodpecker, Mombasa
White-eye, Madagascar	Widowbird, Red-collared	Woodpecker, Mountain Gray
White-eye, Mauritius Gray	Widowbird, White-winged	Woodpecker, Nubian
White-eye, Mauritius Olive	Widowbird, Yellow-mantled	Woodpecker, Olive
White-eye, Mayotte	Wigeon, Eurasian	Woodpecker, Speckle-breasted
White-eye, Montane	Winchat	Woodpecker, Speckle-throated
White-eye, Orange River	Wood-Hoopoe, Black-billed	Woodpecker, Stierling's
White-eye, Pemba	Wood-Hoopoe, Forest	Woodpecker, Tullberg's (Fine-banded)
White-eye, Reunion Gray	Wood-Hoopoe, Grant's	Woodpecker, Yellow-crested
White-eye, Reunion Olive	Wood-Hoopoe, Green	Wryneck, Northern
White-eye, Seychelles	Wood-Hoopoe, Violet	Wryneck, Red-throated
White-eye, South Pare	Wood-Hoopoe, White-headed	Yellowlegs, Greater
White-eye, Taita	Woodpecker, Abyssinian	Yellowlegs, Lesser
Whitethroat, Common	Woodpecker, Bearded	
Whitethroat, Lesser	Woodpecker, Bennett's	

Cardinal Woodpecker

The names used in this list follow those in *Birds of Africa; South of the Sahara* by Ian Sinclair & Peter Ryan (StruikNature/Random House, 2010).

Species marked with a * symbol are non-indigenous invaders that have established feral populations.

256

PACKING CHECKLIST

1. Check the items listed below to be taken with you on your trip. Add additional items in the blank spaces provided. Use this list as a guide. In case of baggage loss, assess the value of items lost and file a claim with your baggage-loss insurance company.

2. Safari clothing can be any comfortable cotton or breathable synthetic clothing and should be neutral in color (tan, brown, khaki, light green). Avoid dark blue and black, as these colors may attract tsetse flies. Note that cotton clothing is also cooler on safari than most synthetic fibers.

3. Please note that all clothes washed on safari may be ironed, so synthetic clothing may be damaged.

4. Please read your itinerary carefully as you may have a strict baggage weight limit (i.e. 33 pounds/15 kg or 44 pounds/20 kg per person), so please pack accordingly.

5. Virtually all safari camps and lodges provide daily laundry services and many provide complimentary shampoo and conditioner, so you can travel with much less clothing and toiletries than you might imagine!

6. Take all medications and valuables on your person or in your carry-on luggage.

WOMEN'S CLOTHING
- ❏ Sandals or lightweight shoes
- ❏ Walking shoes or light weight hiking shoes (not white for walking safaris)
- ❏ Wide-brimmed hat and cap
- ❏ Windbreaker
- ❏ Sweater or fleece
- ❏ 2–3 pr. safari* pants
- ❏ 2–3 pr. safari* shorts
- ❏ 5 pr. safari/sports socks
- ❏ 3 short-sleeve safari* shirts
- ❏ 3 long-sleeve safari* shirts
- ❏ Swimsuit/cover-up
- ❏ 1 pr. casual slacks or skirt
- ❏ 1 or 2 blouses
- ❏ Belts
- ❏ 6 pr. underwear
- ❏ 3 bras
- ❏ 1 sports bra (for rough roads)
- ❏ pajamas

Optional (for dining at a top restaurant or on a luxury train)
- ❏ 1 cocktail dress
- ❏ 1 pr. dress shoes and nylons/panty hose

MEN'S CLOTHING
- ❏ Sandals or lightweight shoes
- ❏ Walking shoes or light weight hiking shoes (not white for walking safaris)
- ❏ Wide-brimmed hat and cap
- ❏ Windbreaker
- ❏ Sweater or fleece
- ❏ 2–3 pr. safari* pants
- ❏ 2–3 pr. safari* shorts
- ❏ 5 pr. safari/sports socks
- ❏ 3 short-sleeve safari* shirts
- ❏ 3 long-sleeve safari* shirts
- ❏ Swim trunks
- ❏ 1 pr. casual slacks

- ❏ 1 sports shirt
- ❏ 6 pr. underwear
- ❏ Belts
- ❏ Pajamas
- ❏ Large handkerchief

Optional (for dining at a top restaurant or on a luxury train)
- ❏ 1 pr. dress slacks, shoes and dress socks
- ❏ 1 dress shirt/jacket/tie

* Any comfortable cotton clothing for safari should be neutral in color (tan, brown, light green, khaki). Evening wear can be any color you like!

257

COLD WEATHER ADDITIONS

For travel in Southern Africa May to August, temperatures may drop below 40°F (5°C)

- ❏ Warm pajamas or thermal underwear to sleep in
- ❏ Warm ski hat covering the ears
- ❏ Scarf
- ❏ Gloves
- ❏ Additional sweater or fleece

TOILETRIES AND FIRST AID

- ❏ Anti-malaria pills (prescription)
- ❏ Vitamins
- ❏ Aspirin/Tylenol/Advil
- ❏ Motion sickness pills
- ❏ Decongestant
- ❏ Throat lozenges
- ❏ Laxative
- ❏ Anti-diarrhea medicine
- ❏ Antacid
- ❏ Antibiotic
- ❏ Cortisone cream
- ❏ Antibiotic ointment
- ❏ Anti-fungal cream or powder
- ❏ Prescription drugs
- ❏ Medical summary from your doctor (if needed)
- ❏ Medical alert bracelet or necklace
- ❏ Band-Aids (plasters)
- ❏ Thermometer
- ❏ Insect repellent
- ❏ Sunscreen/sun block
- ❏ Shampoo (small container)
- ❏ Conditioner (small container)
- ❏ Deodorant
- ❏ Toothpaste (small tube)
- ❏ Toothbrush
- ❏ Hairbrush/comb
- ❏ Razor
- ❏ Q-tips/cotton balls
- ❏ Nail clipper
- ❏ Emery boards
- ❏ Makeup
- ❏ Tweezers

SUNDRIES

- ❏ Passport (with visas, if needed) - *must be valid for at least 6 months after you return home and have sufficient blank 'visa' pages (2 consecutive per country).*
- ❏ International Certificate of Vaccination
- ❏ Air tickets/vouchers
- ❏ Money pouch
- ❏ Credit cards
- ❏ Insurance cards
- ❏ Cell phone and charger
- ❏ Sunglasses/guard
- ❏ Spare prescription glasses/contacts
- ❏ Copy of prescription(s)
- ❏ Eyeglass case
- ❏ Travel alarm clock
- ❏ Small flashlight (torch) and extra batteries
- ❏ Binoculars
- ❏ Sewing kit
- ❏ Small scissors
- ❏ Tissues (travel packs)
- ❏ Handiwipes (individual)
- ❏ Anti-bacterial soap
- ❏ Laundry soap (for washing delicates)
- ❏ Large waterproof bags for damp laundry
- ❏ Maps
- ❏ Business cards
- ❏ Pens
- ❏ Deck of cards
- ❏ Reading materials
- ❏ Decaffeinated coffee/ herbal tea
- ❏ Sugar substitute

CAMERA EQUIPMENT

- ❏ Lenses
- ❏ Digital memory cards
- ❏ Camera bag or backpack
- ❏ Lens cleaning fluid
- ❏ Lens tissue/brush
- ❏ Extra camera batteries
- ❏ Flash
- ❏ Flash batteries
- ❏ Battery charger and adapters
- ❏ Waterproof bags for lenses and camera body
- ❏ Beanbag, small tripod or monopod
- ❏ Extra video camera batteries
- ❏ Video charger
- ❏ Outlet adapters (universal)
- ❏ Cigarette lighter charger (optional)

GIFTS & TRADES

- ❏ T-shirts
- ❏ Pens
- ❏ Inexpensive watches
- ❏ Postcards from your area/state
- ❏ Children's magazines and books
- ❏ Small acrylic mirrors
- ❏ Balloons
- ❏ School supplies

OTHER

- ❏ ....
- ❏ ....
- ❏ ....
- ❏ ....
- ❏ ....

MY AFRICAN SAFARI JOURNAL

On the following pages is a day-by-day account of my safari, with descriptions of the landscapes and weather, wildlife sightings, the way we traveled, the food we ate and the people we met.

Name: ....

Destinations and Dates: ....

....

....

....

....

Did you know? On a still night, a lion's roar can be heard from a distance of about 5 miles (8 km).

Did you know? A giraffe has the same number of vertebrae in its neck as a human - seven.

Did you know? Monkeys communicate primarily through 'pulling faces' (facial expressions).

Did you know? Several female ostrich lay their eggs in the same ground scrape; each egg can weigh up to 3 pounds (1.3 kg).

Did you know? Crocodiles cannot chew their food and must swallow small rocks to aid digestion.

Did you know? An elephant's trunk has more than 100,000 muscles and is used to breathe, pick things up, make noises, drink and smell.

Did you know? Fewer that 900 Mountain Gorillas survive, with the population split between the Virunga range (shared by Rwanda, D.R.Congo and Uganda) and Bwindi Impenetrable Forest (Uganda).

Did you know? Spotted Hyenas have 11 recognized calls: whoop, fast-whoop, low-whoop, giggle, yell, growl, rattling-growl, grunt, groan, whine and soft-squeal.

....

....

....

....

....

....

....

....

....

....

....

....

....

....

....

....

....

....

....

....

....

....

....

....

Did you know? Vultures are able to soar to a height of 36,000 feet (over 10 km) above the ground.

Did you know? Among the extinct African mammals that have been identified from their fossilized bones is a species of giant warthog that was almost the size of a hippo.

Did you know? The Baobab does not produce 'annual rings' like most other trees, but some specimens are certainly over 1500 years of age.

Did you know? Every zebra has a unique pattern of stripes. Just as no two human fingerprints are alike, no two zebras are the same.

Did you know? The Cheetah is the world's fastest mammal, able to reach a speed of 45 mph (72 km/h) within 2.5 seconds. But its top speed of up to 64 mph (103 km/h) can be sustained only briefly.

Did you know? In a vertical stoop, a Peregrine Falcon is able to reach a speed of 240 m.p.h (400km/h).

Did you know? Over 250,000 wildebeest die during their annual Serengeti migration, but the population remains stable as 500,000 calves are born each year.

Did you know? Galagos (bushbabies) urinate on their hands and feet to leave scent trails on branches.

Did you know? Hippos can stay underwater for up to 5 minutes without coming up for air.

Did you know? Baboon troops can number up to 200, but there are usually between 30-40 members; females always outnumber males.

Did you know? Owls do not build nests, but simply lay their eggs in cavities or in the unused nest of another bird.

Did you know? Banded Mongooses are known to groom Warthogs, consuming ticks, fleas and other skin parasites.

Did you know? The Secretarybird gets its name from the long quill-like feathers that protrude from the back of its head (in the past, office secretaries used quill pens, not computers!).

Did you know? The Bat-eared Fox can hear termites moving underground - using its large ears as sound parabolas.

Did you know? Female elephants spend their entire lives in tight family groups made up of mothers, grandmothers, aunts, sisters and daughters.

Did you know? Young Ground Pangolins ride on their mother's back for the first few weeks of life.

Did you know? The Kori Bustard is regarded as the heaviest flying bird. Males can weigh up to 48.5 pounds (22 kg).

Did you know? Wild Dog packs are led by an 'alpha' male and female, with other members in a strict hierarchical order.

....
....
....
....
....
....
....
....
....
....
....
....
....
....
....
....
....
....
....
....
....
....
....
....

Did you know? A dramatic aerial display of twists, turns and rolls is what the Lilac-breasted Roller and its relatives have been named for.

Did you know? The dung of hyena turns snow white when dry. With their powerful jaws they are able to crunch and digest large bones.

....

....

....

....

....

....

....

....

....

....

....

....

....

....

....

....

....

....

....

....

....

....

....

....

....

Did you know? Buffalo are bulk feeders of tall, coarse grass and thus play a vital role in the savannah grazing succession, reducing wild pasture to a height favored by more selective herbivores.

RESOURCES

We have endeavored to make the information that follows as current as possible. However, Africa is undergoing constant change. My reason for including the following information, much of which is likely to change, is to give you an idea of the right questions to ask – not to give you information that should be relied on as gospel. Wherever possible, a resource has been given to assist you in obtaining the most current information.

AIRPORT DEPARTURE TAXES
Ask your Africa tour operator, go online or call an airline that serves your destination, or the tourist office, embassy or consulate of the country (ies) in question, for current international and domestic airport taxes that are not included in your air ticket and must be paid with cash before departure. International airport departure taxes often must be paid in U.S. dollars or other hard currency, such as the Euro or British pounds. Be sure to have the exact amount required – often change will not be given. Domestic airport departure taxes may be required to be paid in hard currency as well, or in some cases, may be payable in the local currency.

At the time of this writing, international airport departure taxes for the countries in this guide are listed below.

Country	Taxes due	Country	Taxes due
Botswana	*	Rwanda	* / **
Congo, Rep.	* / **	Seychelles	*
Ethiopia	*	South Africa	*
Kenya	*	Tanzania	*
Malawi	* / **	Uganda	*
Mauritius	*	Zambia	* / **
Mozambique	* / **	Zimbabwe	* / **
Namibia	*		

* Included in price of air ticket.
**Exceptions apply for charter flights.

BANKS
Banks are usually open Monday through Friday mornings and early afternoons, sometimes on Saturday mornings, and closed on Sundays and holidays.

Most hotels, lodges and camps are licensed to exchange foreign currency. Quite often, the best place to exchange money is at the airport upon arrival.

CREDIT CARDS/ATMS/TRAVELER'S CHECKS/CASH

Major international credit cards are accepted by most top hotels, restaurants, lodges, permanent safari camps and shops. Visa and MasterCard are most widely accepted. American Express and Diner's Club are also accepted by most first-class hotels and many businesses. However, American Express is not often taken in more remote areas and camps. ATMs are in many locations in South Africa and in most major cities in other countries, but are not readily accessible when you are out on safari. Visa is the most reliable card to use at ATMs. MasterCard might not be accepted as well as other international ATM/credit cards. Only local currency can be withdrawn at an ATM and in limited amounts. It is advisable to contact your bank before you travel and let them know that you will be using your ATM card/credit card in a foreign country so your card is not blocked while attempting to withdraw money. Confirm that the card will work in ATMs in the countries you will be visiting. ATM fraud is a common occurrence, so keep your card and PIN safe. Travelers checks are hardly accepted anywhere in Africa, which is why it is important to carry cash in hard currencies – preferably US Dollars, Euros or British pounds. Ways to obtain additional funds include having money sent by telegraph international money order (Western Union), telexed through a bank or sent via international courier (i.e. DHL).

CURRENCIES

Current rates for many African countries can be found on the Internet. **For U.S. Dollars, bring only bills that are not older than 2010, as the older bills are not accepted in many African countries.** The currency of Namibia is on par with the South African Rand. The South African Rand may be accepted in Namibia, however, the currency of Namibia is not accepted in South Africa. The currencies used by the countries included in this guide are as follows:

Botswana	1 Pula =100 thebe	Rwanda	1 Rwanda Franc = 100 centimes
Congo, Rep.	1 Central African Franc = 100 centimes	Seychelles	1 Seychelles Rupee = 100 cents
Ethiopia	1 Ethiopian Birr =100 cents	South Africa	1 Rand = 100 cents
Kenya	1 Kenya Shilling =100 cents	Tanzania	1 Tanzania Shilling =100 cents
Malawi	1 Malawi Kwacha = 100 tambala	Uganda	1 Uganda Shilling = 100 cents
Mauritius	1 Mauritius Rupee = 100 cents	Zambia	1 Zambia Kwacha = 100 ngwee
Mozambique	1 Metical = 100 centavos	Zimbabwe	1 U.S. Dollar =100 cents
Namibia	1 Namibian Dollar =100 cents		

CURRENCY RESTRICTIONS

For some countries in Africa, the maximum amount of local currency that may be imported or exported is strictly enforced. Check for current restrictions by contacting the tourist offices, embassies or consulates of the countries you wish to visit. In some countries, it is difficult (if not impossible) to exchange unused local currency back to foreign exchange (i.e., U.S. Dollars). Therefore, it is best not to exchange more than you feel you will need.

CUSTOMS

US Customs:
For current information on products made from endangered species of wildlife that are not allowed to be imported, contact Traffic (USA), World Wildlife Fund, 1250 24th St. NW, Washington, DC 20037, tel. (202) 293-4800, and ask for the leaflet "Buyer Beware" for current restrictions, and/or visit www.worldwildlife.org/pages/buyer-beware.

Canadian Customs:
For a brochure on current Canadian customs requirements, ask for the brochure "I Declare" from your local customs office, which will be listed in the telephone book under "Government of Canada, Customs and Excise", or visit www.Travel.gc.ca/customs/what-you-can-bring-home-to-canada.

DIPLOMATIC REPRESENTATIVES IN AFRICA FOR UNITED STATES OF AMERICA

BOTSWANA:
http://botswana.usembassy.gov/
Tel: 267 31 395-3982
After hours: 267-31 395-7111
Fax: 267 31 318-0232
United States Embassy, Embassy Drive, Gov. Enclave, P.O. Box 90, Gaborone, Botswana.

CONGO REPUBLIC:
http://brazzaville.usembassy.gov/
Tel: 242 06 612-2000
Email: brazzavilleACS@state.gov
American Embassy, 70-83 Section D Maya-Maya Boulvard Brazzaville, Congo Republic.

EGYPT:
http://egypt.usembassy.gov/
Tel: 20 2 2797-3300
Fax: 20 2 2797-3200
United States Embassy, 5 Tawfik Diab St., Garden City, Cairo, Egypt.

ETHIOPIA:
http://ethiopia.usembassy.gov/
Tel: 251 11 130-6000
After Hours: 251 11 130-6911
Fax: 251 11 124-2401
Email: pasaddis@state.gov
United States Embassy, Entoto Street, P.O. Box 1014, Addis Ababa, Ethiopia.

KENYA:
http://nairobi.usembassy.gov/
Tel: 254 20 363 6000
Fax: 253 20 363 6157
United States Embassy, United Nations Avenue. P.O. Box 606, Village Market Nairobi, Kenya.

MADAGASCAR:
http://antananarivo.usembassy.gov/
Tel: 261 20 23 48000
After Hours: 261 34 49 32854
Fax: 261 23 480 35
United States Embassy, Lot 207A, Andranoro, 105 Antananarivo, Madagascar

MALAWI:
http://lilongwe.usembassy.gov/
Tel: 265 1773 166
Fax: 265-1 771 142
United States Embassy, P.O.Box 30016, 16 Jomo Kenyatta Road, Lilongwe 3, Malawi.

MAURITIUS:
http://mauritius.usembassy.gov/
Tel: 230 202-4400
Fax: 230 208-9534
Email: usembass@intnet.mu
United States Embassy, 4th Floor, Rogers House, John Kennedy Ave., P.O. Box 544, Port Louis, Mauritius.

MOZAMBIQUE:
http://maputo.usembassy.gov/
Tel: 258-21 49-27-97 Fax: 258 21 49 01 14
Email:consularmaputo@state.gov/
United States Embassy, Avenida Kenneth
Kaunda 193, Caixa Postal 783, Maputo,
Mozambique.

NAMIBIA:
http://windhoek.usembassy.gov/
Tel: 264 61 295 8500
Email:consularwindo@state.gov
United States Embassy, Ausplan Bldg.,
14 Lossen St., Private Bag 12029,
Windhoek, Namibia.

RWANDA:
http://rwanda.usembassy.gov/
Tel: 250 252 596 400 Fax: 250 52 580 325
Email: consularkigali@state.gov
United States Embassy, 2657 Avenue de la
Gendarmerie, PO Box 28, Kigali, Rwanda.

SEYCHELLES:
www.seychellesembassy.com/
Tel: 248 422 5256 Fax: 248 422 5189
US Consular Agency, Suite 23,2nd Floor,
Oliaji Trade Centre, Victoria, Mahe,
Seychelles.

SOUTH AFRICA:
http://southafrica.usembassy.gov/
Johannesburg Consulate, 1 Sandton Drive,
P.O. Box 787197, Sandton 2146, South Africa
Tel: 27 11 290 3000   Fax: 27 11 884 0396
Cape Town Consulate:
Tel: 27 21 702-7300 Fax: 27 21 702-7493
2 Reddam Ave, Westlake 7945, Private
Bag x26, Tokai 7966, South Africa.

TANZANIA:
http://tanzania.usembassy.gov/
Tel: 255 22 266 4000
Fax: 255 22 229 4970
Email: drsacs@state.gov
United States Embassy, 686 Old
Bagamoyo Road, Msasani, P.O. Box 9123,
Dar es Salaam, Tanzania.

UGANDA:
http://kampala.usembassy.gov/
Tel: 256 414 306 001
Fax: 256 414 259 794
Email: kampalawebcontact@state.gov.
United States Embassy, 1577 Gaba Road,
Kansanga, Box 7007, Kampala, Uganda.

ZAMBIA:
http://zambia.usembassy.gov/
Tel: 260 0 211 357 000
Fax: 260 0 211 357 224
Email: consularlusaka@state.gov
United States Embassy, Kabulonga
Road, Ibex Hill, P.O. Box 31617, Lusaka,
Zambia.

ZIMBABWE:
http://harare.usembassy.gov/
Tel: 263 4 250593/4 ext. 211
Email: consularharare@state.gov
United States Embassy, 172 Herbert
Chitepo Ave., P.O. Box 3340, Harare,
Zimbabwe.

FOR CANADA

BOTSWANA:
Tel: 267 31 390 4411
Consulate of Canada, Ground Floor,
Mokolwane House, Fairgrounds, P.O.
Box 2111, Gaborone, Botswana.

CONGO REPUBLIC: *no embassy in
Brazzaville but served by* The Embassy
of Canada, 17 Pumbu Avenue, Gombe
Commune, Kinshasa, Dem.Rep.Congo.
Tel: 243 99 60 21 500
Email: knsha@international.gc.ca.

EGYPT:
www.canadainternational.gc.ca/egypt
Tel: 20 2 2791 8700   Fax: 20 2 2791 8860
Email: cairo@dfait-maeci.gc.ca
The Embassy of Canada, Nile City
Towers, 2005 (A), Corniche El Nile,
South Tower, 18th Floor, Cairo, Egypt
11221.

Resources

ETHIOPIA:
www.canadainternational.gc.ca/ethiopia
Tel: 251 11 371 0000
Fax: 251 11 371 0040
Email: addis@international.gc.ca
The Embassy of Canada, Wereda 23
Kebele 12, House #122, Addis Ababa, Ethiopia.

KENYA:
www.canadainternational.gc.ca/kenya
Tel: 254 20 366 3000
Fax: 254 20 366 3900
Email: nrobi-cs@international.gc.ca
High Commission of Canada, Limuru Road, Gigiri, P.O. Box 1013, 00621 Nairobi, Kenya.

MADAGASCAR:
Tel: (261 20) 22 397 37
Fax: (261 20) 22 540 30
Email: consulat.canada@moov.mg
Consulate of Canada, Immeuble Fitarata, Ankorondrano, Antananarivo 101, Madagascar.

MAURITIUS:
Tel: (230) 212-5500
Fax: (230) 208-3391
Email: canada@intnet.mu
Consulate of Canada, 18 Jules Koenig Street, P.O. Box 209, Port Louis, Mauritius.

MOZAMBIQUE:
www.canadainternational.gc.ca/mozambique
Tel: (258 21) 492 623
Fax: (258 21) 492 667
Email: mputo@international.gc.ca
The High Commission of Canada, Avenida Kenneth Kaunda, No. 1138, Box 1578, Maputo, Mozambique

SEYCHELLES:
The Canadian High Commission has no representation in the Seychelles. Contact the Canadian Embassy in Dar es Salaam, Tanzania.

SOUTH AFRICA:
www.canadainternational.gc.ca/southafrica
Tel: 27 12 422 3000
Fax: 27 12 422 3052
Email: pret@international.gc.ca
High Commission of Canada, Private Bag X13, 1103 Arcadia St., Hatfield 0028, Pretoria, South Africa.

TANZANIA:
www.canadainternational.gc.ca/tanzania
Tel: 255 22 216 3300
Fax: 255 22 211 6897
Email: dslam@international.gc.ca
High Commission of Canada, 38 Mirambo St., P.O. Box 1022, Dar es Salaam, Tanzania.

UGANDA:
Tel: 256 414 348 141 Fax: 256 414 349 484
Email: kampala@canadaconsulate.ca
Consulate of Canada, Jubilee Insurance Centre, 14 Parliament Ave., P.O. Box 37434, Kampala, Uganda.

ZAMBIA:
http://zambia.gc.ca
Tel: 260 21 1 250 833
Fax: 260 21 1 254 176
Email: lsaka@international.gc.ca
High Commission of Canada, 5199 United Nations Ave., P.O. Box 31313, Lusaka, Zambia 10101.

ZIMBABWE:
www.canadainternational.gc.ca/zimbabwe
Tel: (263 4) 252181/5
Fax: (263 4) 252186
E-mail: hrare@international.gc.ca
The Embassy of Canada, 45 Baines Ave., P.O. Box 1430, Harare, Zimbabwe.

DUTY-FREE ALLOWANCES
Contact the nearest tourist office or embassy for current, duty-free import allowances for the country(ies) that you intend to visit. The duty-free allowances vary; however, the following may be used as a general guideline: 1–2 liters (approximately 1–2 qt. /33.8-67.4 fl. oz.) of spirits, one carton (200) of cigarettes or 100 cigars.

293

ELECTRICITY

Electric current is 220–240-volt AC 50 Hz. Three-prong square or round plugs are most commonly used, but two-prong round plugs are also frequent. Universal adapter plugs are available for sale at most airports and offer a good solution to having an adapter that should work in all countries. If there is one sold specifically listing "Africa" then that would be the better choice.

HEALTH

Malarial risk exists in all of the countries included in this guidebook (except for Lesotho and much of South Africa), so be sure to take your malaria pills (unless advised by your doctor not to take them) as prescribed before, during and after your trip. Contact your doctor, an immunologist or the Centers for Disease Control and Prevention in Atlanta (toll-free tel. 1-888-232-3228, toll-free fax 1-888-232-3299, Website: www.cdc.gov) or the appropriate source in your own country for the best prophylaxis for your itinerary. Use an insect repellent. Wear long-sleeve shirts and slacks for further protection, especially at sunset and during the evening.

Bilharzia is a disease that infests most lakes and rivers on the continent but can be easily cured. Do not walk barefoot along the shore or wade or swim in a stream, river or lake unless you know for certain it is free of bilharzia. Bilharzia does not exist in salt water or in fast-flowing rivers or along shorelines that have waves. A species of snail is involved in the reproductive cycle of bilharzia, and the snails are more often found near reeds and in slow-moving water. If you feel you may have contracted the disease, go to your doctor for a blood test. If diagnosed in its early stages, it is easily cured.

Wear a hat and bring sun-block to protect yourself from the tropical sun. Drink plenty of fluids and limit alcohol consumption at high altitudes. In hot weather, do not drink alcohol and limit the consumption of coffee and tea unless you drink plenty of water. For further information, U.S. citizens can obtain a copy of *Health Information for International Travel* from the U.S. Government Printing Office, Washington, DC 20402.

INOCULATIONS

See "Visa and Vaccination Requirements" on page 302.

INSURANCE

Travel insurance packages often include a combination of emergency evacuation, medical, baggage, trip interruption and trip cancellation. I feel that it is imperative that all travelers to Africa cover themselves fully with an insurance package from a reputable provider. Many tour operators require guests to be fully insured, or to at least have emergency evacuation insurance as a requirement for joining a safari. The peace of mind afforded by such insurance far outweighs the cost. Ask your Africa travel specialist for information on relatively inexpensive group-rate insurance.

MEASUREMENT CONVERSIONS

The metric system is used in Africa. The U.S. equivalents are listed in the following conversion chart.

1 inch =	2.54 centimeters (cm)
1 foot =	0.305 meter (m)
1 mile =	1.60 kilometers (km)
1 square mile =	2.59 square kilometers (km^2)
1 quart liquid =	0.946 liter (l)
1 ounce =	28 grams (g)
1 pound =	0.454 kilogram (kg)
1 cm =	0.39 inch (in.)
1 m =	3.28 feet (ft.)
1 km =	0.62 mile (mi.)
1 acre =	0.4 hectares
1 km^2 =	0.3861 square mile (sq. mi.)
1 l =	1.057 quarts (qt.)
1 g =	0.035 ounce (oz.)
1 kg =	2.2 pounds (lb.)

TEMPERATURE CONVERSIONS

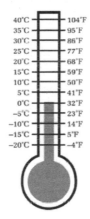

40°C	104°F
35°C	95°F
30°C	86°F
25°C	77°F
20°C	68°F
15°C	59°F
10°C	50°F
5°C	41°F
0°C	32°F
−5°C	23°F
−10°C	14°F
−15°C	5°F
−20°C	−4°F

TEMPERATURE CONVERSION FORMULAS

To convert degrees Centigrade into degrees Fahrenheit:
Multiply Centigrade by 1.8 and add 32.

To convert degrees Fahrenheit into degrees Centigrade:
Subtract 32 from Fahrenheit and divide by 1.8.

295

PASSPORT OFFICES
To obtain a passport in the United States, contact your local post office for the passport office nearest you. Then call the passport office to be sure you will have everything on hand that will be required (www.travel.state.gov/).

PHONES
International Dialing Country Codes:
(from the USA, dial 011 + code + number)

Botswana	267	Mauritius	230	South Africa	27
Rep. Congo	242	Mozambique	258	Tanzania	255
Ethiopia	251	Namibia	264	Uganda	256
Kenya	254	Rwanda	250	Zambia	260
Malawi	265	Seychelles	248	Zimbabwe	263

Cell phones:
Your cell phone provider will be able to assist you with the possibility of using your own phone while in Africa; however obtaining international roaming service can be expensive. You will need to have your phone unlocked by your cell phone company in order to use it abroad. In most major cities you will be able to purchase a SIM card and air time which may be exchanged for your normal SIM card. Remember though that reception in the bush may not be possible. Satellite phones are only available to rent in the Johannesburg Airport in South Africa, so if you feel you need one, you may want to rent one for your trip prior to leaving home. A quad band phone that is programmed for worldwide use is considered best.

SHOPPING IDEAS
Do not purchase items that are illegal to import into your own country or illegal to transport through your onward destinations.
Botswana: Baskets, wood carvings, pottery, tapestries and rugs. There are curio shops in many safari camps, hotels and lodges.
Congo, Republic: Wood carvings, malachite, copper goods, semiprecious stones and baskets.
Ethiopia: Traditional clothes and textiles, weavings, carvings, ethnic artifacts, wooden headrests, spices/coffee, silver and gold jewelry and paintings with both modern and religious influences.
Kenya: Makonde and Akomba ebony wood carvings, soapstone carvings, colorful kangas and kikois (cloth wraps) and beaded belts. In Mombasa, Zanzibar chests, gold and silverwork, brasswork, Arab jewelry and antiques.
Malawi: Wood carvings, woven baskets.
Mauritius: Intricately detailed, handmade model sailing ships of camphor or teak, pareos (colorful light cotton wraps), knitwear, textiles, dolls, tea, rum and spices.
Namibia: Semiprecious stones and jewelry, karakul wool products, wood carvings, ostrich eggshell necklaces and beadwork.
South Africa: Diamonds, gold, wood carvings, dried flowers, wire art, wildlife paintings and sculpture, and wine.
Tanzania: Makonde carvings, meerschaum pipes and tanzanite.
Uganda: Fabrics, bark-cloth and wood carvings.
Zambia: Wood carvings, statuettes, semiprecious stones and copper souvenirs.
Zimbabwe: Carvings in wood, stone and Zimbabwe's unique verdite, intricate baskets, wildlife paintings and sculpture, ceramic ware, and crocheted garments.

SHOPPING HOURS

Shops are usually open Monday through Friday from 8:00 or 9:00 a.m. until 5:00 to 6:00 p.m. and from 9:00 a.m. until 1:00 p.m. on Saturdays. Shops in the coastal cities of Kenya and Tanzania often close midday for siesta. Use the shopping hours given above as a general guideline; exact times can vary within the respective country.

THEFT

The number one rule in preventing theft on vacation is to leave all unnecessary valuables at home. What you must bring, keep on your person or lock in room safes or safety deposit boxes when not in use. Carry all valuables on your person or in your carry-on luggage – do not put any valuables in your checked luggage. Consider leaving showy gold watches and jewelry at home. Theft in Africa is generally no worse than in Europe or the United States. One difference is that Africans are poorer and may steal things that most American or European thieves would consider worthless. Be careful in all African cities (like most large cities in North America) and do not go walking around the streets at night.

TIME ZONES

EST = Eastern Standard Time (east coast of the United States). GMT = Greenwich Mean Time (Greenwich, England). * Time difference could vary 1 hour depending on daylight savings time

EST + 6/GMT + 1
Congo

EST + 8/GMT + 3
Ethiopia, Kenya, Tanzania and Uganda

EST + 7/GMT + 2
Botswana, South Africa, Malawi, Zambia, Mozambique, Zimbabwe, Namibia and Rwanda

EST + 9/GMT + 4
Mauritius, Seychelles and Madagascar.

TIPPING

A 10% tip is recommended at restaurants for good service where a service charge is not included in the bill. For advice on what tips are appropriate for guides, safari camps and lodges, ask the Africa specialist booking your safari. Guides are usually tipped separately and other lodge or camp staff are usually tipped as a unit.

VACCINATIONS

Check with the tourist offices or embassies of the countries you wish to visit for current requirements. If you plan to visit one or more countries in endemic zones (i.e., in Africa, South America, Central America or Asia), be sure to mention this when requesting vaccination requirements. Many countries do not require any vaccinations if you are only visiting the country directly from the United States, Canada or Western Europe; but, if you are also visiting countries in endemic zones, there may very well be additional requirements.

Then check with your doctor, and preferably an immunologist, or call your local health department or the Centers for Disease Control in Atlanta, GA (toll-free tel. 800-232-4636, Website: www.cdc.gov) for information. They may recommend some vaccinations in addition to those required by the country you will be visiting.

Make sure you carry with you the International Certificate of Vaccinations (Yellow Card) showing the vaccinations you have received. Malarial prophylaxis (pills) are highly recommended for all the countries included in this guide, except for parts of South Africa.

VISA AND VACCINATION REQUIREMENTS

Travelers from most countries must obtain visas to enter some of the countries included in this guide. You may apply for visas with the closest diplomatic representative or through a visa service well in advance (but not so early that the visas will expire before or soon after your journey ends) and check for all current requirements. Travelers must obtain visas (either before travel or on arrival) and have proof that they have received certain vaccinations for entry into some African countries.

VISA REQUIREMENTS				VACCINATIONS
COUNTRY	U.S.	Canada	UK	
Botswana	No	No	No	*see notes
Congo, Rep of	Yes	Yes	Yes	Yellow Fever
Ethiopia	Yes	Yes	Yes	*see notes
Kenya	Yes	Yes	Yes	*see notes
Malawi	Yes	Yes	Yes	*see notes
Mauritius	No	No	No	*see notes
Mozambique	Yes	Yes	Yes	*see notes
Namibia	No	No	No	*see notes
Rwanda	Yes	Yes	Yes	Yellow Fever
Seychelles	No	No	No	*see notes
South Africa	No	No	No	*see notes
Tanzania	Yes	Yes	Yes	*see notes
Zanzibar (Tanzania)	Yes	Yes	Yes	*see notes
Uganda	Yes	Yes	Yes	Yellow Fever
Zambia	Yes	Yes	Yes	*see notes
Zimbabwe	Yes	Yes	Yes	*see notes

Notes
1. Passports must be valid for at least six (6) months beyond your intended stay.
2. Please make sure that you have sufficient blank VISA pages (not the endorsement/amendment pages right at the back of the passport). If needed, a new passport should be obtained well in advance of your trip.
3. * : Yellow Fever Vaccination: proof of having the vaccination is required if arriving from a country with risk of Yellow Fever.
4. Optional vaccinations: Hepatitis A, Hepatitis B, Typhoid, Tetanus, Polio and Meningitis.

WILDLIFE CONSERVATION ASSOCIATIONS

African Wildlife Foundation, 1400 16th St. NW, Suite 120, Washington, DC 20036; tel. 202 939-3333. Headquartered in Nairobi, Kenya, African Wildlife Foundation (AWF) is a leading international conservation organization focused solely on Africa. AWF is a nonprofit organization and registered as a 501(c)(3) in the United States. **www.awf.org**

Bushlife Conservancy supports the conservation of wildlife in Mana Pools by assisting in funding the anti-poaching teams and supporting National Parks employees for the betterment of the park. Elephant poaching is a serious problem in the area and contributions to the conservancy go a long way to protecting these magnificent animals and other species as well. The Great Elephant Census, funded by Paul Allen of Microsoft, showed numbers in the Zambezi Valley down 40% to about 12,000 from 20,000. To Give a Gift to Save the Mana Pools Elephants and help conserve our important natural resource for the benefit of generations to come, please contact Global Wildlife Conservation (GWC): Sam Reza, Financial Manager, sreza@globalwildlife.org tel. 512 593-1883.

David Sheldrick Wildlife Trust was established in 1977 in Kenya and has been involved in a variety of activities to conserve wildlife; most notable is its work with elephant and rhino orphans. USA Representative: US Friends of the David Sheldrick Wildlife Trust, 25283 Cabot Road, Suite 101, Laguna Hills, CA 92653, USA. **www.sheldrickwildlifetrust.org**

Dian Fossey Gorilla Fund International, 800 Cherokee Avenue, S.E., Atlanta, GA 30315; tel. 404 624-5881 or 1 (800) 851-0203. **www.gorillafund.org**

Maasailand Preservation Trust works in conjunction with ol Donyo Lodge and 4,500 Maasai shareholders. Lions are regularly killed by the locals for preying on their livestock. The outreach program pays compensation for cattle losses due to predators and positive results are the rise in the lion population. **www.maasailand.wildlifedirect.org**

Mother Africa Trust was established in 2011 and, in addition to hosting volunteers on purpose-driven safaris, undertakes a wide variety of research, conservation and humanitarian development projects. The Trust works in the Matobo Hills, Hwange wildlife area and the city of Bulawayo, all in Zimbabwe. Focus activities include a children's home, Southern Ground Hornbill breeding research, a home for abused women and children in addition to supporting several rural schools. Address: 23 Old Gwanda Road, Granite Site, Hillside, Bulawayo, Zimbabwe; tel: 263 9 243 954. **www.mother-africa.org**

Save the Rhino Trust (SRT) mission is to "serve as a leader in conservation efforts in the Kunene and Erongo regions, including monitoring, training and research focused on desert-adapted black rhino, in order to ensure security for these and other wildlife species, responsible tourism development, and a sustainable future for local communities." P.O. Box 2159, Swakopmund, Namibia; tel. 264 (64) 400166. **www.savetherhinotrust.org**

Wildlife Conservation Network is dedicated to protecting endangered species and preserving their natural habitats. By supporting innovative conservationists and their projects, they are able to develop new approaches that work with the local communities. Current wildlife projects in Africa include African Wild Dog, Cheetah, Lion and African Elephant. Address: 209 Mississippi St., San Francisco, CA 94107, USA; tel. 415-202-6380 **www.wildlifeconservationnetwork.org**

Wilderness Safaris Wildlife Trust seeks to make a difference in Africa, to its wildlife and its people. These projects address the needs of existing wildlife populations, seek solutions to save threatened species and provide education and training for local people and their communities. A portion of each guest's fare while staying in Wilderness Safaris camps and lodges is allocated to this Trust. Donations to the Trust can be tax-deductible through a 501(c)(3) facility. Address: 373 Rivonia Boulevard, Rivonia, Johannesburg, South Africa Tel: 27 11 807 1800. **www.wildernesstrust.com**

LANGUAGES
French (Central Africa)
General Expressions

English	French	Phonetics
good morning	bonjour	bonjor
good day	bonjour	bonjor
good night	bonne nuit	bon nuee
How are you?	Comment allez-vous?	koman-tallay-voo
very well	très bien	tray-beeuh
good-bye (go well)	au revoir	o-revwour
mister	monsieur	muh seeuh
madam	madame	madam
yes/no	oui/non	wee/no
please	s'il vous plait	seal-voo-play
thank you	merci	mear see
very much	beaucoup	bo-koo
today	aujourd'hui	o jord wee
tomorrow	demain	duhma
yesterday	hier	ee year
toilet	toilette	twalet
left	gauche	gosh
right	droite	drwat
I want	je dèsire	juh dezeer
How much?	Combien?	komb ya
How many?	Combien?	komb ya
Where is?	Ou est?	oo-ay
When?	Quand?	kon
to eat	manger	mon-jay
food	nourriture	nureetur
water	eau	o
coffee	cafè	kafe
tea	thè	te
milk	lait	lay
beer	bière	be-year
bread	pain	pun
butter	beurre	burr
sugar	sucre	sukr
salt	sel	cell
pepper	poivre	pwavr
hot/fire	chaud/feu	show/fuh
cold	froid	frwa
ice	glace	glass

French: Numbers

English	French	Phonetics	English	French	Phonetics
one	un	uh	eleven	onze	ownz
two	deux	duh	twenty	vingt	vuh
three	trois	trwa	thirty	trente	trwant
four	quatre	katr	forty	quarante	karant
five	cinq	sank	fifty	cinquante	sank-ant
six	six	sees	sixty	soixante	swa-sant
seven	sept	set	seventy	soixante-dix	swa-sant dees
eight	huit	wheat	eighty	quatre-vingt(s)	katr-vuh
nine	neuf	nuhf	ninety	quatre-vingt(s)-dix	katr-vuh dees
ten	dix	dees	hundred	cent	san
			thousand	mille	meal

French: Mammal Names

English	French	Phonetics
Aardvark	fourmillier	foor mee lye
Aardwolf	protèle	protel
Antelope, Roan	hippotrague rouanne	eepotrahguh-rwan
Baboon	babouin	bah bwa
Bongo	bongo	bongo
Buffalo, Cape	buffle d'Afrique	bufl-dafreek
Bushbaby, Greater	galago à guelle epaisse	galago-ah-kuh-aypass
Bushbuck	antilope harnaché o	nteelop-ahrnah shay
Bushpig	potamochère d'afrique	potahmoshare-dafreek
Caracal	caracal	kahrahkahl
Cheetah	guépard	gu-epahr
Chimpanzee	chimpanzé	shamponzay
Civet	civette	see vet
Colobus	colobe guereza	kolob guerezah
Duiker	cephalophe	sefahlof
Eland	élan	aylon
Elephant	elephant d'afrique	aylayfon-dafreek
Gazelle, Grant's	gazelle de Grant	gahzel duh grant
Gazelle, Thomson's	gazelle de thomson	gahzel duh tomson
Genet, Large-spotted	genette à grandes taches	juhnet-ah-grand-tash
Gerenuk	gazelle giraffe	gahzel giraf
Giraffe	giraffe	giraf
Gorilla	gorille	goreeyuh
Hare, Scrub	lièvre des buissons	lee-evr de bueessan
Hartebeest	bubale	bubal
Hedgehog	hérisson du cap	ayreessan du kap
Hippopotamus	hippoptame	eepopotahm
Hog, Giant Forest	hylochère géant	ee-lo-share gayan

English	French	Phonetics
Honey Badger	ratel	rahtel
Hyena, Brown	hyène brune	yen brun
Hyena, Spotted	hyène tachetée	yen ta shuhte
Hyena, Striped	hyène rayée	yen re ye
Hyrax, Tree	daman d'arbre	dahmon dahrbr
Impala	pallah	pah lah
Jackal, Black-backed	chacal à chabraque	shah kahl-ah-shahbrak
Jackal, Side-striped	chacal à flancs rayé s	hah kahl-ah-flon-ray-ye
Klipspringer	oreotrague	orayo trah guh
Kob, Uganda	cob de Buffon	kob duh bufon
Kudu, Greater	grand koudou	gran koo doo
Lechwe, Red	cobe lechwe	kobe lechwe
Leopard	lèopard	lay opahr
Lion	lion	leeown
Mongoose, Banded	mangue rayée	mangooz-ray-ye
Monkey, Syke's	cercopitheque	sare ko pee tek
Monkey, Vervet	grivet	gree vay
Oribi	ourébie	oo ray bee
Otter, Clawless	loutre à joues blanches	lootr-ah-jeur-blansh
Pangolin	pangolin	pangola
Porcupine	porc-épique	pork-ay-peek
Reedbuck, Common	redunca grande	ruhdunka grand
Rhino, Black	rhinocéros noir	reenosayros nwar
Rhino, White	rhinocéros blanc	reenosayros blan
Serval	serval	sair vahl
Sitatunga	sitatunga	see tah tun gah
Springbok	antidorcas	an tee dor kah
Springhare	lièvre	leeevr
Squirrel, Tree	e'cureuil des bois	aykuroyl-de-bwa
Steenbok	steenbok	steenbok
Topi	damalisque	dah mah leesk
Tsessebe	sassaby	sah sah bee
Warthog	phacochère	fah ko share
Waterbuck, Common	cobe à croissant	kob-ah-krwasson
Waterbuck, Defassa	cobe defassa	kob-defahssah
Wild Dog	cynhyène	seen yen
Wildebeest	gnou bleu	gnu-bluh
Zebra, Plains	zèbre de steppe	zabr-duh-step
Zebra, Grevy's	zèbre de Grévy	zabr-duh-grayvee
Zorilla	zorille	zoreeyl

Swahili (Kenya, Tanzania and Uganda)

General Expressions

English	Swahili	Phonetics
hello	jambo	jä-mbô
How are you?	Habari?	hä-bä-ree
fine, good	nzuri	nzoo-ree
good-bye	kwaheri	kwä-hay-ree
mister	bwana	bwä-nä
madam	bibi	bee-bee
yes/no	ndio/hapana	ndee-ô/hä-pä-nä
please	tafadhali	itä-fä-dhä-lee
thank you	asante	ä-sä-ntay
very much	sana	sä-nä
today	leo	lay-ô
tomorrow	kesho	kay-shô
yesterday	jana	jä-nä
toilet	choo	chô-ô
left	kushoto	koo-shô-tô
right	kulia	koo-lee-ä
I want	nataka	nä-tä-kä
I would like	ningependa	nee-ngay-pee-ndä
How much?	Pesa ngapi?	pay-sä ngä-pee
How many?	ngapi?	ngä-pee
Where is?	iko wapi?	ee-kô wä-pee
When?	lini?	lee-nee
to eat	kula	koo-lä
food	chakula	chä-koo-lä
water	maji	mä-jcc
coffee	kahawa	kä-hä-wä
tea	chai	chä-ee
milk	maziwa	mä-zee-wä
beer	pombe	pô-mbay
bread	mkate	'm-kä-tay
butter	siagi	see-ä-gee
sugar	sukari	soo-kä-ree
salt	chumvi	choo-'m-vee
hot/fire	moto	mô-tô
cold	baridi	bä-ree-dee
ice	barafu	bä-rä-foo

303

Languages

Swahili: Numbers

English	Swahili	Phonetics	English	Swahili	Phonetics
one	moja	mô-jä	eleven	kumi na moja	koo-mee nä mô-jä
two	mbili	mbee-lee	twenty	ishirini	eé-shee-ree-nee
three	tatu	tä-too	thirty	thelathini	thay-lä-thee-nee
four	nne	'n-nay	forty	arobaini	ä-rô-bä-ee-nee
five	tano	tä-nô	fifty	hamsini	hä-m'-see-nee
six	sita	see-tä	sixty	sitini	see'-tee-nee
seven	saba	sä-bä	seventy	sabini	sä'-bee-nee
eight	nane	nä-nay	eighty	themaninit	hay-mä-nee-nee
nine	tisa	tee-sä	ninety	tisini	tee'-see-nee
ten	kumi	koo-mee	hundred	mia	mee-ä
			thousand	elf	ay-l'-foo

Swahili: Mammal Names

English	Swahili	Phonetics
Aardvark	muhanga	moo-hä-ngä
Aardwolf	fisi ndogo	fee-see ndô-gô
Antelope, Roan	korongo	kô-rô-ngô
Antelope, Sable	palahala	pä-lä-hä-lä
Baboon	nyani	nyä-nee
Buffalo	nyati	nyä-tee
Bushbaby	komba	kô-mbä
Bushbuck	pongo	pô-ngô
Bushpig	nguruwe	ngoo-roo-way
Caracal	siba mangu	see-bä mä-ngoo
Cheetah	duma	doo-mä
Chimpanzee	sokwe mtu	sô-kway 'm-too
Civet	fungo	foo-ngô
Colobus	mbega	mbay-gä
Dikdik	dikidiki	dee-kee-dee-kee
Duiker	naya	n-syä
Eland	pofu	pô-foo
Elephant	tembo	tay-mbô
Fox, Bat-eared	mbweha masikio	mbway-hä mä-see-ke
Gazelle, Grant's	swala granti	swä-lä 'grä-ntee
Gazelle, Thomson's	swala tomi	swä-lä tô-mee
Genet	kanu	kä-noo
Giraffe	nguruwe, twiga	ngoo-roo-way, twee-gä
Gorilla	makaku	mä-kä-koo
Hare	sungura	soo-ngoo-rä
Hartebeest	kongoni	kô-ngô-nee
Hedgehog	kalunguyeye	kä-loo-ngoo-yay-yay
Hippopotamus	kiboko	kee-bô-kô
Hog, Giant Forest	nguruwe mwitu dume	ngoo-roo-we mwe-too doo-may
Honey Badger	nyegere	nyay-gay-ray

English	Swahili	Phonetics
Hyena	fisi	fee-see
Hyrax	pimbi	pee-mbee
Impala	swalapala	swä-lä-pä-lä
Jackal	mbweha	mbway-hä
Klipspringer	mbuzimawe	mboo-zee-mä-wee
Kudu	tandala mdogo	tä-ndä-lä 'm-dô-gô
Leopard	chui	choo-ee
Lion	simba	see-mbä
Mongoose	nguchiro	ngoo-chee-rô
Monkey, Vervet	tumbili ngedere	too-mbee-lee ngay-day-ray
Oribi	taya	tä-yä
Oryx	choroa	chô-rô-ä
Otter	fisi maji	fee-see mä-jee
Pangolin	kakakuona	kä-kä-koo-ô-nä
Porcupine	nunguri	noo-ngoo-ray
Reedbuck	tohe	tö-hay
Rhino	kifaru	kee-fä-roo
Serval	mondo	mô-ndô
Sitatunga	nzohe	nzô-hay
Squirrel	kidiri	kee-dee-ree
Steenbok	dondoro	dô-ndô-rô
Topi	nyamera	nyä-may-rä
Tsessebe	nyamera	nyä-may-rä
Warthog	ngiri	ngee-ree
Waterbuck	kuro	koo-rô
Wild Dog	mbwa mwitu	'mbwä mwee-too
Wildebeest	nyumbu	nyoo-mboo
Zebra	pundamilia	poo-nday-'mee-lee-ä
Zorilla	kicheche	kee-chay-chay

Nyumbu

Shona (Zimbabwe)

General Expressions

English	Shona	Phonetics
good morning	mangwanani	mä-gwä-nä'-nee
good day	masikati	mä-see-kä'-tee
good night	manheru	män-ay'-roo
How are you?	makadini?	mä-kä-dee'-nee
very well	ndiripo zvangu	n-dee-ree'-po zwän'-goo
good-bye (go well)	chiendal zvenyu	chee-aan'-däee zwaan'-yoo
mister	baba	bä'-bä
madam	amai	ä-mä'-yee
yes/no	hongu/kwete	oon'-goo/kwâ-tâ
please	ndapota	n-dä-po'-tä
thank you	mazviita	mä-zwee'-tä
very much	kwazvo	kwä'-zo
today	nhasi	nää'-zee
tomorrow	mangwana	män-gwä-nä
yesterday	nezuro	nay-zoo-rö
toilet	chimbuzi	cheem-boo-zee
left	ruboshwar	oo-bô'-shwâ
right	rudyi	roo'-dee
I want	ndinoda	ndee-no'-dä
How much?	Zvakawanda sei?	zwä-kä-wän'-dä
How many?	Zvingani?	zween-gä-nee
Where is?	ndekupi?	nday-koo'-pee
When?	rini?	ree'-nee
to eat	kudya	koo'-deeä
food	chidyo	chee'-deeo
water	mvura	m-voo'-rä
coffee	kofi	ko'-fee
tea	tii	tee
milk	mukaka	moo-kä'-kä
beer	doro	do'-ro
bread	chingwa	cheen'-gwä
butter	bhata	bää'-tä
sugar	shuga, tsvigiri	shoo'-gä, tswee-gee'-ree
salt	munyu	moon'-yoo
hot/fire	inopisa/moto	e-no-pee'-sä/mo'-to
cold	inotonhora	e-no-ton-o-rä
ice	chando, aizi	chän'-do, äee'-zee

Shona: Numbers

English	Shona	Phonetics
one	potsi	po'-tsee
two	piri	pee'-ree
three	tatu	tä'-too
four	ini	e'-nee
five	shanu	shä'-noo
six	tanhatu	tän-ä-too
seven	nomwe	no'-mway
eight	tsere	tsay'-ray
nine	pfumbanmwe	foom-bä'-mway
ten	gumi	goo'-mee
eleven	gumi nerimwechere	goo'-mee nay-ray-mway'-ayayray
twenty	makumi maviri	mä-koo-mee mä-vee'-ree
thirty	makumi matatu	mä-koo-mee mä-tä'-too
forty	makumi mana	mä-koo-mee mä'-nä
fifty	makumi mashanu	mä-koo-mee mä-shä'-noo
sixty	makumi matanhatu	mä-koo-mee mä-tän'-ä-too
seventy	makumi manomwe	mä-koo-mee mä-no'-mway
eighty	makumi masere	mä-koo-mee mä-say'-ray
ninety	makumi mapfumbamwe	mä-koo-mee mä-foom-bä'-mway
hundred	zana	zä'-nä
thousand	chiuru	chee-oo'-roo

Shona: Mammal Names

English	Shona	Phonetics
Aardvark	bikita, chikokoma	bee-kee'-tä, chee-ko-ko'-mä
Aardwolf	mwena	mwi-nä
Antelope, Roan	chengu, ndunguza	chayn'-goo, n-doon-goo'-zä
Antelope, Sable	mharapara	m-ä'-rä-pä-rä
Baboon	bveni/gudo	vay'-nee/goo'-doe
Buffalo	nyati	n-yä-tee
Bushbaby	chinhavira	cheen-ä-vee'-rä
Bushbuck	dzoma	zoo'-mä
Bushpig	humba	hoom'-bä
Caracal	hwana, twana	hwä-nä, twä'-nä
Cheetah	didingwe	dee-deen'-gway
Civet	bvungo, jachacha	voon'-go, zhä-chä'-chä
Duiker	mhembwo	maym'-bway
Eland	mhofu	m-o'-foo
Elephant	nzou	nzo'-oo
Genet	tsimba, simba	tseem'-bä, seem'-bä
Giraffe	furiramudenga	foo-ree'-rä-moo-dayn'-gä
Hare	tsuro	tsoo'-ro
Hartebeest	hwiranondo	whee-rä-nôn'-dô

English	Shona	Phonetics
Hippopotamus	mvuu	m-voo'
Honey Badger	sere, tsere	say'-ray, tsay'-ray
Hyena	bere, magondo	bay'-ray, mä-gôn'-do
Hyrax	mbira	m-be'-rä
Impala	mhara	m-ä-rä
Jackal	hungubwe	hoon-goo'-bwa
Klipspringer	ngururu	n-goo-roo'-roo
Kudu	nhoro	n-o'-ro
Leopard	mbada	m-bä'-dä
Lion	shumba	shoom'-bä
Mongoose	hovo	ho'-vo
Monkey, Vervet	shoko, tsoko	sho'-ko, tso'-ko
Nyala	nyara	n-yä'-rä
Oribi	sinza, tsinza	seen'-zä, tseen'-zä
Otter	binza, chipu, mbiti	been'-zä, chee'-poo, m-be'-tee
Pangolin	haka	hä'-kä
Porcupine	nungu	noon'-goo
Reedbuck	bimha	beem'-hä
Rhino	chipembere	chee-paym-bay-ray
Serval	nzudzi, nzunza	n-zoo'-zhee, n-zoon'-zä
Squirrel	tsindi	tseen'-dee
Steenbok	mhene	m-â-nâ
Tsessebe	nondo	non'-do
Warthog	njiri	n-zhee'-ree
Waterbuck	dhumukwa	doo-moo'-kwä
Wild Dog	mhumbi	moom'-bee
Wildebeest	mvumba, ngongoni	m-voom-bä,n-gon-go'-nee
Zebra	mbizi	m-be-ze
Zorilla	chidembo	chee-daym'-bo

Shumba

Tswana (Botswana)

General Expressions

English	Tswana	Phonetics
good morning	dumêla	doo-may'-lä
good day	dumêla	doo-may'-lä
good night	rôbala sentlê	rô-bä'-lä sin'-kla
How are you?	O tsogilê jang?	o tso-khee-lay zhäng
fine, thank you	ke tsogilê sentlê	ki tso-khee-lay sin'-klâ
good-bye (go well)	tsamaya sentlê	tsä-mä-yä sin'-kla
mister	rrê	r-ra'
madam	mmê	m-mô'
yes/no	êê/nnyaa	a'-a/n-nyä'
please	tswêê-tswêê	tswâ-tswâ
thank you	kea lêboga	ki' ä lay-bo'-klä
very much	thata	tä'-tä
today	gompiêno	khom-pee-a'-no
tomorrow	kamosô	kä-mo'-sô
yesterday	maabane	mä-ä-bä'-ni
toilet	ntlwana ya boithomêlô	n-klwä'-nä yä bo-ee-toe-mô-lo
left	ntlha ya molêma	n-klhä yä mo-lô'-mä
right	ntlha ya go ja	n-klhä yä kho zhä
I want	ke batla	ki bä-klä
How much?	Bokae?	bo-kä'-i
How many?	dikae?	dcc-kä'-i
Which way is?	tsela e kae?	tsela-a-kä'-i
When?	leng?	li'-ng
to eat	go ja	kho zhä
food	dijô	dee'-zhô
water	mêtsi	may-tsee'
coffee	kôfi	ko'-fee
tea	tee	ti'-i
milk	maswi/mashi	mä-shwee/mä'-shee
beer	bojalwa	bo-zhä'-lwä
bread	borôthô	bo-rô'-tô
butter	bôtôrô	bô-tô'-rô
sugar	sukiri	soo-kee'-ree
salt	letswai	li-tswä'-ee
fire (hot)	aa fisa/molelô	ä'-ä fee-sä/mo-li'-lô
cold	a tsididi	ä tsee-dee'-dee
ice	segagane	see-khä-khä'-ni

Tswana: Numbers

English	Tswana	Phonetics
one	nngwe	n ngwâ'
two	pedi	pay'-dee
three	tharo	tä'-ro
four	nne	n-nâ'
five	tlhano	klhä'-no
six	thataro	tä-tä'-ro
seven	supa	soo'-pä
eight	rôbêdi	ro-bay'-dee
nine	rôbongwe	ro-bo'-ngwâ
ten	lesomê	li-so'-mâ
eleven	lesomê le motsô	li-so'-mâ li mo-tsô
twenty	masomê mabêdi	mä-so'-mâ ä mä-bay'-de
thirty	masomê mararo	mä-so'-mâ ä mä-rä'-ro
forty	masomê manê	mä-so'-mâ ä mä'-nâ
fifty	masomê amatlhano	mä-so'-mâ ä mä-klhä'-no
sixty	masomê amarataro	mä-so'-mâ ä mä-rä-tä'-ro
seventy	masomê aa supa	mä-so'-mâ ä soo-pä
eighty	maomê aa rôbêdi	mä-so'-mâ ä ro-bay'-dee
ninety	masomê aa rôbongwe	mä-so'-mâ ä ro-bo-ngwe
hundred	lekgolo	li-kho'-lo
thousand	sekete	si-ki'-ti

Tswana: Mammal Names

English	Tswana	Phonetics
Aardvark	thakadu	tä-kä-doo
Aardwolf	thukhwi	too-khwee
Antelope, Roan	kwalara êtsnêtiha	kw-lä-tä a tsâ'-klhä
Antelope, Sable	kwalata êntsho	kwä-lä'-tä a n-cho'
Baboon	tshwêne	chway'-ni
Buffalo	nare	nä'-ri
Bushbaby	mogwele	mo-khwi'-li
Bushbuck	serôlô-bolhoko	si-rô'-lô-bo-klo-ko
Bushpig	kolobê	ko-lo'-bâ
Caracal	thwane	twä'-ni
Cheetah	letlôtse	li-ngä'-oo li-klô-tsâ
Civet	tshipalore	tse-pä-lo-ri
Duiker	photi	poo'-tee
Eland	phôhu	po'-foo/po'-hoo
Elephant	tlôu	klo'-oo
Fox, Bat-eared	(mo)tlhose	(mo) klho'-si
Genet	tshipa	tse-pä
Giraffe	thutlwa	too'-klwä
Hare	mmutla	m-moo'-klä

English	Tswana	Phonetics
Hartebeest	kgama	khä'-mä
Hedgehog	(se)tlhông	(si) klho'-ng
Hippopotamus	kubu	koo'-boo
Honey Badger	magôgwê/matshwane	mä-khô-khwâ/mä-chwä'-ni
Hyena, Spotted	phiri	pe'-re
Hyrax	pela	pi'-lä
Impala	phala	pä'-lä
Jackal	phokojwê	po-ko-zhwâ
Klipspringer	mokabayane, kololo	mo-kä-bä-yä'-ni, ko-lo'-lo
Kudu, Greater	thôlô	tô'-lô
Lechwe, Red	letswee	li-tswi'-i
Leopard	nkwê	n-kwâ
Lion	tau	tä'-oo
Mongoose, Slender	kgano	khä'-no
Monkey, Vervet	kgabo	khä'-bo
Oribi	phuduhudu kgamane	poo-doo-hoo-doo khä mä-ni
Oryx	kukama	koo-kä'-mä
Otter	kônyana yanoka	kôn-yä-nä yä-no-kä
Pangolin	kgaga	khä'-khä
Porcupine	noko	no'-ko
Reedbuck	sebogata, motsweema	si-boo'-gä-tä, mo-tsway-ay-mä
Rhino	tshukudu	choo-koo'-doo
Serval	tadi	tä'-de
Sitatunga	sitatunga/nankông	si-tä-toon'-gä/nân-ko'-ng
Springbok	tshêphê	tsâ'-pâ
Squirrel, Tree	setlhora	si-klho'-rä
Steenbok	phuduhudu	poo-doo-hoo'-doo
Tsessebe	tshêsêbê	tsâ-sâ-bâ
Warthog	kolobê yanaga	ko-lo-bâ yä nä'-khä
Waterbuck	motumoga	mo-too-mo'-khä
Wild Dog	letlhalerwa	li-klhä-li-rwä
Wildebeest	kgôkông	kho-ko'-ng
Zebra	pitse/yanaga	pe'-tsi
Zorilla	nakêdi	nä-kay-dee

Kubu

Zulu (South Africa)

General Expressions

English	Zulu	Phonetics
good morning	sawubona	sä-woo'-bo-nä
good day	sawubona	sä-woo'-bo-nä
good night	lala kahle	lä-lä kä'-klhay
How are you?	Kunjani?	koon-zhä'-nee
very well	kuhle	koo'-klhay
good-bye (go well)	hamba kahle	häm'-bä kä-klhay
mister	mnumzane	m-noom-zä-ni
madam	nkosazane	n-ko-s-ä-zä'-ni
yes/no	yebo/qua	yay'-bo/qwa
please	ngiyacela	n-gee-yä-câ'-lä
thank you	ngiyabonga	n-gee-yä-bon-gä
very much	kakhulu	kä-koo'-loo
today	namuhla	nä-moo'-klhä
tomorrow	kusasa	koo'-sä-sä
yesterday	izolo	e-zo'-lo
toilet	indlwana	een-dlwä'-nä
left	esokunxele	i-so-koo-nxay'-lay
right	esokudia	i-so-koo'-dlä
I want	ngifuna	n-gee-foo'-nä
How much?	Kangakanani?	kän-gä-kä-nä'-nee
How many?	Zingakanani?	zeen-gä-kä-nä'-nee
Where is?	Zikuphi?	zee-koo'-pee
When?	nini?	nee'-nee
to eat	ukudla	oo-koo'-dlä
food	ukudla	oo-koo'-dlä
water	amanzi	ä-män'-zee
coffee	ikhofi	e-ko'-fee
tea	itiye	e-tee'-yay
milk	ubisi	oo-be'-see
beer	utshwala, ubhiya	oo-chwä'-lä, oo-be'-yä
bread	isinkwa	e-seen'-kwä
butter	ibhotela	e-bo-tay'-lä
sugar	ushukela	oo-shoo'-kay-lä
salt	itswayi, usawoti	e-tswä'-e, oo-sä-oo-tee
hot/fire	ayashisa/umlilo	ä-yä-she'-sä/oom-lee'-lo
cold	ayabanda	ä-yä-bän'-dä
ice	iqhwa	e'-qhwä

Zulu: Numbers

English	Zulu	Phonetics
one	kunye	kuun'-yay
two	kubili	koo-be'-lee
three	kutathu	koo-tä'-too
four	kune	koo'-nay
five	kuhlanu	koo-klä'-noo
six	isithupha	e-see-too'-pä
seven	isikhombisa	e-see-kom-be'-sä
eight	isithobambili	e-see-to'-bäm-be-lee
nine	isithobanye	e-see-to'-bän-yay
ten	ishumi	e-shoo'-me
eleven	ishumi nanye	e-shoo'-me nän-yay
twenty	amashumi amabili	ä-mä-shoo'-me ä mä-be'-lee
thirty	amashumi amathathu	ä-mä-shoo'-me ä mä-tä'-too
forty	amashumi amane	ä-mä-shoo'-me ä mä'-nay
fifty	amashumi amahlanu	ä-mä-shoo'-me ä mä-klhä'-noo
sixty	amashumi ayisithupha	ä-mä-shoo'-me ä ye-see-too'-pä
seventy	amashumi ayisikhombisa	ä-mä-shoo'-me ä ye-see-kom-be-sä
eighty	amashumi ayisithobambili	ä-mä-shoo'-me ä ye-see-to-bäm-be'-lee
ninety	amashumi ayisithoba	ä-mä-shoo'-me ä ye-see-to'-bä
hundred	ikhulu	e-koo'-loo
thousand	inkulungwane	een-koo-loon-gwä'-ni

Zulu: Mammal Names

English	Zulu	Phonetics
Aardvark	isambane	e-säm-bä'-ni
Aardwolf	isingci	e-see'-ngcee
Antelope, Sable	impalampala	ccm-pä läm-pä
Baboon	imfene	eem-fay'-nay
Buffalo	inyathi	een-yä'-tee
Bushbaby	insinkwe	e-seen'-kway
Bushbuck	imbabala	eem-bä-bä'-lä
Bushpig	ingulube	een-goo-loo'-bay
Caracal	indabushe	e-dä-boo-she
Cheetah	ingulule	een-goo-loo'-lay
Civet	impica	eem-pee'-cä
Duiker	impunzi	eem-poon'-zee
Eland	impofu	eem-po'-foo
Elephant	indlovu	een-dlo'-voo
Genet	insimba	en-seem'-bä
Giraffe	indiulamithi	een-dloo-lä-me'-tee
Hare	unogwaja, umvundla	oo-no-gwä'-zä, oom-voon'-dlä
Hartebeest	indluzele, inkolongwane	een-dloo-zay'-lay, eenko-loon-gwä'-ni

313

English	Zulu	Phonetics
Hippopotamus	imvuvu	eem-voo'-boo
Honey Badger	insele	een-say'-lay
Hyena	impisi	eem-pee'-see
Hyrax	imbila	eem-be'-lä
Impala	impala	eem-pä'-lä
Jackal	impungutshe	eem-poon-goo'-tsee
Klipspringer	igogo	e-go'-go
Kudu, Greater	umgankla	oom-gän'-klä
Leopard	ingwa	een'-gwä
Lion	ingonyama, ibhubese	een-gon-yä'-mä, e-boo-bay'-see
Mongoose	uchakide	oo-chä-kee'-day
Monkey, Vervet	inkawu	een-kä-woo
Nyala	inyala	een-yä'-lä
Oribi	iwula	e-woo'-lä
Otter	umthini	oom-tee'-nee
Pangolin	isambane	e-säm-bä'-ni
Porcupine	inungu	e-noon'-goo,
Reedbuck	inhlangu	een-klhän'-goo
Rhino	umkhombe, ubhejane	oom-koom'-bâ, oo-b-zhä'-ni
Serval	indlozi	een-dlo'-zee
Springbok	insephe	een-say'-pay
Squirrel	intshindane	een-tseen-dä'-ni
Steenbok	inqhina	e-qhee'-nä
Warthog	indlovudawana,	een-dloo-voo-dä-wä-nä,
	intibane	een-tee-bä'-ni
Waterbuck	iphiva	e-pee-vä
Wild Dog	inkentshane	een-kane-tsä'-ni
Wildebeest	inkonkoni	een-kone-ko'-nee
Zebra	idube	e-doo'-bay
Zorilla	iqaqa	e-qä'-aä

Indlovudawana

SUGGESTED READING

GENERAL/WILDLIFE/AFRICA

Africa, John Reader, 2001 (USA: National Geographic)

Africa, Michael Poliza, 2006 (USA: teNeues Publishing Company)

Africa in History, Basil Davidson, 2001 (U.K.: Phoenix Press)

African Game Trails, T. Roosevelt, 1983 (USA: St. Martins Press)

African Nights, K. Gallmann, 1995 (U.K.: Penguin Books)

African Trilogy, P. Matthiessen, 2000 (U.K.: Harvill Press)

Africa's Top Wildlife Countries, Mark Nolting, 2009 (USA: Global Travel)

Behaviour Guide to African Animals, Richard Estes, 1995 (USA: Univ. California Press)

Birds of Africa: South of the Sahara, Ian Sinclair et al, 2010 (South Africa: Struik)

Elephant Memories, Cynthia Moss, 1999 (USA: Chicago Univ. Press)

Eyes Over Africa, Michael Poliza, 2007 (USA: teNeues Publishing Company)

Field Guide to the Larger Mammals of Southern Africa, Chris and Tilde Stuart, 1996 (South Africa: Struik)

Field Guide to the Reptiles of East Africa, S. Spawls, K. Howell, R. Drews and J. Ashe, 2002 (U.K.: Academic Press)

Field Guide to the Tracks and Signs of Southern and East African Wildlife. Chris & Tilde Stuart, 2000 (South Africa: Struik)

From Silicon Valley to Swaziland: How One Couple Found Purpose and Adventure in an Encore Career. Rick & Wendy Walleigh (Wheatmark, 2015).

I Dreamed of Africa, K. Gallmann, 1991 (USA: Penguin Books)

The Kingdon Field Guide to African Mammals, Jonathan Kingdon, 1997 (U.K.:Academic Press)

Malaria , A Layman's Guide, Martine Maurel, 2001 (South Africa: Struik)

Pyramids of Life, John Reader and Harvey Croze, 2000 (U.K.: Collins)

Safari Companion, A Guide to Watching African Mammals, Richard D. Estes, 2001 (Chelsea Green Publishing)

Safari Planning Map, Mark Nolting, 2016 (USA: Global Travel)

The African Adventurers, Peter Capstick, 1992 (USA: St. Martins Press)

The End of the Game, Peter Beard, 1996 (USA: Chronicle Books)

The Great Migration, Harvey Croze, 1999 (U.K.: Harvill Press)

The Tree Where Man Was Born, Peter Matthiessen, 1997 (USA: Dutton)

Through a Window, J. Goodall, 2000 (U.K.: Phoenix Press)

Whatever You Do, Don't Run, Chris Roche, 2006 (South Africa: Tafelberg)

When Eagles Roar: the Amazing Journey of an African Wildlife Adventurer, 2014. (Ukhozi Press)

SOUTHERN AFRICA

Complete Guide to Freshwater Fishes of Southern Africa. Paul Skelton, 1993. (South Africa: Struik).

Complete Guide to the Frogs of Southern Africa. L. Preez & V.Carruthers, 2009. (South Africa: Struik)

Complete Guide to the Reptiles of Southern Africa. Graham Alexander & Johan Marais, 2007. (SA:Struik)

Complete Guide to Snakes of Southern Africa. J. Marais, 1992. (SA: Struik)

Discovering Southern Africa, TV Bulpin, 2000 (South Africa: Tafelberg)

Field Guide to Mammals of Southern Africa, C. and T. Stuart, 1991 (South Africa: Struik)

Field Guide to Snakes and Reptiles of Southern Africa, Bill Branch, 1992 (South Africa: Struik)

In the Footsteps of Eve, Lee Berger, 2001 (USA: National Geographic)

Suggested Reading

Living Deserts of Southern Africa,
  Barry Lovegrove, 1993 (South
  Africa: Fernwood Press)
Lost World of the Kalahari, Laurens
  van der Post, 2001 (U.K.: Vintage)
Raconteur Road, Shots into Africa,
  Obie Oberholzer, 2000 (South Africa:
  David Phillip Publishers)
*Robert's Nests & Eggs of Southern
  African Birds,* Warwick Tarboton,
  2011 (South Africa: John Voelcker)
Sasol Birds of Southern Africa,
  Ian Sinclair et al 2011(South Africa:
  Struik)
Trees of Southern Africa, Palgrave, 2002
  (South Africa: Struik)
Walk with a White Bushman, Laurens
  van der Post, 2002 (U.K.: Vintage)
*Wildlife of Southern Africa: A Field
  Guide,* V. Carruthers, 1997 (South
  Africa: Southern)

BOTSWANA
Birds of Botswana. Peter Hancock & Ingrd
  Weiersbye, 2016. (USA: Princeton)
Cry of the Kalahari, Mark and Delia
  Owens, 1984 (USA: Houghton
  Mifflin)
*Hunting with Moon, The Lions of
  Savuti,* Dereck and Beverley Joubert,
  1998 (USA: National Geographic)
Okavango: Sea of Land, Land of Water
  Anthony Bannister & Peter Johnson,
  1996 (South Africa: Struik)
Okavango: Jewel of the Kalahari, Karen
  Ross, 2003 (USA: Macmillan)
*Shell Field Guide to the Common Trees
  of the Okavango Delta,* Veronica
  Roodt, 1993 (Botswana: Shell)
*Shell Field Guide to the Wildflowers of
  the Okavango Delta,* Veronica Roodt,
  1993 (Botswana: Shell)
The Africa Diaries, Dereck and Beverley
  Joubert, 2000 (USA: National
  Geographic)
Wildlife of the Okavango, Duncan
  Butchart, 2016 (South Africa:
  StruikNature)

ZAMBIA and ZIMBABWE
African Laughter, Doris Lessing, 1992
  (U.K.: Harper Collins)
*Don't Lets Go To The Dogs Tonight, An
  African Childhood,* Alexander Fuller,
  2001 (USA: Random House)
Eye of the Elephant, Mark and Delia
  Owens, 1992 (USA: Houghton
  Mifflin)
Kakuli, Norman Carr, 1995 (U.K.:
  Corporate Brochure Company)
Luangwa, Zambia's Treasure, Mike
  Coppinger, 2000 (South Africa:
  Inyathi Publishers)
Mukiwa, Peter Godwin, 1996 (U.K.:
  Picador)
The Leopard Hunts in Darkness (and
  other series), Wilbur Smith,
  1992 (U.K.:MacMillan)
Zambia Landscapes, David Rodgers,
  2001 (South Africa: Struik)

MALAWI
Malawi, Lake of Stars, Vera Garland,
  1998 (Malawi: Central Africana)

NAMIBIA
*An Arid Eden: One Man's Mission in
  the Kaokoveld.* Garth Owen-Smith,
  2011. (South Africa: Gazelle).
Sheltering Desert, Henno Martin, 1996
  (South Africa: Ad Donker)
*Skeleton Coast, a Journey Through the
  Namib Desert,* Benedict Allen, 1997
  (U.K.: BBC)

SOUTH AFRICA
History of South Africa, Frank Welsh,
  Revised and Updated 2000 (U.K.:
  Harper-Collins)
Long Walk to Freedom, Nelson Mandela,
  1995 (U.K.: Abacus, Little Brown)
My Traitor's Heart, Rian Malan, 2000
  (USA: Moon Publications)
On Safari: A Young Explorer's Guide.
  Nadine Clarke, 2012 (South Africa:
  Struik)

The Heart of the Hunter (series), Laurens Van der Post, 1987 (U.K.: Vintage)

The Washing of the Spears: The Rise and Fall of the Zulu Nation, Donald R. Morris, 1995 (U.K.: Pimlico)

Wildlife of South Africa, D. Butchart, 2010 (South Africa: Struik)

EAST AFRICA

A Guide to the Seashores of Eastern Africa, M.D. Richmond (Ed.), 1997, (Sweden: Sida; Zanzibar: Sea Trust)

Africa's Great Rift Valley, Nigel Pavitt, 2001 (USA: Harry N. Abrams)

African Trilogy, Peter Matthiessen, 1999 (U.K.: Harvill Press)

Among the Man-eaters, Stalking the Mysterious Lions of Tsavo, Philip Caputo, 2002 (USA: National Geographic)

Field Guide to the Birds of East Africa, Terry Stevenson and John Fanshawe, 2002 (U.K.: Academic Press)

Field Guide to the Reptiles of East Africa, Stephen Spawls, 2002 (U.K.: Academic Press)

In the Shadow of Kilimanjaro, Rick Ridgeway, 2000 (U.K.: Bloomsbury)

White Hunters, Golden Age of African Safaris, Brian Herne, 1999 (USA: Henry Holt)

KENYA

Big Cat Diary, Brian Jackson and Jonathan Scott, 1996 (U.K.: BBC)

Born Free Trilogy, Joy Adamson, 2000 (U.K.: Macmillan)

Elephant Memories, Portraits in the Wild, Cynthia Moss, 1999 (USA: Chicago University Press)

Flame Trees of Thika: Memories of an African Childhood, Elspeth Huxley, 1998 (U.K.: Pimlico)

I Dreamed of Africa, Kuki Gallmann, 1991 (U.K.: Penguin)

Out in the Midday Sun, Elspeth Huxley, 2000 (U.K.: Pimlico)

Out of Africa, Isak Dinesen, 1989 (U.K.: Penguin Books)

TANZANIA

In the Dust of Kilimanjaro, David Western, 2000 (USA: Island Press)

Journal of Discovery of the Source of the Nile, John Hanning Speke, 1996 (USA:Dover)

Mara Serengeti, A Photographer's Paradise, Jonathan Scott, 2000 (U.K.: Newpro)

Serengeti Lions, Predator Prey Relationships, G. Schaller, 1976 (USA: Univ. Chicago Press)

Serengeti: Natural Order on the African Plain, Mitsuaki Iwago, 1996 (USA: Chronicle Books)

Serengeti Shall Not Die, Bernard and Michael Grzimek, 1960 (U.K.: Hamish Hamilton)

Snows of Kilimanjaro, Ernest Hemingway, 1994 (U.K.: Arrow)

RWANDA

Across the Red River, Rwanda, Burundi and the Heart of Darkness, Christian Jennings, 1999 (U.K.: Indigo)

Gorillas in the Mist, Dian Fossey, 2001 (U.K.: Phoenix Press)

In the Kingdom of Gorillas, Bill Weber & Amy Veder, 2002 (U.K.: Aurum Press)

Lake Regions of Central Africa, Richard Burton, 2001 (USA: Narrative Press)

Year of the Gorilla, The. George Schaller, 2011 (USA:Univ. Chicago Press)

UGANDA

Uganda: The Land and Its People, Godfrey Mwakikagile, 2009. (UK: New Africa Press)

Suggested Reading

ETHIOPIA
Blue Nile, Alan Moorehead, 2000.
 (UK:Hamish Hamilton)
Birds of the Horn of Africa. Nigel
 Redman et al., 2011 (UK: Helm)
*Notes From The Hyena's Belly: An
 Ethiopian Boyhood.* Nega Mezlekia,
 2001. (USA: Picador)

CONGO
African Silences. Peter Matthiessen,
 1992. (USA: Random House)
Birds of Central and Western Africa. Ber
 van Perlo, 2003. (USA: Princeton).
Congo Journey, Redmond O'Henlon,
 1996 (U.K.: Hamish Hamilton)
*Forests of Central Africa: Nature and
 Man.* Jean Pierre Vander Weghe,
 2004. Ecofac (SA: Protea
 Book House)
Forest People, The. Colin Turnbull, 1994
 (U.K.: Pocket Books)
*King Leopold's Ghost, Story of Greed and
 Heroism in Colonial Africa,* Adam
 Hochschild, 2000 (U.K.: Macmillan)
*The Road from Leopold to Kabila, A
 Peoples History.* Nsongola-Ntalaja,
 2002 (U.K.: Zed Books)
Facing the Congo, Jeffrey Taylor, 2001
 (U.K.: Little Brown)
Poisonwood Bible. Barbara Kingsolver,
 1998. (USA: Harper Flamingo)
*Travels in the White Mans Grave,
 Memoirs from West & Central Africa.*
 Donald McIntosh, 2001 (U.K.: Abacus)

MADAGASCAR
*Birds of Madagascar: a photographic
 guide.* Pete Morris et al., 2000.
 (UK: Pica Press).
*Field Guide to the Amphibians and
 Reptiles of Madagascar.* Frank Glaw
 & Miguel Vences, 2007. (Frosch
 Verlag)
Madagascar: A Natural History. Ken
 Preston-Mafham, 1991. (USA:
 Facts on File)

Madagascar Wildlife: A Vistor's Guide.
 Hilary Bradt et al., 1996.
 (USA: Globe Pequot)
*Mammals of Madagascar: A Complete
 Guide.* Nick Garbutt, 2007.
 (UK: A&C Black).
Natural History of Madagascar. Steven
 Goodman & Jonathan Benstead,
 2007. (USA: Univ. Chicago Press)

INDIAN OCEAN ISLANDS
Birds of the Indian Ocean Islands. Ian
 Sinclair et al., 2004. (South Africa:
 Struik)
Birds of the Seychelles. Adian
 Skerrett and Tony Disley, 2011.
 (UK: Christopher Helm)
*Coral Reef Fishes: Indo-Pacific &
 Caribbean.* Ewald Lieske & Robert
 Myers., 1994. (UK: Harper Collins)
Empires of the Monsoon. Richard Hall,
 1998. (UK: HarperCollins)
*Lost World: The Marine World of
 Aldabra and the Seychelles.* Thomas
 Peschak, 2010. (South Africa: Africa
 Geographic)
Wildlife of Seychelles. John Bowler, 2006.
 (UK: WildGuides)

MARK W. NOLTING

Mark Nolting is the author of *Africa's Top Wildlife Countries* (8th edition), an award-wining guide book that is considered the quintessential guide for planning a safari by the travel industry. He has also authored the *Safari Planning Map: East & Southern Africa* (2nd edition), the only safari map of its kind in the world, and this, the *African Safari Field Guide* (7th edition).

Nolting was born in 1951 in Minneapolis, Minnesota. He graduated from Florida State University in 1974. A year later he decided to take a "walkabout" and spent three years working his way around the world. This trip included six months in Africa during which he toured several parks and reserves and fell in love with the "safari experience."

He worked in the USA for five years, and then returned to Africa and traveled for two years through 16 countries, from Cairo to Cape Town, gathering material for his books and establishing contacts with safari companies and tour guides. On his return to the United States in 1985, he wrote the first editions of his books and established The Africa Adventure Company.

Mark enjoying the trained African elephant experience near Stanley's Camp in the Okavango Delta, Botswana.

Mark watching over the Great Migration, Serengeti, Tanzania.

In July 1992 he married Alison Wright, whom he had met a few years previously at a safari camp she was running in Zimbabwe. In July 1993, they had their first child, Miles William Nolting, and in 1996, their second child, Nicholas Hamilton Nolting. Both Miles and Nicholas have each been on over a dozen family safaris with Mark and Alison and have visited virtually all the top safari countries. These trips have given both Mark and Alison huge insights into travel with children.

He has received the *Condé Nast Traveler* magazine award as one of the World's Top African Travel Specialists for over a dozen years and has been on *Travel+Leisure*'s A-List for many years as well.

He has had a number of television appearances including a recent interview on the Wall Street Journal's Lunch Break with Tanya Rivero.

Mark has been on hundreds of safaris over the past 30 years, and continues to travel to Africa several times a year to update information and explore new areas, and especially enjoys taking his family on safari. Hard-to-find information on Africa is always at his fingertips, and he loves to take the time to talk to people about the many adventures that can be found on this exciting continent.

The Publishers

DUNCAN BUTCHART

A keen observer of the natural world, Duncan has made a career for himself as an illustrator, writer and specialized ecotourism consultant. He has produced all of the watercolor illustrations and natural history texts for this book.

Duncan has worked as a specialist nature and bird guide in South Africa, Botswana, Zimbabwe and Namibia, and acted as a mentor to over 200 safari guides in six countries whose wildlife observations and field studies he edited and published in five editions of the *Ecological Journal* and two *WildWatch* annuals (1999-2007) for Conservation Corporation Africa (now &Beyond).

Butchart never goes anywhere without his sketchbook or camera and is the author of numerous books including *Wildlife of South Africa* and *Wildlife of the Okavango*. He lives in South Africa but has traveled widely and published articles on the birds and other wildlife of Tanzania, Uganda, Kenya, Gabon, Borneo, Thailand, Costa Rica, Peru, Brazil and Australia.

Butchart provides interpretation services to the ecotourism industry through his company Nature Works: www.dbnatureworks.com.

Index of Featured Species

Index

Index

Africa Adventure Company Making A Difference

Zimbabwe Schools: We continue to sponsor 450 children at three schools near Hwange as part of the Children in the Wilderness feeding program. We identify children from here to also sponsor their high school education. Our annual donation is used to support monthly payments for internet connection.

Tanzania Schools: Schools we have partnered with are located near Arusha, Tarangire and Karatu.

Tanzania Scholarships: We have an education fund for over 35 children of the Tanzania guides who take our clients on safari.

Kenya Schools and Scholarships: AAC has an ongoing sponsorship commitment a Maasai Camp assistant to attend College in Nairobi as he works towards his guiding license.

Tanzania Guides: We give an annual Guide of the Year award to recognize a wildlife naturalist who has excelled at the highest level. Ephata Lotashu and Hillary Mandia are the recent winners!

Botswana Guides: We sponsor the opportunity for camp guides to work up their specialist knowledge providing them with private guiding opportunities that our lucky clients enjoy on a complimentary basis.

Children in the Wilderness: An inspirational project for local children to attend and be hosted for 3 days in Wilderness camps in their five regions. We focus on and support the Zimbabwe children.

Mana Pools Bushlife Conservancy: We give a yearly donation on behalf of all the clients we have booked at Vundu Camp for their on-going work with the park rangers and wild dog research.

Mother Africa Organization: We continue to donate and support their community and conservation projects in Matobo Hills.

Wilderness Wildlife Trust: We are major supporters of Wilderness Safaris in Botswana, Namibia, Zimbabwe, Zambia and South Africa. Beyond the outstanding safari experience they deliver, we know that for every bed-night we book with them, a portion of the price goes to the Wilderness Wildlife Trust. This is a true commitment to sustainable photographic tourism.

THE
AFRICA ADVENTURE
COMPANY   EST. 1986

10 Great Reasons to Travel with Africa Adventure Company

1. We wrote the definitive guide book on safaris to Africa. The President of our company, Mark Nolting, has written the quintessential book on traveling to Africa, "Africa's Top Wildlife Countries" - a testament to our level of expertise and dedication to giving you up-to-date information.

2. We specialize ONLY in Africa While many companies offer trips all over the world our work is focused only on Africa. This has enabled us to become experts in designing African safaris, foster close relationships within the industry and benefit from special pricing on the trips we feature. Our insider knowledge of Africa is unsurpassed. We'll provide you with special access to places, guides and events that are unavailable to travelers who book online.

3. Award winning CUSTOMIZED travel planning. We pioneered customized safari travel in Africa. After 25 years it was thrilling to have *TRAVEL + LEISURE* select a smaller, bespoke company in their 2012 World's Best Awards. We were recognized again in 2015/2014! The prestigious recognition landed us in the "world's best safari outfitter" category and is testament to our excellent customer service and expert knowledge.

4. One of the world's top Travel Specialists. We offer first hand, unbiased advice. All of our consultants go back to Africa every year to stay on top of product knowledge, so there is always someone who has been where you are going! *CONDE NAST TRAVELER* has recognized us as one of the World's Top Travel Specialists and Tour Outfitters - for 12 years in a row including 2015!

5. Affordable independent and private safaris. Many people expect private and independent safaris to be very expensive, but our clients are delighted to discover that they do not have to join a group of strangers in order to afford a great customized safari. Independent travel has never been easier.

6. Value-added adventure! Offering safari trips to over 15 African countries, there are hundreds of parks and game reserves, safari activities and a wide range of accommodations to choose from. We do not have to tie you into one line of properties and destination. Rather we match the ones to best fit your travel style with exclusive access to some of the best guides.

7. Sustainable tourism and eco conservation. In recognition of our commitment for over 28 years, **NATIONAL GEOGRAPHIC** selected us as one of the Best Travel Adventure Travel Companies on Earth. We have whole-heartedly promoted local ground operators and guides, eco accommodations and community projects that are supporting the merits of low-impact travel and the survival of habitats.

8. Safari trips with a purpose. Our award winning travel planning is based on more than game viewing; there is purpose to making a difference! We are very involved in many African communities, giving back to conservation projects, and supporting guides at grass roots level. At the community level we assist student education through funding of scholarships. For conservation, a percentage of bookings revenue in a variety of camps goes to supporting local projects. And we run and support guide initiatives recognizing wildlife naturalists who excel at the highest level. Because of our involvement, we were awarded the Tanzania Tour Operator Humanitarian Award by the Tanzania Tourist Board.

9. Our In-House air department Our IATA/ARC in-house air department completes the planning process with flight arrangements. By booking your air with us, we can assist if flights are changed or cancelled. And should there be a travel emergency, we can be reached 24/7.

10. Our clients come back for more! Over 70% of our business is repeat clients and referrals! What a testament to the quality of our services, and of course, the incredible beauty and wildlife of Africa!

IATA

2601 East Oakland Park Boulevard, Suite 600 * Fort Lauderdale, Florida 33306 U.S.A
Tel: 800.882.9453 * Tel: 954.491.8877 * Fax: 954.491.9060
email: safari@AfricanAdventure.com * www.AfricanAdventure.com

The Africa Adventure Company Award Winners

The Africa Adventure Company is proud of the reputation we have earned on the African continent over the past 30 years. We continue to offer the best value prices and best personal service and would love to work with you to plan and book your "safari of a lifetime" experience!

Sept 2015 - Travel + Leisure - Mark Nolting was named on the A-List 2015 for a 7th year in a row! Thousands of agents were evaluated and the highly selective list is the best in the business. Mark's insider knowledge of the top local guides across Africa and enabling clients a face -to-face adventure with elephants, rhino and lions on walking expeditions makes him a top pick!

July 2015 - Travel + Leisure - We're very honored to be recognized once again by *Travel + Leisure's* "World's Best Awards" on the Top Safari Outfitters list. Readers voted on thousands of travel experiences and tour operators and selected The Africa Adventure Company as one of the World's best. For more than 30 years, it has been our pleasure to craft trips of a lifetime for our clients. We are honored to be one of the Top 5 Safari Outfitters. Receiving this award for the 3rd time since its inception confirms our ongoing dedication to providing some of the best safaris in the world.

July 2015 - Congratulations to Mark Nolting of The Africa Adventure Company for his 12th year being selected as one of the *146 Top Travel Specialists* by *Conde Nast Traveler!* We have been listed as their chosen *Tour Operator for Family Safaris* (2015-2003)

Africa Adventure Company's *"Eyes on Elephant"* Zimbabwe trip was selected as one of this year's National Geographic Traveler magazine's prestigious *"50 Tours of a Lifetime"* for 2011. The honorees have been chosen for being the most authentic, most innovative, most immersive, best -guided and most sustainable tours of the year.

The Tanzania Tourist Board (TTB) has honored The Africa Adventure Company with the *Tour Operator Humanitarian Award 2011* for their ongoing contribution to local communities in Tanzania.
September 2012. Congratulations - "Hongera"! On behalf of the Tanzania Tourist Board (TTB), we are pleased to inform you that **Africa Adventure Company** has been selected to receive the **Tanzania Tourist Board Product Development Award for 2012** in recognition of the <u>**8-Day Culinary Tanzania Safari.**</u>

OTHER PUBLICATIONS FROM GLOBAL TRAVEL

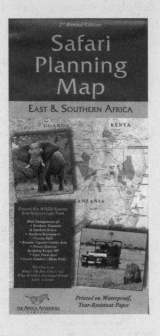

The complete guide for anyone traveling to Africa, and the best guidebook for planning your safari as it:
* Highlights and compares over 100 wildlife reserves in
Africa's best wildlife countries
* Includes invaluable charts such as "When's the Best Time to Go" and "What Wildlife is Best Found Where?"
* Grades safari camps and lodges for easy selection and highlights the ones that offer the best safari experience
*Beautifully depicts the safari experience with 533 striking photos and 73 easy-to-read maps in 616 pages of color!

Available in paperback and e-book formats

$27.95

This Safari Planning Map helps make the planning of the safari of a lifetime easy!
This beautifully illustrated full-size (26" x 38") map includes all the top wildlife countries and reserves – providing an overall perspective on where you can go on safari.
Also included are enlargements of:
* Northern Tanzania & Southern Kenya
* Northern Botswana to Victoria Falls
* Rwanda/Uganda Gorilla Area
* Kruger Area Reserves
* Cape Town Area
* Lower Zambezi – Mana Pools

$11.95